# MONEY AND MOTIVATION

# MONEY AND MOTIVATION

## An Analysis of Incentives in Industry

### By WILLIAM FOOTE WHYTE

New York State School of Industrial and Labor Relations, Cornell University

**AND**

Melville Dalton, Donald Roy, Leonard Sayles
Orvis Collins, Frank Miller, George Strauss
Friedrich Fuerstenberg, Alex Bavelas

HARPER & ROW, PUBLISHERS
NEW YORK, EVANSTON, AND LONDON

# CONTENTS

v

# PART IV

## A Theory of Economic Incentives and Human Relations

# PREFACE

In a sense this book has had two beginnings. The first beginning came when I was at the University of Chicago on the Committee on Human Relations in Industry. Orvis Collins, Melville Dalton, and Donald Roy also were in or around the university at that time working toward their Ph.D.'s. Dalton was working as an incentive applier or checker in one department of a steel mill. Roy was spending his eleven months as an operator on the "drill line" in another nearby factory and Collins was a part-time production worker in a third plant. During this period Collins and Roy kept work diaries in which each day after work they recorded their experiences and observations of the day. Dalton's job gave him more freedom to move around the plant and a natural reason to work with pencil and paper, so that he was able to record some of his interviews and observations during the working day.

These three work situations had at least one thing in common: individual piecework as the method of payment. Also in each case the familiar phenomenon of restriction of output was to be observed.

In so far as their factory work schedules would permit, we tried to get Collins, Dalton, and Roy together to discuss their experiences and observations. Out of these discussions grew the idea of an article "Restriction of Output and Social Cleavage in Industry" (Collins, Dalton, and Roy, *Applied Anthropology*, Vol. 5, No. 3).

Later I was able to bring the three men together again on a more ambitious project, a book dealing with worker reactions to incentive systems. It was to be based primarily upon the three factory situations they knew so well. We went at this with some enthusiasm and a number of chapters did get written, but somehow we were never able to put together a book that satisfied any of us. At last after about six months of work, we reluctantly abandoned the project. At the time it seemed that this had all been waste motion.

However, we did not abandon our interest in the problem. In succeeding months Dalton (now at the University of California at Los Angeles) published two articles: "Worker Response and Social

Background" (*Journal of Political Economy*, August 1947) and "The Industrial Rate Buster: A Characterization" (*Applied Anthropology*, Winter 1948). Later Roy (now at Duke University) came out with "Quota Restriction and Goldbricking in a Machine Shop" (*American Journal of Sociology*, Vol. LVII, No. 5, March 1952).

In the following years I was also spending some of my time working on incentive problems with special reference to situations where a plant-wide formula was applied. This interest led to "Incentive for Productivity" (*Applied Anthropology*, Vol. VII, No. 2, Spring, 1948) and to "Union Management Cooperation: The Toronto Case" (*Applied Anthropology*, Vol. VI, No. 3). My case study of transition from conflict to cooperation in Inland Steel Container Co. (*Pattern for Industrial Peace*, New York: Harper & Brothers, 1951) also dealt at some length with incentive problems in the context of union-management relations. Finally I had published a general statement on "Economic Incentives and Human Relations" (*Harvard Business Review*, Vol XXX, No. 2).

In the meantime I had been associated with a line of research that was to fill in another part of this book. First Leonard Sayles and then George Strauss came to Cornell to work with me at the New York State School of Industrial and Labor Relations on a research project, supported by the Grant Foundation, to study human relations in unions. They approached the study of the union through an examination of the groupings of workers who make up its membership. They found these groupings importantly influenced by the technology of the plant, the structure of the management organization and the pay systems that are in operation. This last item necessarily led us to an examination of incentive systems from a different angle—that of intergroup relations. Sayles then published an article on "The Impact of Incentives on Inter-Group Work Relations" (*Personnel*, Vol. XXVIII, No. 6, May 1952). (Sayles is now at the University of Michigan, while Strauss is at the University of Buffalo.)

That was the situation when this book had its second beginning. Conception occurred in my bathtub. I rarely take the *American Sociological Review* for bathtub reading, but this time I had it with me because I was interested in an article just published by Roy on "Work Satisfaction and Social Reward in Quota Achievement" (Vol. XVIII, No. 5). I read the piece with mounting excitement and yet with some sense of regret. Wasn't it too bad, I told myself, that we had never been able to push to a conclusion our book on incentives when there was so much rich data available? Suddenly the thought struck me that perhaps the book had already been partially written. Perhaps it would now be possible to take the published material we had and, with relatively little additional effort, make this the book we once hoped to write.

While I seriously underestimated the work that would be involved in fitting all the parts together, the pattern of organization that suggested itself at that time proved adequate for the new project.

The Collins, Dalton, and Roy material seemed to fit naturally together in the first part on the relations between the individual and his work group. I received an unexpected windfall for the intergroup relations discussion when Roy sent along an article he had written for the *American Journal of Sociology* dealing with intergroup cooperation. I remembered an incentive case that Sayles and I had often discussed in relation to departmental case studies he had made while at Cornell. I asked him to write this case for me. When I went over the plans for the book with George Strauss, he told me about an experiment that Alex Bavelas had carried through in a factory but which had not yet been written up. This I felt cast new light on intergroup problems and we were fortunate in getting Professor Bavelas' permission to have George Strauss write up the case from classroom notes for later review and correction by Bavelas.

I then learned that the plant-wide incentive formula that I had examined in one case had been introduced into a second plant of the same company with rather different results. This invited a comparison, and here we were able to undertake new field work. Frank Miller of our School of Industrial and Labor Relations and Friedrich Fuerstenberg, a Fulbright scholar from Germany, wrote the case study which appears as the second part of Chapter 12.

I am indebted to W. R. Dymond, who did the first research report on the Lever Brothers case.

We would have liked to have been able to undertake a new field study of a Scanlon Plan plant but found it impossible to work out arrangements to do so. Therefore I had to be content with summarizing and analyzing a number of reports on the Scanlon approach. Here I profited particularly from the work of George Shultz of the Massachusetts Institute of Technology.

While I was preparing the manuscript I was fortunately invited by Rensis Likert to present my ideas to a management group brought together for a seminar of his Foundation for Research in Human Behavior. The discussions there with his research associates and with the management people were invaluable in the further development of my ideas. They also encouraged me in the project, for the response of this group seemed to promise a wide interest in the book.

I should clarify the question of responsibility for various parts of the book. This is a group project in the sense that I have made widespread use not only of the data but also of the interpretations of my collaborators. However, I have added my own interpretations, and, since it has been impossible to get us all together to discuss the final manuscript, there may well be points at which one or another of the coauthors would disagree with me. I must therefore take full responsibility for the conclusions presented throughout the book. Also, the introduction and the theoretical section (Part IV) are entirely my own writing, although, of course, the case studies developed by my collaborators made such a theoretical statement possible.

For valuable suggestions on background reading, I am particularly indebted to Robert Aronson of the New York State School of Industrial and Labor Relations. For advice on readings and on questions of theory I am indebted to Donald Cullen and Henry Landsberger of the same college, to Urie Bronfenbrenner and Alexander Leighton also at Cornell, and to Conrad M. Arensberg of Columbia University. I am also indebted to Douglas MacGregor of the Massachusetts Institute of Technology for his help. The criticisms and suggestions of George Strauss were especially helpful in revision of the manuscript. For suggestions on theoretical aspects, I am indebted to Chris Argyris of Yale University.

I was fortunate in having a teaching schedule at the New York State School of Industrial and Labor Relations that made it possible for me to devote a large part of my time for about nine months to the preparation of this book. I am also indebted to the Grant Foundation, which supported the Sayles and Strauss studies and also the case study of the plant-wide incentive made by Frank Miller and Friedrich Fuerstenberg.

In connection with the beginning of the project I am also much indebted to my former colleagues, Burleigh B. Gardner, Everett C. Hughes, and W. Lloyd Warner, who did so much to encourage work along these lines while I was with them a member of the Committee on Human Relations in Industry.

June Price has given invaluable assistance in typing the manuscript through its various revisions. Maxine Crispell also has helped with part of the typing.

Finally, I am indebted to Kathleen Whyte for her criticisms and suggestions.

WILLIAM F. WHYTE

*Ithaca, New York*

## COLLABORATORS' NOTE OF APPRECIATION TO WILLIAM F. WHYTE*

The contributors to this volume share a common debt. Each of us has known Bill Whyte as teacher, colleague, or friend.

He has given us an appreciation for the values and methods of field research as well as the "wherewithal" in terms of endless encouragement, moral and financial support, and, most of all, the striking example of his own work. For many years his office and his home have been an open forum for the discussion of field "tactics" as well as research data.

No comment on his contributions is needed. An examination of indexes in the literature of industrial relations, the field of sociology, and related disciplines will suggest the influence of his work. These are well known. Rather we want his readers to know more about Bill Whyte, the person.

Many of the studies included in this book owe much more to Bill than author credits would indicate. He has always taken satisfaction in having his students, whom he guided and inspired, submit the final manuscript. While his name appeared only in the preface or footnote, his effort and support appear in every line.

* The following contributors to this volume did not sign this statement either because correspondence with them was impractical or, as in the case of Professor Bavelas, he was not a student of Professor Whyte: Alex Bavelas, Orvis Collins, Friedrich Fuerstenberg.

However, Bill has never required conformity from those who collaborate with him. He has expected individual thinking as much as he has expected independent writing. Indeed his students are probably better known for their lack of common agreement than for a system or a model that is mutually accepted. Bill has stimulated independent thought and research by practicing, not moralizing upon, the role of the free scholar.

Few social scientists quarrel with the idea that students and researchers need field experience, the "feel" of the factory, store, and community. But the outside world is often threatening, and guides to field research are few and far between. Bill Whyte has few rivals in encouraging students to test out their ideas and their skills in the world of reality. His training in interviewing, observation, and the less easily defined abilities of establishing and maintaining relationships in ongoing organizations have been invaluable to all of us.

In almost every instance he has built enduring relationships with the people and institutions with which he has come into contact in research—whether they were management or union, initially friendly or hostile. These friendships have been based on the almost intuitive recognition that his personal integrity and values were beyond reproach. Simply put, Bill Whyte has never used his knowledge or contacts for personal aggrandizement.

Finally, Bill has inspired clear writing to complement the ideas expressed. Readable English may seem like a minor objective in the light of the major social problems still unsolved. Yet by stimulating people to read his prolific writings, by, in fact, being successful in communicating the results of his studies, the audience for and the impact of his work has been enormously increased.

For these deceptively simple virtues then, the ones we talk so much about and practice so rarely, democratic leadership and communication, Bill Whyte has earned our gratitude and respect.

MELVILLE DALTON
FRANK MILLER
DONALD ROY
LEONARD SAYLES
GEORGE STRAUSS

# MONEY AND MOTIVATION

# 1

# Economic Incentives and Human Relations

This book is about 5 M's of factory life: men, money, machines, morale, and motivation.

We are examining the effect of money incentives upon the behavior of the men who operate the machines. We find that money incentives sometimes seem to work, in stimulating production, and sometimes show little effect. Why these differences?

Even where the incentive seems to work, in most cases its success is only partial, for workers set a ceiling on production well below the limits of their physical capacities. Why this restriction of output?

Often, whether the incentive works or not, it seems to give rise to all sorts of worker-management and union-management conflicts. What is the fighting all about?

We are also examining problems of morale and motivation. It is often assumed that high morale and high productivity go together, that if the workers have high morale they will also be highly productive. That depends upon what we mean by "morale." If we mean by high morale only that the workers are well satisfied with their jobs and think well of management, then high productivity does not necessarily follow. People may simply be happy to be members of the organization and have no urge to contribute to its goal of production. They may be confident that management will take care of them and be reasonably well content with this dependent, paternalistic relationship.

There is something lacking in any definition of morale that is limited to job satisfaction and acceptance of management. If we are to find relationships between morale and productivity we need to broaden our conceptions of morale. In effect, *we need to put motivation into morale.*

Some have suggested that *participation* on the part of workers will provide them with the motivation to contribute to the organization. But different people mean different things by "participation." What sort of participation does in fact provide motivation toward productivity?

In this book we shall concentrate upon money incentives. If we were to consider all the various facets of morale and motivation in industry we would be writing a textbook or a series of general books upon human relations in industry. To bring research knowledge more effectively to bear, we shall focus upon men, money, and machines. However, it is one of the themes of this book that we cannot explain men's reaction to money without studying their relations with each other. Thus we will inevitably be led into considering some problems of morale and motivation. They will provide background for our study, while economic incentives will be in the primary focus of our attention.

Our task is to build a new model, socioeconomic man to replace the discredited economic man who has held sway in the incentive systems most common in industry today. Before the new man can be built, we shall have to examine the old man and the theory he represents.

As represented by F. W. Taylor and his followers in the scientific management movement, managerial thinking begins with one of the basic assumptions of orthodox economic theory: that man is a rational animal concerned with maximizing his economic gains. Of course, no economist believes this assumption to be true to the facts, but the tendency has been to reason from the assumption as if it were close to actuality.

If we assume that man's goal in the factory is to make money, then it naturally follows that we can get him to produce more if we pay him in accordance with the amount he produces. Thus the theory of economic motivation leads directly to the development of a piecework incentive system.

The second major assumption is that each individual responds to economic incentives as an isolated individual. Under such conditions there would be no need to investigate the effect of fellow workers upon the individual under consideration. While most management people realize that this individualism is never quite to be found, there is a tendency to think that people should respond in this individualistic fashion and that management should encourage them to do so.

The third major assumption is that men, like machines, can be treated in a standardized fashion. While individual variations are recognized, it is assumed that there is a "one best way" to do a job so that variations in method of work can and should be eliminated. There are expected to be variations in speed and endurance, but by studying fast and slow workers an average is to be obtained for "the standard workman." The theories of scientific management are based upon standards: standard hours, standard machines and standard workmen, and so on. For example, an incentive engineer's handbook defines the standard hour in this way: "a unit of measurement of the amount of work expected of an operator or a piece of equipment in one actual hour at a pace equivalent to standard performance." It is interesting to observe the way in which machines and workers tend to be linked together as part of the equipment of the factory.

Management also seems to assume that machines and workers are alike in that they are both normally passive agents who must be stimulated by management in order to go into action. In the case of the machines, management turns on the electricity. In the case of workers, money takes the place of electricity.

Since the theory requires a system of economic incentives, it also requires people and procedures and policies to administer this system. If the worker is to be paid in terms of the amount of work accomplished, then it is necessary to have some standards of the amount of work expected. Management must arrive at a price to be paid for each unit of production. The price is generally established through the work of time-study men. Their first task is to see to it that the job is being done according to the most efficient methods. They then are expected to time selected workers on the actual job operation. The price per piece is set on the basis of these measurements.

Management generally adds two guarantees to make the system more attractive to the workers. In the first place, his regular hourly pay is guaranteed whether or not he makes the standard. Let us assume that his regular pay is $1.50 an hour and that the standard on this operation is 10 pieces an hour, which would mean a price for him of 15 cents apiece. Then, if he produced only 8 pieces he would still get his guaranteed $1.50, but if he produced 12 pieces he would earn $1.80.[1]

The second guarantee involves rates or prices set for the particular job. It is generally understood that the rate or price is not to be changed unless there has been a significant change in the machine or method of operation which would justify the establishment of a new rate. This is designed to assure the worker that he can produce an unlimited amount with no fear that in the future he will have to produce more pieces on the same job with the same methods to make the same money.

In spite of such guarantees, we find almost universally that workers set a quota on what constitutes a fair day's work and refuse to go beyond this amount even when it is well within their ability to do so. This situation exists whether the plant is unionized or not. It exists where the workers hate and distrust management, as we shall see in the cases described by Donald Roy. It exists even in cases where the workers evince considerable loyalty for the company and for management in general.[2]

The conflicts that we shall point to in the administration of incentive systems are not, for the most part, discoveries of our own. Some of them were discussed forty years ago by R. F. Hoxie in his book on *Scientific Management and Labor*.[3] Furthermore, many factory management people will certainly find similar problems in their own experience.

Does the fault lie perhaps with the use of poor techniques in administering incentive systems? If management just used the "right" methods of time study and rate setting, would the problems be solved? The fact that these problems have existed down through

[1] There is a bewildering variety of incentive schemes in existence today. The example here is of what is known as a straight-line or 100 per cent incentive, where the same price is paid for each piece. There are systems where a smaller price is paid after the standard has been reached and there are others which pay a higher price beyond the standard. The straight-line incentive is probably the most common today, and we will deal with that. However, we will seek to avoid the complications of the technical side of incentive systems since this is a book on morale and motivation rather than one on incentive systems per se.

[2] F. J. Roethlisberger and W. J. Dickson, *Management and the Worker* (Cambridge: Harvard University Press, 1939).

[3] London: D. Appleton & Company, 1915.

the years, in similar form, in a great variety of factories, suggests to us that the fault cannot lie solely with poor techniques. The persistence and generality of the problems suggests that there is something basically wrong with the policies and procedures on which piece-rate systems are based.

If this is so, we may also assume that there is something wrong with the theory of worker motivation upon which the policies and procedures are based. A basic reexamination of theory and practice seems to be in order.

In the first place, we should recognize that scientific management theorists seem to accept without question an arbitrary assumption regarding man's motivation which economists themselves do not take to represent reality. D. H. Robertson, the noted British economist, stated the case against the economic man more than thirty years ago in these words:

A high wage will not elicit effective work from those who feel themselves outcasts and slaves, nor a low wage preclude it from those who feel themselves an integral part of a community of free men. Thus the improvement of this element of the supply of labour is an infinitely more complex and arduous task than if it depended upon wage alone, but at the same time a task more possible of fulfilment by an impoverished world.[4]

The same point was made more than forty years ago by Frank Gilbreth, one of the pioneers of scientific management:

It should be stated here emphatically that there is nothing that can permanently bring about results from scientific management and the economies that it is possible to effect by it unless the organization is supported by the hearty cooperation of the men. Without this there is no scientific management.[5]

Such a statement suggests that we ought to study the conditions under which the "hearty cooperation of the men" is attained. Unfortunately this has never been a matter of serious concern to most of the scientific management practitioners. They have assumed that this cooperation existed and have then gone on to build up their systems. Or else they seem to have assumed that a proper

[4] "Economic Incentives," *Economica*, October 1921, p. 244.

[5] "Units, Methods and Devices of Measurement Under Scientific Management," *Journal of Political Economy*, Vol. XXI (July 1913), p. 623. Georges Friedmann drew this to my attention.

administration of the system would create the hearty cooperation.

To make progress on this problem we must refuse to assume the existence of cooperation and instead focus our attention upon the conditions under which cooperation is attained. We will not abandon our interest in incentive systems. We will try instead to develop a theory which will tie together the economic incentive and the human relations pattern existing in the plant.

It may be argued at this point that we are wasting our breath in destroying the straw man of scientific management. Does anybody really believe in this theory of motivation any more? The answer seems to be that most people will deny that they hold such a belief and yet will then have difficulty in abandoning the belief. For example, an industrial engineer made this statement to Melville Dalton:

We know that money alone won't move a man to work. You've got to have good supervision and the will to work. We can't measure a man's illness or the pain of his hangover. We don't have a psychologist to study the workers and chart each man's periodic grouch. We know that all the workers have a low feeling and a high feeling. But that's the variable that we haven't attempted to measure. If we would consider it, we could probably say that in the long run his highs would cancel out his lows. For us to measure such things, we would need a corps of specialists—psychologists, physiologists, and what not running around out in the shops. You know how long the old boy up in the front office would stand for that stuff, and if he did you can imagine how you'd palm that off on the stooges from Big Town when they came snooping around.

The engineer begins by rejecting economic man but ends by embracing him. He recognizes that money is not all-important and points to certain other factors that may operate on the worker. But then he immediately dismisses these other factors by assuming that they either cancel each other out or cannot be measured anyway. Finally comes a practical objection: even if these other factors could be measured, the task would require such a corps of specialists that top management would never be willing to make the effort.

This may be a fairly representative reaction. It also fits in with one theory concerning the growth of scientific knowledge. James B. Conant[6] has argued that in the natural sciences a theory is not

[6] *On Understanding Science* (New York: Mentor Books), p. 48.

abandoned as soon as it is found to be inadequate in explaining the phenomena in question. The old theory hangs around and to a considerable extent shapes man's thinking until there evolves a new theory which makes a more adequate explanation of the phenomena. Until this reformulation takes place, men fall back upon the old theory even when they explicitly recognize its inadequacy.

This general statement may apply to men of action as well as to men of science. Even the practical businessman who likes to say that he is not burdened down by theory operates on certain implicit assumptions about human behavior. You may point out to him that these assumptions are incorrect, and he may even admit that this is the case without in effect abandoning the assumption.

Therefore, we are not just burying a straw man. That man is still alive in spite of all the criticisms leveled against him. The economic man will be laid to rest only when we are able to build a new model socioeconomic man. That requires a new theoretical statement regarding the motivation of man in the industrial production process.

Before we can make that theoretical statement we shall examine a number of cases that illustrate various aspects of the incentive problem. The general statements we make are based upon cases— cases that have been intimately studied by researchers who were holding down regular jobs in the plants or who were interviewing and observing the men in action. The material here will be familiar to many people, but we shall seek to present it in terms of a pattern that will make both worker and manager behavior more readily understandable.

We shall begin by examining the worker in relation to his own group and in relation to management. We shall see him as he is introduced to the system and reacts to it and to the people who apply it.

We shall then go on to study intergroup relations, for the plant is made up of a number of groups which affect each other. Thus, in considering the impact of an incentive upon one particular group we cannot treat the group as if it were in isolation.

In the first two parts of this book we shall be dealing primarily with individual piece-rate systems. In the third part we shall turn to a consideration of the plant as a whole, and finally to some recent efforts to establish an incentive that pays off in terms of the performance of the total organization.

We shall seek to explain each case as we go along, but in the concluding chapters we shall attempt to pull these various theoretical comments together in order to make a systematic theoretical statement.

This will be no finished theory. Our statements will be tentative and we shall not be able to tie them together as well as we would wish. Nevertheless, we are convinced that there is a theoretical pattern emerging out of the many studies that have been made. If we are successful at least in stating the main outlines of this pattern, others can modify and further develop our schemes. We hope also that this will lead to new practical approaches that will be useful to union officers as well as to management people in resolving the many knotty problems they face in the administration of incentive systems.

# PART I

## THE WORKER AND HIS WORK GROUP

# 2

# The Worker Meets the System

How is the new worker introduced to the piecework system?
He receives an orientation from management and of course he receives more informally an orientation from fellow workers. Management makes an effort to explain the technical aspects of the system to him. Some systems are so complicated that it is difficult to explain to the worker how his pay is figured, but in any case it is assumed that management must give him some of this technical information.

The orientation, however, is not entirely technical. Management and fellow workers are concerned about how the new man will think and feel about this system. An indoctrination process accompanies the technical explanations. Here we see a new worker (Orvis Collins, a research man serving as a participant observer in the factory) being inducted into the factory way of life by an old and experienced worker. They are discussing the talk regularly given to new employees by Mr. Heinzer, the factory superintendent.

JOE: Well, I suppose you've been up to see Heinzer. Gosh! I remember when I went up to see him.

COLLINS: What did you talk about?

JOE: It was a hot August afternoon and we all sat around there in a big circle. Heinzer did the talking. He just went on and on about the company, and what a good place the company is to work at, and how democratic it is here, and how everybody can talk to anybody they please about any gripe, and how he wanted to hear about it if there was anything we didn't like. He just went on and on.

COLLINS: What else?

JOE: He told us about how the piecework system was set up so that nobody could hang on anybody else's shirttail. He said it was every man for himself. He said, "You've got your friends. Sure! But you're not going to give them anything unless they give you something in the bargain in return." He went on this way:

"Now say that you want to buy a suit and you have a friend who is in

11

the clothing business, you might go in and say, 'Look here, Joe, I'm looking for a suit and I want to pay about $25 for it. What have you got?' Joe shows you what he has in stock and you're pretty well satisfied with one and you say, 'I'll come in Monday with the money, Joe.' And you go out, but while you're walking down the street you see this other suit in the window. Just the same suit Joe offered you for $30, but this outfit only wants $25. All right, young man, which suit do you buy?"

Heinzer looked right at me, and I knew what he was getting at. So I thought for a minute and I said, "I'll buy the $30 suit and lose the extra $5 if I can help a friend out."

Heinzer didn't know what to say. He took off his hat and wiped his forehead with his handkerchief. Then he said, "But that isn't good business, young man."

I said, "When it comes to buying a suit from a friend or from some other fellow, I'll buy from a friend, and I don't care about business." (We knew we were both talking about piecework.)

Heinzer thought for a long time and then he said, "But that's not the way the world is run. Now what would you do if you were walking down the street with your wife and met another friend, and this fellow was wearing the identical suit with the one you had on and your wife was with you and his wife was with him, and your wife said to this fellow, 'Why, that's just like Joe's suit, how much did you pay for it?' And the fellow said, 'I paid $25 for it at such and such a store and bought my wife a new hat with the five dollars I saved by not trading at our mutual friend's store.' (He had fancy names for all these people worked out and everything and you could tell that he had been working up this story for a long time but I'll bet this is the first time he had to use it this way.)

I said to Heinzer, "Whoa, just a minute! My wife wouldn't say such a thing. My wife isn't selfish. She would want me to do the right thing by my friend." That ended Heinzer's talk.

He just said, "I guess that'll be all for today, boys." As we walked out, he said to me, "That's all right, son. I like a man who can give a straight answer." Like hell he does.[1]

What is going on here? This is obviously not a cold factual statement regarding the mechanics of the incentive system. The Heinzer talk is really a statement on ethics. He is not talking simply about the world as it is but about the world as it ought to be.

Although the superintendent does not realize it, he is expressing a view of life that Max Weber, the German sociologist, has called the Protestant ethic.[2] According to this view of the world, man not

---

[1] Orvis Collins, Melville Dalton, and Donald Roy, "Restriction of Output and Social Cleavage in Industry," *Applied Anthropology*, Vol. V, No. 3.

[2] See *The Protestant Ethic and the Spirit of Capitalism*, translated by Talcott Parsons (New York: Charles Scribner's Sons, 1930).

only *is* an isolated competitive individual; he also *should* be thus individualistically oriented. He *should* want to work hard and get ahead. He *should* want to make money. Furthermore, money should not be viewed simply as a means to some other end, such as the enjoyment of life. The acquisition of money is believed in almost as an end in itself. Making money is simply a good thing and people should be encouraged to do it.

The worker in this dialogue takes a different ethical view of the world. He would like to make money, to be sure, but he also recognizes other important values. He looks upon himself as part of a group. He feels certain obligations to friends. He is unable to act the part of the acquisitive individualist that management seems to be thrusting upon him.

This contrast is, of course, too neat. We do not claim that one instance illustrates typical management and worker views. We find some workers who are highly acquisitive and individualistic. (We will meet some of them later.) We also find many management people who recognize and are willing to cultivate and deal with group ties among workers. Other management people, who seem to be urging upon workers an extreme individualism, do not practice that same individualism in their dealings with fellow management people.

However, even if the contrast is too extreme, it serves to set the problem for us. The piece-rate system is geared to an acquisitive, competitive, individualistic worker. The workers have these characteristics in varying degrees but in the factory they do not work in isolation from each other. Most individuals fit into some group that has real meaning for them and real influence upon their behavior. We face, then, the problem of reconciling a system designed for isolated individuals to a situation where men live and work in groups.

# 3

# Setting the Rates

The rate-setting process is crucial to the operation of any incentive program. If rates are set too tight or too loose, then we run into the difficulties to be described in the next chapter. If rates could be set "right," then management would get its production with a minimum of conflict.

How, then, does the time-study man go about setting rates that will be right?

The textbooks and monographs on time study present detailed instructions and advice on the technical side of the measuring and rate-setting process. They discuss which sorts of operators should be selected for measurement, how many observations should be made, what to do with the occasional very slow or very fast time, and so on. On the technical side, the experts present highly conflicting approaches to the problem.[1] But even if we could imagine all these technical issues being resolved, the time-study man would still face serious problems in the relations between himself and the men whose work he is measuring.

As Burleigh Gardner has pointed out, workers in most factories look upon the time-study man as an enemy. His presence in the department is to be feared. It is assumed that his objectives and those of the workers are in conflict, so they must make it difficult for him to do his job. This requires of workers a high degree of ingenuity and even of dramatic skill.

Gardner illustrates with this example:

In one case, a group, who worked together in assembling a complicated and large sized steel framework, had worked out a system to be used only when the rate setter was present. They found that by tightening certain bolts first, the frame would be slightly sprung and all the other bolts would

[1] See Solomon Barkin, "Diversity of Time Study Practice," *Industrial and Labor Relations Review*, Vol. VII, No. 4 (July 1954), pp. 537-549.

bind and be very difficult to tighten. When the rate setter was not present, they followed a different sequence and the work went much faster.[2]

The following examples were taken from the work diary of Donald Roy, who spent eleven months as a drill press operator in a steel fabricating plant, where he had a base rate of 85 cents per hour. Here we see an experienced worker, Starkey, advising Tennessee, a relatively inexperienced man, in the ways of coping with the time-study man.

In the first case the indoctrination deals with the difficult art of going slow under the watchful eye of the rate setter. Starkey begins in this way:

"If you expect to get any kind of a price, you got to outwit that son-of-a-bitch! You got to use your noodle while you're working, and think your work out ahead as you go along! You got to add in movements you know you ain't going to make when you're running the job! Remember, if you don't screw them, they're going to screw you! . . . Every movement counts!"

"Another thing," said Starkey, "You were running that job too damn fast before they timed you on it! I was watching you yesterday. If you don't run a job slow before you get timed, you won't get a good price. They'll look at the record of what you do before they come around and compare it with the timing speed. Those time-study men are sharp!"

"I wasn't going very fast yesterday," exclaimed Tennessee. "Hell, I was going as slow as I could without wearing myself out slowing down."

"Well, maybe it just looked fast, because you were going so steady at it," said Starkey.

"I don't see how I could of run it any slower," said Tennessee, "I stood there like I was practically paralyzed!"

"Remember those bastards are paid to screw you," said Starkey. "And that's all they got to think about. They'll stay up half the night figuring out how to beat you out of a dime. They figure you're going to try to fool them, so they make allowances for that. They set the prices low enough to allow for what you do."

"Well, then, what the hell chance have I got?" asked Tennessee.

"It's up to you to figure out how to fool them more than they allow for," said Starkey.

"The trouble with me is I get nervous with that guy standing in back of me, and I can't think," said Tennessee.

"You just haven't had enough experience yet," said Starkey. "Wait until you have been here a couple of years and you'll do your best thinking when those guys are standing behind you."

[2] *Human Relations in Industry*, (Riehard D. Irwin Inc. Illinois: 1945), pp. 164-165.

Now Starkey provides further instruction in the art of getting a slow timing for a fast job. He explains the possible adjustments of speeds and feeds on his machine.

"I was timed once on some levers like the ones you're running. I got a price of $4 a hundred, and I could make about $2 an hour! But I didn't run them the way they were timed. When the time-study man came around, I set the speed at 180. I knew damn well he would ask me to push it up, so I started low enough. He finally pushed me up to 445, and I ran the job later at 610. If I'd started out at 445, they'd have timed it at 610. Then I got him on the reaming, too. I ran the reamer for him at 130 speed and .025 feed. He asked me if I couldn't run the reamer any faster than that, and I told him I had to run the reamer slow to keep the hole size. I showed him two pieces with oversize holes that the day man ran. I picked them out for the occasion! But later on I ran the reamer at 610 speed and .018 feed, same as the drill. So I didn't have to change gears—And then there was a burring operation on the job too. For the time-study man I burred each piece after I drilled and reamed, and I ran the burring tool by automatic feed. But afterwards, I let the burring go till I drilled 25 pieces or so; and I just touched them up a little by holding them under the burring tool.—Hell, I used to make out in five hours, easy, on that job."

Now Starkey draws the conclusion from these observations:

"Always keep in mind the fact that you can't make money if you run the job the way it's timed. They time jobs just to give you your base rate if you kill yourself trying to make it, no more. You've got to get the job timed below the speeds and feeds you can use later. Whenever a piece is timed at maximum speeds and feeds, there's no hope! You have as much chance as a snowball in hell!"

"Yeah, but what if they make you speed it up to maximum speed? What are you going to do then?" asked Tennessee.

"You got to be tough with them!" said Starkey. "Remember those guys don't know their ass from a hole in the ground as far as these machines are concerned. When they tell me to speed up to about what I figure I can run the job, I start to take my apron off, and tell them, 'All right, if you think it can be run that fast, you run it!' They usually come around."

Now Starkey provides a lesson in the advanced course as he describes how to make a machine break down when the time-study man is pressing you for more speed. Here he describes Ray Ward, one of the real heroes of the department, a man so smart that the time-study people finally refused to match wits with him.

"Ray knew his drills," said Starkey. "He'd burn up a drill every four or five pieces when they were timing him, and say the speed was too high for the tough stuff he was running. Tough stuff, my ass! They'd lower the speed and feed to where he wasn't burning up the drills, then afterwards he'd speed up and cut through that tough stuff like cheese."

"What I want to know," said Tennessee, "is how in hell could Ward burn up the drills like that? You can't just burn up a drill when you feel like it."

"It's in the way you grind the drill," said Starkey. "Roy used to grind his own drills, and he'd touch them up before they timed him. The wrong kind of a grind will burn up a drill at a lower speed than the drill can take if it's ground right for the job."

"Oh," said Tennessee.

"There are all sorts of ways to skin a cat," said Starkey, "and Ray knew 'em all. He could start with the head or the tail or any one of four feet. Ray knew all the tricks! I used to have to laugh at the way he got up a sweat when they were timing him. He'd jump around the machine like a monkey on a string, with the sweat just pouring off him! His shirt used to get soaking wet, and he'd have to wring it out afterwards! And when they finished timing him, he'd stagger away from the machine a little, like he'd given everything he had in him. But of course it got to a point where he wasn't fooling anybody any more, except maybe some new time-study man that came along, and the time-study department would have him tipped off about Ray. I never did see Ray sweat a drop when he was actually running a job; he was always about 40 pounds overweight, the laziest guy I ever did see. He'd move a box up to the machine and putter around all day like he was making mud pies or something."

In addition to these methods described by Starkey, there are, of course, other short cuts that the workers devise for use after the time-study man leaves. In many of these departments workers have hidden an arsenal of secret weapons—jigs and fixtures—that can be used to do the job faster than the rate at which it was timed. These devices are a great tribute to the ingenuity of the American work-man. They evidence a knowledge of machine operation that could be exceedingly valuable to management, but the knowledge is carefully hidden so that it may be used in the battle against the time-study man.

## THE GUESSING GAME

What does such a situation mean for the functions of the time-study man? As we see him here, he is not operating as a technician. Instead, he is engaged in a guessing game with the workers that he is timing. He is trying to guess how much the workers are fooling him and to compensate for this estimate in the rate he proposes to management.

The time-study man is supposed to be setting a rate on the exact methods to be used in doing the job. He has learned that the men are trying to fool him, so he estimates that they are not working at 100 per cent efficiency and sets his rate accordingly. The workers then find that they cannot "make out" on the job if they do it according to the methods on which they were timed, so they change the methods.

In this situation we can have cases where the time-study man apparently sets a good rate, where actually the rate turns out to be good because the men are not doing the job as they were when it was timed. So, even when he is right, the time-study man may be right for the wrong reason.

But if he is too high or too low in his estimates, the time-study man is in a good deal more trouble. If he sets the rate too loose, he gets no complaints from workers. They make their bonus but they produce only up to a certain point and it becomes evident to everybody familiar with the department that the men are having a lot of time to waste. Labor costs then are much higher than management thinks they should be, and the time-study man looks bad in management's eyes.

On the other hand, if the time-study man guesses that he is being fooled more than is actually the case he sets the rate too tight, and that is no solution either. With rates that are too tight, management does not get production and is also harassed by complaints from workers and by union grievances in unionized situations.

What can management do with a rate that is too tight? It can order the time-study man to restudy the job to see whether possibly his original estimate might have been a mistake. But is this restudy to be an operation in which the time-study man brings to bear the knowledge and skills of his technical training? Or is he to juggle his figures in an attempt to come out at a point which will be reasonably satisfactory to both workers and management. Perhaps the latter course leads to less trouble in the department, but the rate setter who takes it throws into question the value of the training he has had.

For years now industrial engineers have been trying to gain professional standing for their occupation. F. W. Taylor, the pioneer of the field, gave this discipline the instructive title "scientific management." It was then under the banner of science that these new techniques, including time study, were to gain acceptance in industry. As Taylor saw it, scientific management would eliminate the necessity for collective bargaining, since rates would be set upon scientific principles. If now the time-study man gets into bargaining and compromising in order to get a rate settled he leaves his technical training far behind him—but where else is he to go?

Readers may have been impressed by the bitterness of the feeling between workers and time-study men reflected in the examples given by Donald Roy. They may be inclined to ask whether such situations are typical of American factories. That is an impossible question to answer in terms of the research so far done. Our impressions are that the situation observed by Roy had in it a good deal more conflict than we would find in the average factory. On the other hand, let us not discard the examples on these grounds. In factory after factory we have seen the same conflicts. Even if the conflict is less severe, we observe the same sorts of tactical maneuvers on the part of workers or time-study men. The examples in the Roy cases simply serve to highlight the rate-setting problem as it appears quite generally in American industry.

# 4

# Quota Restriction and Goldbricking

Restriction of output is not a simple, uniform phenomenon. It occurs, with different sorts of behavior, on different types of jobs.

To see the pattern in restriction, let us examine the experience of Donald Roy on the drill line. Here we can confine ourselves to the last six months of his eleven-month employment period, for this represents a time when he was sufficiently skilled to make bonus on approximately two jobs out of every three (65.6 per cent). And, of course, he had the skill to go well beyond the quota if he had cared to do so.

In this situation, anything beyond the guaranteed day rate of 85 cents per hour represents making bonus. Roy worked on a wide variety of jobs, and each one had its own rate set by time study. Throughout the period he kept a record of his earnings on each job run.

If we assume that the operator is working with uniform effort on jobs with rates varying randomly from loose to tight, then we would expect a distribution of earnings in something like a normal, bell-shaped curve. That is, we would find that the operator who earned over the day rate two-thirds of the time would have the peak number of his jobs perhaps in the earnings interval $1.05-$1.14, with steadily diminishing numbers of jobs below and above that, going as low as 55 cents and as high as $1.54.

Instead, we find a radically different distribution as illustrated in Figure I. As the graph indicates, we have here two distributions of jobs. Below the "make out" line, the distribution is irregular, but the peak of 9.1 per cent of jobs run falls in the 45-54 cent interval. It is noteworthy here that only 1.1 per cent of the jobs fall in the 75-84 cent interval where the operator had almost "made out."

On the "make out" side of the graph, we find less than two per cent of the jobs falling into each of the first three earnings intervals.

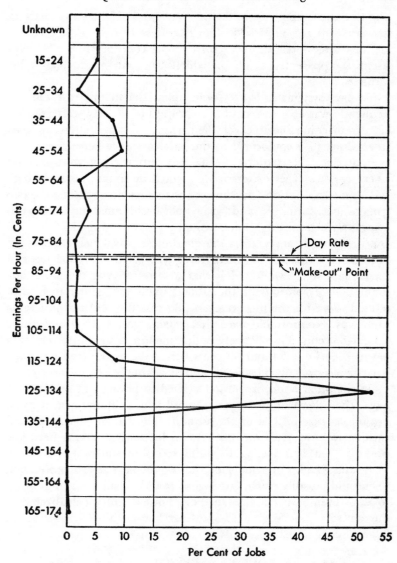

Fig. I. A Pattern of Piece Work Earnings

The line then jumps up to 8.4 per cent for $1.15-1.24 and soars to 52.3 per cent for $1.25-1.34. The line then dips back to zero for the next three intervals and records .2 per cent for $1.65-1.74—representing apparently a job on which Roy had miscalculated his earnings.

We have systematic figures only upon Roy in this case, but he frequently was able to record the earnings of the day shift man on his own machine and to check the earnings of other fellow workers. In all cases, they conformed to the pattern we see here.

What does this pattern mean? Roy interprets it in this way: There are two types of restriction, which he terms "goldbricking" and "quota restriction." In the eyes of the operators there were two types of jobs: "stinkers" and "gravy jobs," with anything in between being only a transitory phenomenon.

With 85 cents an hour as the guaranteed day wage, earnings of $1 an hour seemed to be the dividing line between a good job and a poor job. If the workers felt that $1 an hour was the most they could possibly earn with the utmost skill and effort, then they refused to try for the incentive. In that case they did not just relax to an easy, comfortable pace that might have yielded something close to 85 cents. They actively put on the brakes to hold production down to between 20 and 50 cents below the guaranteed day rate. That behavior Roy classifies as "goldbricking."

On the other hand, if the job seemed to promise $1 and a little more, then the operators went to work with skill and ingenuity to exploit its possibilities to the utmost. Thus a job that promised earnings of, say, $1.04 did not remain for long at that figure. The workers soon found ways to build it up to somewhere between $1.15 and $1.29. On some jobs this would be the top production they could possibly reach. Other jobs would promise earnings of up to $2 or even $3 per hour. On these, however, they held back production so as not to go over $1.29 per hour. This Roy classifies as "quota restriction."

## QUOTA RESTRICTION

When the operator is new on the job he may not receive explicit instructions from fellow workers as to how much he is to make. To be sure, he hears of the dangers of rate cutting and the evil practices of the time-study men as he joins in the conversation with other workers. But at first he may be so lacking in skill that there is no chance of his exceeding the quota.

When the new man gains skill, so that it looks as though it will soon be possible for him to go beyond the quota, he then receives more specific and detailed instructions. Roy reports the situation in this way:

From my first to my last day at the plant I was subject to warnings and predictions concerning price cuts. Pressure was the heaviest from Joe Mucha, day man on my machine, who shared my job repertoire and kept a close eye on my production. On November 14, the day after my first attained quota, Joe Mucha advised:

"Don't let it go over $1.25 an hour, or the time-study man will be right down here! And they don't waste time, either! They watch the records like a hawk! I got ahead, so I took it easy for a couple of hours."

Joe told me that I had made $10.01 yesterday and warned me not to go over $1.25 an hour. He told me to figure the setups and the time on each operation very carefully so that I would not total over $10.25 in any one day.

Jack Starkey defined the quota carefully but forcefully when I turned in $10.50 for one day, or $1.31 an hour.

Jack Starkey spoke to me after Joe left. "What's the matter? Are you trying to upset the applecart?"

Jack explained in a friendly manner that $10.50 was too much to turn in, even on an old job. "The turret-lathe men can turn in $1.35," said Jack, "but their rate is 90 cents, and ours 85 cents."

Jack warned me that the Methods Department could lower their prices on any job, old or new, by changing the fixture slightly or changing the size of the drill. According to Jack, a couple of operators (first and second shift on the same drill) got to competing with each other to see how much they could turn in. They got up to $1.65 an hour, and the price was cut in half. And from then on they had to run that job themselves, as none of the other operators would accept the job.

According to Jack, it would be all right for us to turn in $1.28 or $1.29 an hour, when it figured out that way, but it was not all right to turn in $1.30 an hour.

Well, now I know where the maximum is—$1.29 an hour.

In this situation Roy did not observe any "rate busters," workers who refused to abide by the informally established ceiling. How they would have been dealt with is indicated in the story about the men who competed with each other until they were making $1.65 an hour. When the job was reengineered and the price cut, the other men refused to work on it, thus forcing the former competitors to stay with the "stinker." It is also clear from the story that such behavior was distinctly frowned upon and men who violated the group's standards would at least be ostracized from the group if not more severely punished.

### GOLDBRICKING

Goldbricking behavior was equally well organized. In effect the workers were bargaining with management over the rate.

Roy gives this report based on his work diary:

The hinge-base fight is an example of deliberate restriction on a major job that was regarded as poorly priced. This fight went on for at least nine months at the machine operated by Jack Starkey. During this period three men worked second shift on Jack's machine in the following sequence: Ed Sokolsky, Dooley, and Al McCann.

*December 19.* Ed Sokolsky and Jack Starkey have not been doing well. Ed cusses intermittently and leaves his machine for long periods of time. The foremen find the machine idle, and Steve bellows about it. Ed calls the piece he is working on a "stinker." I know it is, because Ed is free with his advertising of the "gravy" he finds.

Ed seems to have constant trouble with his jig, a revolving piece attached to the side of the table. Two disks seem to stick together, and Ed is constantly (every day or so) using the crane to dismantle the jig (a very heavy one). He sands the disks and oils them, taking several hours for the cleaning operation. Steve saw the dismantled jig again tonight and bellowed, "Again?" Steve does not like it.

Paul, the setup man, gets concerned, too, when he finds the jig torn down and Ed away somewhere. He says, "Where the hell's Ed?" in a provoked manner.

*February 10.* I noticed that Ed was poking along and asked him if he had a good job. He shook his head, saying that he was making but 46 cents an hour, turning out 2 pieces an hour that paid 23 cents each.

*February 26.* Jack Starkey told me tonight that, although his job on the hinge bases was retimed, there was no raise in price. The price is still 23 cents.

I said, "All you've got to turn out is 5 an hour to make $1.15."

"I'd just like to see anybody turn out 5 of these an hour," said Jack, "with a tolerance of 0.0005!"

Later, Ed Sokolsky said that he and Jack were turning out about 24 pieces in a 10-hour period (2.4 an hour), that the job had been retimed several times, but no raise in price had been given.

Ed and Jack asked for a price of 38 cents. Ed said that they could turn out 3 an hour, but, until they got a decent price, they were turning out 2 an hour.

Toward the end of the evening I noticed that Ed's machine was idle, and Ed was sitting on a box, doing nothing.

"What's the matter, did they stop the job on you?" I asked.

"I stopped it," said Ed. "I don't feel like running it."

*March 20.* Dooley worked on the hinge bases again tonight. He admitted that he could barely make out on the job, but "Why bust my ass for day rate? We're doing 3 an hour or less until we get a better price!"

This 3-an-hour-or-less business has been going on several months. The price is 23 cents; so Dooley and Jack turn in 69 cents an hour (or less).

*May 15.* McCann said that Starkey was arguing all day over the price of the hinge bases. The methods men maintain that they can't raise the price "because the jacks that the parts go on sell for $14 apiece." They plan to retool the job and lower the price. According to McCann, Jack told them that if he didn't get a decent price he was going to make out on the job but scrap every one of the pieces.

"Jack fights it out with them," said McCann. "He'll stay right with the machine and argue. I get disgusted and walk away.

"Jack turned out 28 today," McCann went on. "That's too many, nearly 3 an hour. He'll have to watch himself if he expects to get a raise in price."

Starkey was running the hinge bases again tonight. I remarked, "I see you're in the gravy again."

His reply was, "Yeah! 69 cents an hour!"

McCann did not seem to enjoy the hinge bases either. He looked bored, tired, and disgusted all evening. His ten hours is a long stretch at day work. He cannot make out early and rest after eleven o'clock (for four hours), but has to keep on the machine until three.

*August 14.* Al McCann was working on the hinge bases tonight, one of the jobs that he and Jack are protesting as to price. Gil (the foreman) sat and stood behind Al for at least an hour, and I could see that Al did not like it. He worked steadily, but with deliberate slowness, and did not look at Gil or speak to him. Al and Jack have agreed to restrict production on the hinge bases until they get a better price, and Gil was probably there to see what Al could really do. I think that Al and Jack could make out on the job, but not at $1.25 an hour, and they cut production to less than 80 cents an hour.

*August 16.* Al told me that they had won a price raise on the hinge bases, from 23 to 28 cents, and another raise to 31 cents.

"But it's still not high enough. As it is now we can make exactly 93 cents an hour. We're trying to get 35 cents. We can turn out 1 in exactly 16 minutes. That's not 4 an hour. We've been giving them 3 an hour."

At the 31-cent price and at the output rate of 3 pieces per hour the men were turning in 93 cents per hour or $7.44 per 8-hour day. Since the special base rate as experienced operators on a machine handling heavy fixtures was $1.10 per hour, they were earning 17 cents an hour less than they were paid.

Roy reports the end of the hinge-base fight in these words from his diary:

Al said tonight that he was making out on the hinge bases, that he got disgusted Friday, speeded up the tools, and turned in 31 pieces for earnings of $9.60 (3⅞ pieces per hour, or $1.20 per hour earnings).

"It was easy, just as easy as the frames. Now I'm kicking myself all over for not doing it before. All I did was to change the speed from 95 to 130. I was sick of stalling around all evening, and I got mad and decided to make out and let the tools burn up. But they made it all right, for 8 hours. What's the use of turning in 93 cents an hour when you can turn in $1.25 just as easy? They'd never raise a price you could make 93 cents on anyhow. Now maybe they'll cut it back."

Tonight Al made out easily in 6 hours, though he stretched the last few pieces to carry him until 10:30.

We can make two observations on the basis of this case. We see, in the first place, the war of conflicting pressures regarding the piece-rate price. Convinced that the piece rate is too low, the workers stand together to hold down production to hurt management and thus force an increase in the price. After many months the pressure is eventually successful in raising the price from 23 up to 31 cents apiece. Even this does not seem to be enough to the men, but now the price has risen to a point where they realize that if they really work at it they can make more than their base rate. How long, then, should they go on holding back production and fighting for a still better price? They now have to weigh the chances of getting a further adjustment from management against the losses that they are suffering in their pay envelope. The point is finally reached where some individual tires of the struggle over rates and decides to see what he can do on the job. If he is successful in making quota earnings or near quota earnings, then the fight is over and the new rate has in effect been accepted.

It is also instructive to note that the private estimates of the operators as to the production they could achieve were on the conservative side. When they were holding back production they did not really believe it possible to turn out a piece in less than 16 minutes. When they once decided that there was no further point in holding back, when they went ahead and bent all their efforts toward production, they found that they could make quota earnings—and not in eight hours but in six. Apparently men are not good estimators as to what they can do on a machine when the estimates are made at a time when they are not really trying for production.

In this situation we see the conflict fought out directly with management by the workers themselves. In other situations we might find the union prominently involved in the struggle, pressing grievances against piece rates. In this situation, while the men were represented by a union, they had no faith in it and preferred to handle their problems themselves. But even in cases where union stewards and officers are active in the struggle against management's administration of the incentive program, it is evident that the union has not created the conflict. The union is simply one important channel through which the conflict is expressed.

# 5

# Gains and Losses of Piecework

How effective is the piecework incentive? To measure its effectiveness in productivity terms we would have to compare production under piecework with production in the same situation without piecework. (Also we should throw against the piecework side of the scale all the costs of administering the system, which sometimes come to substantial amounts even when only direct costs are considered.) While we cannot make any firm comparisons between a real and a hypothetical situation, our examination of Roy's earning record suggests certain tentative conclusions regarding piecework as an incentive.

It is only in a fraction of the jobs—perhaps one-third of those assigned—that the piecework provides an incentive to tap the full productive capacities of workers. In this case the incentive really works only on those jobs that seem to promise earnings slightly over 15 cents beyond the day rate. On jobs that promise less, the incentive becomes actually a *de*centive, with the workers holding back *below* an easy, comfortable pace. On jobs that promise substantially more, the promise is never exploited beyond the quota of $1.29.

Would management be satisfied with a machine that functioned at about 33 per cent efficiency?

Of course, we must not generalize for all of American industry from Roy's drill line. A plant which has a large number of separate rates, with a variety of jobs and rates being offered to the same workers, can expect more rate problems than a plant where the rates are fewer and the production runs longer, so that more time is available for working out mutually acceptable rates. Furthermore, here the bitterness of the conflict between workers and management made effective action upon rate problems impossible. In

28

Chapter 11 we shall examine a case in which piece-rate problems were settled reasonably amicably.

However, let us not carry our reservations to the point of ruling out the case altogether. The pattern of production that Roy reports is one that seems to conform very well with our observations in a number of other plants, although nowhere do we have the detailed production and earnings data that Roy presents. The quota restriction phenomenon has been noted again and again, being perhaps best documented in the classic Western Electric study, *Management and the Worker*, by Roethlisberger and Dickson.[1] Nor does gold-bricking seem to be unique to the drill line. We often find workers holding back on tight rates in an effort to pressure management into making changes. We are left then with a fraction of the jobs on which the incentive works with full efficiency. In Roy's case that fraction seemed to be about 33 per cent. In other cases it will be perhaps 50 per cent, but, whether 33 or 50, there remains a large gap between physical possibilities and actual achievement.

The theoretical economic losses to workers are also substantial. On every "quota" job, Roy worked for a short time full speed to see how much he could make if he really went after the incentive. He then compared that potential figure with the actual quota earnings to establish a figure of "hours loafed per quota day." Perhaps the potential figure is high, since Roy might not have been able to maintain this top speed consistently. On the other hand, had he tried consistently to exploit all the possibilities in the job he might well have discovered short cuts that led to still higher earnings. In any case, the figure is only an estimate, but it is large enough to be impressive.

If we take the last six months of Roy's experience on the job, and count earnings about $1.15 as representing quota earnings, we find that Roy made the quota about 61 per cent of the time. If we now confine our attention to this 61 per cent of jobs, we find that Roy made the quota by actually working 6.61 hours out of 8. He took 1.39 hours for loafing out of each 8-hour day. But even in this six-month period, as his skill increases, we find him able to work less and less. The March figure of "hours loafed per quota day" is .88, while the August figure is 2.06. By the end of the

[1] Cambridge: Harvard University Press, 1939.

period, then, Roy is earning his quota by working less than 3 hours out of every 4. If we could imagine the worker working full time at the same rate of speed, he would be earning $1.68 per hour instead of around $1.25. If we throw the 39 per cent of hours worked when he only received his base pay of 85 cents together with the 61 per cent of hours on which he made quota earnings, we get an actual earnings figure of about $1.09 per hour. If we turn the 61 per cent of quota hours into potential earnings of $1.68 per hour, we have an average earnings figure of about $1.36 per hour. Twenty-five cents an hour represents the difference between "what was" and our imaginary "what might have been."

This 25 cents an hour does not represent a dead loss. In a sense, we can say that workers are trading that quarter for certain other values. Let us see what these values are.

Our discussion of the struggle between workers and time-study men seems to paint a completely negative picture of factory life under the incentive—except for the money that is offered. Can we, indeed, assume that piecework offers absolutely nothing to workers except the possibility of greater earnings? If this were so, then life in the factory would be a punishing and never-ending sacrifice endured solely for the purpose of having money to spend outside. Even if we cannot truly picture the factory as a recreational club, we must recognize that this picture of unrelieved frustration is one-sided.

As he has brought us some of the grimmer aspects of life under the incentive, Donald Roy has also discovered some of the rewards that lie hidden in the system. He found these rewards even in a factory department where worker-management conflict was present in extreme form.

In his eleven months on the drill line, Roy was first impressed with worker preoccupation over the economics of the incentive system. Contrary to what he had read in the literature of human relations research, he found workers apparently constantly thinking about and talking about money. He was first prepared to accept the notion that money was their main and overwhelming concern until he began noticing instances where the same men who talked so much of money displayed an apparent disregard for their earnings. He found men taking days off from work especially when daywork jobs were scheduled but also sometimes when good piecework jobs were to be done. He found men sometimes leaving work early by an hour or as much as half a day for personal reasons that did not appear really pressing. He found them sometimes even laying off work to avoid doing a piecework job that they disliked even though it would yield quota earnings.

All this did not prove that money was unimportant, but it suggested that Roy look for other satisfactions involved in factory life. He describes this search in the following way.

### Roy's Account

In the beginning the writer [Roy] was slightly contemptuous of the shop's incentive system, considering it neither mature in its appeal as a motivational device nor honest in its claims to be a method of elevating the wage level of industrial workers. Though his sympathies were with the operators, and he observed their codes and procedures to the best of his ability, either through sympathy or to avoid their censure, he failed to understand their keen interest in achieving quota production and their intense concern over piecework prices. He laid his own indifference to quota attainment, or "making out," to the fact that machine operation was not his permanent work, not knowing at the time that the others, for the most part, did not consider it their permanent work either.

The writer's attitude changed from mere indifference to the piecework incentive to a determination not to be forced to respond, when failure to get a price increase on one of the lowest paying operations of his job repertoire convinced him that the company was unfair. Light scorn for the incentive system turned to bitterness.

Several months later, however, after fellow operator McCann had instructed him in the "angles on making out," the writer was finding values in the piecework system other than economic ones. He struggled to attain quota "for the hell of it," because it was a "little game" and "keeps me from being bored." He felt that he was the only one motivated by such considerations, thinking that the other operators were being induced to work for higher pay in the manner of the horse led to pull the wagon by a carrot dangling in front of his nose.

In addition to escaping the monotony of factory labor by "playing a game," the writer found that there were physiological advantages in speeding up. He found that fast rhythmical work seemed less fatiguing, although the reduction in fatigue may have been closely related to the reduction of boredom. He discovered further that the same job that had bored and wearied him as a "time study," or nonpiecework operation now interested him and gave him exhilaration on piecework.

The writer made occasional diary comments on such values of piecework for the remainder of his stay in the shop. Recorded comparisons between piecework and daywork experience keep telling the same story:

Dooley watched me set up for the frames, and remarked, "You can make out on that if you want to break your neck."

This "breaking my neck" was a welcome relief to the monotony of time study on the replacers. I was so sleepy I could hardly keep awake before I started on the frames, but at eleven o'clock I felt bright and wide awake. This set me to thinking in a new light about the value of the piecework system.

My legs were very tired tonight. Slow jobs like this one seem to wear me out far more than the fast ones. I mentioned this to Johnny.

He said, "That's the way with me. I've got to keep my mind occupied or I get bored, and it wears me out. I can't stand around either."

"When I am going hell bent for election on a good piecework job, the evening passes very swiftly and I do not realize that I am tired until it is all over. On these daywork jobs I get so bored I could stand in the aisle and yell; and my knees feel tired from standing in one spot so long."

During the course of his employment in the shop the writer discovered that other operators felt the same way, in fundamental respects, about piecework. Mike Koszyk, radial drill man, was one who found that time sped along on piecework and dragged on daywork.

Mike compared daywork with piecework the other day.

"On piecework I hear that time clock behind me go 'clock 'click, 'clicking off the minutes. But on daywork I know it's no use looking around to see what time it is, because the hands won't have moved any."

Al McCann was another who brightened up on good piecework operations.

McCann was given an order of the car replacers tonight. When he received the order, he was disgusted, saying, "Guess I'll be staying home tomorrow."

But after working an hour on the replacers McCann suddenly noted, "I'm making money!" He had done 13 an hour at 10 cents apiece. Immediately he brightened up and went at his work with vigor.

McCann expressed his feelings toward his work in terms of making money. However, he once passed up an opportunity to gain three days' pay during an inventory shutdown. Also, he insisted on other occasions that he didn't "care about money."

Could the process of striving for and achieving such a goal as quota production carry its own reward? Could continual reference to making money represent merely the use of symbols of accomplishment deeply rooted in our economic ideology? Has such symbolization so permeated shop communication that machine operators find it difficult to explain in other terminology their true feelings about quota attainment?

Perhaps we might find the key to piecework incentive in Dewey's distinction between "having an experience" and mere "experiencing things."[2] The difference between a quota-yielding piecework job and daywork, in operator experience, might be the difference between activity that purposefully utilizes resources and overcomes obstacles in moving toward an anticipated consummation and activity that constitutes mere happenings, with but temporal or mechanical connection between them—a succession of events beginning at no particular place and ending at no particular place. In other words, between experience characterized by intention, organization, and completion—a self-imposed and finished task, problem, or game—and experience that is aimless, unintegrated, and concluded with mere cessation of activity.

It would seem that the attainment of quota marked the successful completion of a task or solution to a problem in which the outcome was largely controllable by the operator, although chance factors were important determinants of results. Making quota called for the exercise of skill and stamina, and it offered opportunity for self-expression. The element of uncertainty of outcome provided by ever-present possibilities of bad luck made quota attainment an exciting game played against the clock on the wall, a game in which the elements of control provided by the application of knowl-

---

[2] John Dewey, *Art as Experience* (New York: Minton, Balch, and Company, 1934), pp. 35-57.

edge, ingenuity, and speed heightened interest and led to exhilarating feelings of accomplishment. Although operators constantly shared their piecework experience as a chief item of conversation, and always in terms of making money or not making money, they could, in reality, have been communicating game scores rather than financial successes or disappointments. It is doubtful if any quota-attaining operator ever believed that he had been making money in the sense of improving appreciably his financial status. Had anyone been able to communicate accurately such a conviction he would have been laughed out of the shop.

The make-out game broke the monotony of repetitive work and made the long day pass. Although on daywork the operator had only the pause at lunchtime to break up the meaningless flow of time, he had in his piecework game an hour-by-hour series of completions that served to mark his position in relation to the larger completion of the day's work. For the operator engaged in a good piecework job time moved in a rapid succession of intervals toward the final hour of quitting the plant.

But operator interest in quota piecework seemed to have its diminishing returns. McCann, for instance, expressed feelings of boredom on one job that was a never-failing source of premium pay; his claim was that he had performed this particular operation so much that he could do the work in his sleep. His experience suggests that making out on piecework could be a stimulating game only as long as the job represented a real challenge to the operator, only as long as the element of uncertainty was present in the activity's outcome.

If making out lost its value as a game when operator control over the job became so complete that winning degenerated into mere routine, it also lost such value if the element of uncertainty became too predominant over the element of control. That is, if bad luck became too frustrating to the application of skill, the job became nerve-racking. For instance, on one operation the work involved such a high rate of tool breakage at unpredictable intervals that quota attainment seemed to be more a matter of luck than of skill. The nervous strain suffered by the  writer and other radial-drill men who shared this operation made the job assignment a thoroughly unwelcome one.

Even in a setting of authoritarian administration and worker-management conflict, the make-out game induced job interest and productive effort. In fact, during the period of his greatest work effort and enjoyment of the employment of skill and energy, the writer's hostility toward his supervisors was on the increase and his antagonism toward the company was at least not decreasing.

It should not be surprising that effort on good piecework jobs could accompany hostility toward management even if making out did not provide the pleasure of playing a game, for quota attainment in its connections with intergroup and intragroup relations provided social rewards. For one thing, making out meant a reduction in the rate of interaction with supervisors. When an operator achieved his quota, or showed signs that he was in the process of doing so, he was let alone. Pressures from foremen and superintendents were applied only when performance fell short of day rate. Furthermore, as soon as an operator produced his quota his time was his own. Making out in six hours meant two hours of freedom —hours which he could, and usually did, spend in pleasant association with his fellows.

But reference to manipulation of the rate and direction of social interaction does not tell the whole story of the significance of make-out freedom in operator-supervisor relations. If he happened to be inclined to express his aggression toward his foreman, the made-out operator could use his freedom toward that end. Instead of shutting off communication, he could initiate action, for a change, by flaunting his freedom in the supervisor's face. The writer derived keen satisfaction during the latter months of his employment, the months of his peak skill, in conspicuous loafing in the presence of supervision after quota attainment. Since worker inactivity, even after the completion of a fair day's work, seemed to violate a traditional supervisory precept of keeping the appearance of being busy even if there is nothing to do, making out in four or five hours could be used as a way of getting even with foremen for the pressures they applied at times when quota was unattainable.

When operator relations with the despised time-study men are considered, the connection between quota attainment and intergroup conflict stands out quite clearly. In the conflict that characterized relations between machine operators and the Methods Department, making out was victory for the former. The greater the ease in making out, the less time it took to achieve quota, the greater the beating administered the men who set the piece rates.

Thus, a game could be played not only against time but also against personalized opponents. The operator watched the clock as he expended his skill and energy, but sometimes the otherwise guileless face of the timepiece on the wall took on the crafty features of the time-study man. At other times imagery of the opponent would shift to the scowling face of the foreman when the triumphant operator sat with folded arms in conspicuous idleness beside his completed work, waiting for a restive boss to say something. Of course, no such flaunting of success took place in the presence of time-study men or members of the administrative hierarchy above the status of shop superintendent. Since both job timers and top plant officials appeared mainly in daylight hours, making but sporadic appearances at night, only night shift operators dared to celebrate victory openly. The day men had to deny themselves such bold flourishes.

When operator response to piecework is examined for its significance in intragroup relations, it can be said that the make-out game was played before sympathetic and appreciative audiences. One satisfaction provided the operator by successful piecework activity lay in the approval of his fellows, in informal work group prestige. Any operator could gain recognition by making out on work that carried a piecework price that was difficult to beat or by cutting down appreciably the time required for making out on any job. Such achievement earned approbation from fellow workers whether freely, grudgingly, or perfunctorily given. The operator would be asked during the shift how he was doing, and at the end of the shift it was always "Did you make out?" If no one asked the question, the successful operator could always make an announcement.

On the other hand, failure to make out on jobs that had been established by the work group as quota operations meant loss of prestige, unless such failure could be explained by reference to factors outside the control of the operator or by insistence that the defection was deliberate. Such explanations were always offered. [End of Roy's account.][3]

[3] Taken from Donald Roy, "Work Satisfaction and Social Rewards in Quota Achievements," *American Sociological Review*, Vol. XVIII, No. 5 (Oct. 1953). Copyright 1953, American Sociological Society.

## CONCLUSIONS

Roy's account makes it clear that, while money is important, it is not the only reward in a piecework situation. We can identify at least three additional sources of reward:

1. *Playing the game.* Repetitive factory jobs may seem to have no inherent meaning to the worker. He may think of his work as simply an endless series of meaningless motions. Piecework when quota appears to be attainable provides meaning to the job in the form of a goal to shoot at. But note that this goal does not seem to be present in every piecework job. Roy finds the game going on only when the outcome is reasonably possible but not completely certain. When quota earnings seem clearly unattainable, the goal does not seem to be present for the worker and he abandons the game. On the other hand, if the outcome is completely predictable and certain, then the work again can become monotonous and meaningless. Finally, if quota achievement or failure of such achievement depends predominantly upon chance factors outside of the worker's control, then he experiences frustration instead of satisfaction.

2. *Escape from management pressure.* When the worker is earning over his base rate on piecework, he can get the supervisor to let him alone. This reduction of supervisory pressures seems an important source of satisfaction. But it is not only absence of pressure that is involved. The worker gains control over his own time and also gains an opportunity to express his aggression toward supervisors and time-study men by conspicuous loafing or at least by loafing as conspicuously as he dares.

3. *Escape from fatigue.* We also find that the worker who is making his quota on piecework generally experiences less fatigue than when he is working on daywork or holding back production on a job that does not offer quota attainment. On the face of it this seems to be a paradoxical conclusion: the worker works harder but is less tired. This observation, however, is well in line with recent research in industrial psychology. We now know that fatigue is by no means exclusively a physiological phenomenon. The fatigue experienced by a worker is a combination of physiological and psychological factors. We should therefore expect that the man

who is working along at a steady pace on a task that has a mean-
ingful goal for him will experience less fatigue than the same man
when he is working much more slowly on a task which simply
represents a meaningless repetition of motions.

This bears upon a management assumption noted in the first
chapter: that man is naturally a passive animal who would do
nothing if he were not stimulated toward activity through some
sort of reward. On the contrary, we find that man is naturally an
active animal who is happier when he is doing something than
when he is just standing around and doing nothing. This does not
mean, of course, that hard work just naturally has more appeal to
employees than light work. It does suggest that complete idleness
is not rewarding at all and that an unnaturally slow pace can be
fatiguing.

Even as we recognize these rewards available under piece rates,
we should not assume that they are present in every piecework job.
We have noted the conditions under which the worker can be playing a game on his piecework job and the conditions under which
no such game activity can go on. Similarly, there are jobs which
provide opportunities for escape from supervisory pressure and
others that do not. There are piecework jobs that provide relief
from fatigue; there are other jobs which do not promise quota
achievement, where the workers go to considerable and painful
effort to slow down to a wholly unnatural pace.

Nevertheless, some important rewards are offered to workers
under piecework even when the conditions appear highly unfavor-
able. Can the satisfactions involved in playing the piecework game
be preserved in our factories at the same time that the attendant
conflicts are reduced? Can we provide a goal for production which
will be accepted by workers as well as by management?

# 6

## Restricters and Rate Busters

We have now examined worker responses to an individual incentive system. Donald Roy's reports have presented vividly the life of the shop as it involves workers and the system.

This picture alone, however, might seem to suggest that all workers responded in the same way to management's incentives. This is not the case, of course. If we look for differences we find them, and we find that they are apparently not random differences but have a definite pattern.

Some people seem to work as if the incentive were not present at all. Some respond to the incentive and make considerable efforts to earn the financial bonuses, but still stop short of a point informally recognized by the group as the ceiling on production. And then in some plants there are a few individuals—known to their fellow workers as rate busters—who pay no attention to the ceiling at all. In fact, they seem to be going all out to produce just as much as they possibly can.

How can we explain these differences among men? One sort of explanation would involve an intensive personality analysis, for a man's response to the incentive is no doubt intimately tied up with his whole personality. But since such personality analyses on this problem have not yet been made, let us see to what extent these men differ from each other along dimensions that can be discovered by the social researcher.

The case to be reported here was studied by Melville Dalton. Dalton's case is built out of research materials he gathered while he was working in a large machine shop of one of the plants in a giant corporation. He was a checker, or incentive applier. It was his job to calculate the amount each worker had produced and therefore the amount of incentive pay he had earned. This job brought him into intimate contact with the men of the department. Since

39

he did not set the rates himself, he was not subject to the suspicion that tends to attach to time-study men. Over a period of four years of association with these men he was able to develop a remarkable research record.

The department consisted of 300 production workers. He limited his study to those who had had seven or more years of experience within the department on this type of work—84 men in number. This was for the purpose of cutting down on the variations in productivity that would be related to differences in individual skill. Also attitudes toward incentive were found to be relatively constant only among those machinists who had had time to achieve their maximum skill level. That is, those below that point shifted their attitudes with their daily successes or failures under the incentive, while those with stable skill had a general attitude one way or the other toward the incentive. Of course, among these 84 men individual skill differences remained, but it could at least be assumed that the man had had enough experience on the job so that he was not comparing experienced with inexperienced men. Furthermore, Dalton found that in the years before the incentive system was introduced the company had established classifications of A and B machinists. Dalton found that some of the men who had an A machinist classification were among the lowest producers, while some of the B classification were producing at a much higher rate. While this again did not mean that skill differences were eliminated, it showed that the observed production differences could not be explained on the basis of skill alone. There must be other factors involved.

For these 84 men, Dalton gathered production earnings records for a period of two years. At the same time he was going about observing and interviewing the men to try to learn what might explain the differences he observed.

In this shop, bonus earnings began at 66 per cent. The production ceiling informally agreed upon by most workers was 150 per cent. There were 9 men out of the 84 who exceeded this ceiling and were labeled by the work group as "rate busters." (They were also the only ones in the total department of 300 who went over the ceiling.) There were 25 men who averaged below 100 per cent and can be said to have been motivated little, if at all, by the incentive earnings. (Performance near 100 per cent was considered by the men "a good honest day's work.") The "middle performers," who were over 100 per cent but always observed the group ceiling of 150 per cent, totaled 50 men.

## CONTRASTING ATTITUDES

For purposes of contrast, let us examine the two extremes in productivity. Take the case of a worker whose mean performance over a period of two years is only 52 per cent. He admits he was once interested in making bonus.

But no more. You've got to keep your nose to the wheel. You can't stop for a visit, or you'll lose everything you've made. And even if you're willing to work like hell, you can't be sure of making anything. If I come out here and be a mule for eight hours, I want something to show for it. Suppose you plan on making so much bonus every pay—so you can buy a car or something. You'd have to ball the jack the whole turn and every turn. Inside of a week you wouldn't have a friend in the shop. And even if things was fixed so you could make your regular bonus by working like hell—I still wouldn't want it if I had to make somebody sore to get it or have the whole shop down on me. Don't misunderstand me. I'd like a little bonus. But they don't give it away, and I won't pay the price they want—be a ——.

Contrast this with the statement of one of the top performers:

I'm out here to make money. If any of these damn loafers think they can stop me, let them try it. I keep my bills paid an' don't owe anybody a damn cent. I mind my own business and look after my job. I'm always on time. I never lay off an' I don't sneak out early. The company can count on me, so why the hell should I care what a bunch of damn snoopy bums think of me?

Such striking differences do not come about by accident. They can be accounted for in a perfectly objective manner by comparing social backgrounds and present social activities of the two groups. We also find that the response to economic symbols is not an isolated phenomenon but rather fits in with a pattern of responses by the individual to his social and economic environment.

## FAMILY BACKGROUNDS

Most of the bottom production group were sons of unskilled industrial workers and grew up in large cities where for years they had been active in boys' gangs. Such activity tends to build loyalty to one's own group and opposition to authority—whether from parents or from management. Four of the rate busters grew up on farms or in small towns where they lived under the close supervision of parental authority and had little time or opportunity to develop gang activities and the accompanying loyalty to the gang.[1] One man was the son of a farmer who went to the city and became a huckster. Another was the son of a village barber and also spent much time in the cotton fields of his future father-in-law. One was the son of a shipping manager in the paper industry in Sweden. Another's father was a sanitary engineer and contractor in Scotland.

In this case, at least, the social and family backgrounds of rate busters contrasted sharply with that of the other men. In contrast to the urban, working-class experience of the others, the rate busters grew up either on farms or in urban lower-middle-class families— both types of family generally being strongholds of the belief in economic individualism. These men, then, learned early to respond to economic incentives in a manner which set them apart from their fellows.

### SOCIAL PARTICIPATION

In terms of present social participation, the restricters are the men who lead an active social life in the shop. Furthermore, they lead a highly active group life outside of work. The rate busters are, of course, socially isolated from other workers in the shop. Outside of work we find these men also largely isolated. With two exceptions, the nine men do not belong to any clubs, nor do they participate much in informal activities outside of the immediate family. One of the exceptions is a man who is active in the Masons, where he participates with those above him in social status and in the structure of the industrial organization. While further research is needed to fill out the picture of the rate buster, these findings suggest that he is either a lone wolf in factory and community or else an individual with a strong drive toward social mobility, who thus cuts himself off from the others on the same level and seeks association with those of superior status.

In off-the-job activities, the bottom production group is devoted

---

[1] This finding fits together with that of Whyte upon the pro- and antiunion attitudes of workers in terms of their social background. See "Who Goes Union and Why," *Personnel Journal*, December 1944.

to hobbies such as engine modeling, photography, microscopy, and the collecting of guns or fine tools—all pursuits that bring in no economic return and require the spending of money. (Of course, these interests also serve to stimulate social activity with people of like interests.) On the other hand, with one exception, the rate busters do not have such hobbies and regard them as frivolous wastes of time and money. (The exception, the active Mason, had a hobby of model boatbuilding.)

## SPENDING AND SAVING

The two groups contrast not only in attitudes toward making money but also in spending attitudes and behavior. A worker who heads charity drives in the plant pointed the contrast in this way:

When I was working for the Red Cross and Community Chest drives, Reynolds, Pat, Jack, and Ludlow (top producers) were all tight as hell to get anything from. I always went to them first because I knowed they was making a lot of bonus, but they just didn't want to give. They'd always buy a lot of war bonds, though. That was good, but they wasn't giving anything.

Then when I'd made the rounds to Perky, Jean, Carl and guys like that, I'd always get the quota and I didn't have to drag it out of them. That's funny, too. They don't make any bonus to speak of. You've checked all them guys, and you know that when they hit 100 per cent, it's something to write home about.

The rate busters each earned from $4500 to $6000 a year in 1944 and 1945. Dalton's records on four of them in the years 1942-1946 show that each one bought at least $4000 worth of bonds in that period. Two of them vied with each other to keep their names at the top of the honor roll for plant bond purchases—but, even so, they bought more at the bank than in the plant. As one explained, "You lose interest buying them here in the plant—you have to wait two weeks after they're paid for till they're made out and you start drawing interest." So extraordinarily acquisitive were these two men that a difference of approximately $\frac{1}{10}$ of 1 per cent in interest was important. Such differences are, of course, important in business life, but few workers think in such terms.

The restricter appears to be the man who lives in the present, spending money on himself or others in carrying on his social activities. The rate buster shuns activities that cost money, and seeks to build up his savings or invest in property of recognized marketable value.

## POLITICS AND PROPERTY

In political orientation, the contrast is marked. Of the 25 men whose mean performance was below 100 per cent, 22 were Democrats—and New Deal Democrats—while eight of the rate busters were Republicans and the ninth might be classified as a "regional Democrat." That is, he had grown up in the traditionally Democratic area of Texas, but his political views were those of conservative southern Democrats such as Harry Byrd. (Over 70 per cent of the men in the shop were Democrats. There were both Republicans and Democrats in the group producing between 100 and 150 percent.) When the total department was divided politically, Dalton found the Republicans averaging 123.3 per cent and the Democrats 95.8 per cent (a critical ratio of 4.0).

Dalton adds this comment: "When the father's occupation was examined, the Republicans appeared to have come from a higher socioeconomic level than the Democrats. The latter were sons of laborers or nonskilled workers more often than the Republicans who, in most cases, were sons of skilled workers, large farm owners, or supervisors."

The differing reactions toward property are shown in the distribution of home ownership. When only American-born workers were considered, it was found that 17 of 19 Republicans were homeowners as compared with 23 of 36 Democrats (22 of 27 foreign-born workers owned their homes).

Here party affiliation is indicative of profound differences in outlook upon life, and is recognized as such by the workers themselves. The rate-busting Republicans look upon the restricting Democrats as lazy, irresponsible individuals, who are dishonest in withholding their production from management. The counteropinion was expressed in this way by one low-producing Democrat: "I've never seen a Republican yet that wasn't a hog. They don't care about anybody but themselves. [Pointing to a Republican rate buster] Hans over there would rape his grandmother for a five-spot."

## RELIGION AND IDEOLOGIES

These productivity differences seem to have some relation to religion—or at least to church participation. Among 98 practicing Catholics in the department as a whole, there was not a single rate buster, although many of these men had the necessary skill. One of the rate busters had been born a Catholic, but he never went to church. Only one of the other eight men went to church with any regularity.

There may be here a tendency for Catholicism to go with closer attachments to social groups. Emile Durkheim, in his classic study,[2] explained the relatively low rate of suicides among Catholics in terms of a higher degree of integration of individuals into the group life of church and family. However, for purposes of this study, the basic contrast is probably not that between Catholics and Protestants but rather that between people who belong to groups and people who do not. The rate busters, with the single exception of the active Mason, do not participate in any groups, either on the job or in the community. They are as individualistic in religion as they are at the machine.

While the rate buster's work behavior conforms, superficially, to the assumptions of orthodox economic theory, it is clear that he does not simply respond to economic symbols and seek in a rational manner to maximize his earnings. He responds to other symbols at the same time; in fact, he responds to a pattern of symbols, which has been well described by Max Weber in *The Protestant Ethic and the Spirit of Capitalism*.[3] He sees the world in terms of individualistic competition. He believes that hard work is a cardinal virtue, that the satisfactions gained without hard work are ephemeral if not positively sinful. It is immoral, therefore, not to give one's full effort to the employer. Acquisition is considered an end in itself, and the acquisition of money is a mark of virtue. That is the kind of world in which the rate buster believes and for the support of that world he looks to the Republican Party.

On the other hand, the restricters recognize that they are living

[2] Emile Durkheim, *Suicide*, trans. by John A. Spaulding and George Simpson, ed. with an introduction by George Simpson (Glencoe: Free Press, 1951).

[3] New York: Charles Scribner's Sons, 1930.

in a competitive world, but they feel it is necessary and right for them to limit such competition as much as possible and substitute cooperative group effort. Loyalty to one's fellow workers is to them the cardinal virtue. They look to the Democratic Party to safeguard this way of life.

At the two extremes we seem to have two distinct types, in terms of response to economic symbols: the country born (or middle-class born) lone wolf, Republican, money-saving and investing worker without outside interests versus the city born, gregarious, New Deal Democratic, spending worker with hobbies that cost money and bring no economic return. (This should not imply that the *businessman* Republican is an unsocial individual.)

While these two types are in conflict with each other, there is no conflict for either type in interpretation of economic symbols. The rate busters would probably be high producers even on day rates, but the incentive no doubt serves to encourage them to bend every effort toward maximum production. The men who fall below 100 per cent are so determined not to respond to the incentive that they probably produce somewhat less than they would on day rates.

## THE MEN IN THE MIDDLE

Between the two extremes we find the majority of the workers. As might be expected, most of them combine in themselves characteristics of both extreme types. That is, one man may be a country-born Republican who saves his money but belongs to several clubs outside of work and participates in the informal plant society, while another may be a city-born Democrat whose range of social contacts outside and inside the plant is small but who does not go against the group.

The middle performers are pulled both ways, as is indicated by this quotation from an elderly machinist who averaged 125 per cent over a two-year period:

I worked under the same damn system forty-five years ago and thought when I left that I was done with it. Nobody gets any good from an incentive system. It makes bad feelings among the workers, between the workers and the checkers (personnel who apply the incentive) and between workers and the bosses.

Now you take that son-of-a-bitch over there (nodding toward a rate buster), the incentive system made him what he is. He's got a bad principle and the system brought it out. He'd cut the workingman's throat for a nickel. I've told him to stay away from my machine and not to speak to me because I'd feel insulted. I value my fellow worker's opinion above the dollar.

This incentive business gets hold of you before you know it. My health is as good as it ever was, yet last summer I got so damned nervous because of the aggravation that I spent seven weeks in the hospital. That ate up all the bonus I ever made.

The thing that's so damn aggravating is that one job pays twice as much as it should and the next only one-fourth what it should. What you make you lose. And when you get one that pays high, the boss comes around and rides your ass to get it out right away—and you have to kill it. When it runs low, I raise hell with the checker and he takes it to the engineers. They promise to do something about it. Then they say their hands are tied and they can't change it.

We need not necessarily accept this worker's explanation of the cause of his illness. Other things may well have been involved. Nevertheless, he expresses clearly his inner conflict. On the one hand, he is motivated to respond strongly in production to the incentive symbols. Why else would he fight with management personnel when he feels he is unable to make what he should? But at the same time he has a strong loyalty to the work group, so that he is conscientious about keeping his production within the informally prescribed limits even when he is tempted to make more money. He looks upon the incentive system simply as a management tool to manipulate him and his fellows. He resents being manipulated, and he responds—*partially*—to the tool he fights against. It is no wonder that a man who seeks to move in opposite directions at the same time must work under nervous tension.

As psychiatrists are giving increasing attention to the relation between emotional conflicts and stomach ulcers, it seems significant that none of the top or bottom performers were troubled by this ailment, while nine of the fifty middle performers were being treated for ulcers or incipient ulcers.

For the top and the bottom producers the incentive system presents no conflict. The rate busters have renounced the group; the bottom producers have renounced the incentive. It is the men who set a high value on both money and group ties that are pulled in opposite directions. (Of course, the number of cases here is far too small to support any firm conclusions on emotional tension and psychosomatic illness. The cases should be considered suggestive rather than conclusive.)

## LEARNED RESPONSES TO ECONOMIC SYMBOLS

That response to economic symbols is a product of a process of social learning is highlighted by Dalton's findings on native- versus foreign-born machinists. The 27 foreign-born had a mean performance of 90.6 per cent as against a mean of 108.7 per cent for the 56 American-born (critical ratio of 3.5). This difference could not be explained in terms of years of experience, for the foreign-born averaged 24.8 as against 22.8 for the native-born. Dalton also found no evidence of discrimination in assignment of "fat" jobs that was directed particularly against the foreign-born. He explains the differences rather in these terms:

The immigrant is apparently concerned more with anchoring himself in his new environment than with consumption of the luxury items that attract the native machinists. With the foreign-born, security investment is a much more important driving force than the emulation investment of the American-born. And, when the two drives are compared, the latter, as Veblen has so well shown, may be the more compelling. This was apparent in the shop. Where the American-born will have pop, candy, and fancy lunches at every turn the year around and would feel shame before the work group without them, the foreign-born worker will contentedly eat his liver sausage. He will also wear his old clothes into the plant and in some cases does not even change them, while the American "dresses up" for his entrance and exit. Behavior outside the plant follows similar directions.

It all adds up to this:

The response to economic symbols is a learned response. It cannot be separated from other aspects of the individual's personal and social development. His responses will be conditioned by his relations with family and community in the growing-up process, by the status of his family and the drive for mobility that he does or does not learn in earlier life, by the systems of belief on individualism-vs.-group loyalty, on politics, and on the values of money that he learns in the course of his experience, and finally by the present pattern of social participation that he follows.

Does this mean that, for practical purposes, the job of anticipating worker responses is too complex for handling? The executive does not need to explain the responses of each worker. It is enough for him to be able to predict what most people will do. In this connection it should be emphasized that the theory of motivation at present generally applied in industry promotes full effort from probably less than 10 per cent of the work force. In the sorts of situations we have been describing, the other nine-tenths of the force will refuse, more or less, to respond in full measure. Therefore, it is important practically as well as scientifically to develop a theory that will apply to more than one of ten men.

# PART II

## INTERGROUP RELATIONS

# 7

# Intergroup Cooperation

So far we have been examining the relations of the individual to his work group, against the background of worker-management relations. It is, of course, an oversimplification to think of the factory as a structure in which the individual is related to his group and the work groups are in turn related to the total organization. We must also examine the relations of groups to each other, for, as Roy puts it, "The larger institutional structures form networks of interacting groups."[1]

Intergroup relations form no simple pattern. We may see cooperative or conflict relations between groups, and furthermore the nature of the relations may change through time so that cooperation in one period gives way to conflict in the next.

We shall not attempt to examine all the factors that determine the pattern of intergroup relations in the factory. We shall concentrate upon the impact of the incentive system upon intergroup relations—and upon the impact of intergroup relations on the functioning of the incentive system.

Our first case shows how work groups cooperate with each other in undermining management's control of the incentive system. Here we are back on the "drill line" with Donald Roy.

## Roy Speaking

The objective of the cooperative efforts was to enable the drill line operators to make out on the incentive. It might seem, at first glance, that support extended to operators during their periods of intensive application to "getting the work out" would represent cooperation *with* and not *against* management. However, operators

[1] This statement and the case material to follow are taken from Donald Roy, "Efficiency and 'the Fix,'" *American Journal of Sociology*, Vol. LX, No. 3 (Nov. 1954). Copyright 1954, Univ. of Chicago.

and their "allies" joined forces in certain situations in a manner not only at unmistakable variance from the carefully prepared designs of staff experts, but even in flagrant violation of strongly held managerial "moral principles" of shop behavior. In short, machine operators resorted to "cheating" to attain their quotas; and since much of this imposturing involved the collusion of other shop groups, not as mere "accessories after the fact" but as deeply entangled accomplices, any managerial suspicion that swindling and conniving, as well as loafing, were going on all the time was well founded. If worker conviction that the echelons of management were packed with men addicted to the "dirty deal" be additionally considered, it might appear that the shop was fairly overrun with crooks.

However that may be, we are only concerned with showing that the kind of effort made by operators and their aids to expedite production, when they did try to expedite it, represented in many respects conflict with management.

One belief that was universally accepted by members of the writer's work group may be phrased thus: "You can't make out if you do things the way management wants them done." This gem of shop wisdom thus negatively put is hardly a prescription for action, but its obverse, "You've got to figure the angles," gave all hands plenty to do.

However, the sophistication of the time-study men usually measured up to the strategy employed against them. The canniest operators often gave of their best in timing duels only to get "hopeless prices" for their pains.

This is not to say that the hopeless price was always truly hopeless. Since the maintenance of an effective control over job timing and hence price setting was an uncertain, often disheartening, matter, operators were forced to develop skills for turning bad into good. Under the shaping hands of the "angle-applicators" surprising metamorphoses sometimes took place. Like the proverbial ugly duckling who finally feathered out into a beautiful swan, piecework jobs originally classified in operator vernacular as "stinkers" came to give off the delightful aroma of "gravy." Without going into the particulars of various types of operations employed one might say that jobs were "streamlined." This streamlining was, of course, at times "rough on the tools" and adverse in its effects on the quality of output. The jettisoning of quality called, necessarily, for a corresponding attention to ways and means of shielding supervisors and inspectors from awareness of the sacrifices made, and consequently brought into further play the social graces of equivocation, subterfuge, and prestidigitation.

Still, the adroitness of the machine operators, inventing, scheming, and conniving unto themselves to make quotas attainable, was not enough. Many stinkers would not yield before the whitest heat of intelligence or the most cavalier disregard for company property. An appreciable incidence of failure should not be surprising when it is kept in mind that the black arts of making out were not only responses to challenge from management, but also stimulations, in circular interaction, to the development of more effective countermagic in the timing process.

It is to be expected that a group of resourceful operatives, working with persistent intent to make out at quota levels, and relying heavily upon illegal practices in such endeavors, would be alert to possibilities of assistance from groups that were able and willing to give it and would not hesitate at a further flouting of rules and regulations in cultivating such assistance. It is also to be expected that the upholders of a managerial rational and moral order would attempt to prevent the institution of corruptive connections and would take action to stamp out any subversive organization that did manage to develop. During the eleven-month observation period of this study, machine operators, including the drill line men, were enjoying the cooperation of several other shop groups in an illegal facilitation of the make-out process. The activity of this "intergroup network" proved effective in modifying certain formally established shop routines, a too-close attachment to which would handicap the operators. The "syndicate" also proved adequate to meet the problem of circumventing each of a series of "new rules" and "new systems" introduced by management to expurgate all modifications and improvisations and force a strict adherence to the rules.

The shop groups that conspired with the operators were, namely, the inspectors, the tool crib men, the time checkers, the stockmen, and the setup men. With a single exception, these "service" groups stemmed from lines of authority distinct from the one for which the operators formed the base. The one exception was the setup group; it was subordinate to the same set of officials in the production line of authority that controlled the operators.

## SEQUENCES OF OPERATOR INTERACTION WITH SERVICE GROUPS IN THE WORK ROUTINE

The machine operator's performance of each individual job, or order, assigned to him involved formal relationships with service groups in well-defined sequences or routines. The recognized routine in effect at the time the writer began his observations involved the following sequence of formal contacts:

First, the operator received his work order from the time checker. Next, he presented the work order to a tool crib attendant at the window of the crib, which was conveniently located along one of the main traffic arteries. For this he received blueprints, jigs, cutting tools, and gauges. At the same time, that is, immediately after or before approaching the crib attendant, sometimes while waiting for crib service, the operator showed his work order to a stock chaser as a requisite to receiving materials to work on. The stock chaser, after perusing the order slip, occasionally with additional reference to the blueprint, hailed a trucker to direct him to bring the necessary stock to the operator's machine. If there was no delay in contacting a stock chaser or in locating and moving up the stock, a load of materials awaited the operator upon his arrival at his machine with equipment from the tool crib.

The operator then proceeded with the work of "setting up" the job, an activity that usually called for the assistance of a setup man. If called upon for help, setup men stayed with the operator until a piece was turned out that would satisfy an inspector as to quality of workmanship. In appraising a finished piece, the inspector consulted the blueprint brought from the crib for work specifications and then performed operations of measurement with rules, gauges, micrometers, or more elaborate equipment. The inspector might or might not "accept" the first piece presented for his judgment. At any rate, his approval was requisite to the next step in the operator's formal interactional routine, contacting the time checker to punch "off setup" and "on production."

The operator ordinarily had further "business" contact with a setup man during the course of production. Even if the job did not "go sour" and require the services of a trouble shooter, the setup man "dropped around" on his own initiative to see how the work was progressing. Likewise, the operator had further formal contact during the course of his job with inspectors and tool crib attendants. Each inspector made periodic "quality checks" at the machines on his line; and the operator might have to make trips to the tool crib to get tools ground or to pick up additional tools or gauges. Also, the operator might have to contact a stock chaser or trucker for additional loads of materials called for in the work order.

Upon completion of the last piece of his order the operator tore down his setup, returned his tools to the tool crib, and made a final report to the time checker. Should the job be uncompleted at the close of a shift, the operator merely reported the number of pieces finished to a checker, and the latter registered a final punch-out. The setup was left intact for the use of the operator coming in to work the next shift.

## MAJOR JOB CATEGORIES

A noting of certain variations in types of jobs assigned to operators will be pertinent to a discussion of intergroup collusion in the modification of formal work routines. These variations could be classified into four categories; (1) piecework; (2) time study; (3) rework; and (4) setup.

Each piecework job carried a price per 100 pieces, determined by the timing operations mentioned earlier. Time-study and rework jobs carried no prices. The time-study category included:

(a) new jobs that had not yet been timed;

(b) jobs that had once carried a piecework price.

As the label indicates, rework jobs involved the refinishing of pieces that had been rejected, either by inspectors or in the assembly process, and were considered salvageable by reprocessing.

Since time-study and rework jobs carried no piecework prices, operators engaged in these two types of work were paid "day rate," that is, according to an hourly base rate determined in collective bargaining.

Not a fourth type of job, but measured separately in time and payment units, were the setup operations. Piecework jobs always carried piecework setups; failure to equal or exceed base rate on setup did not jeopardize chances to earn premium on "production," and vice versa. Time-study jobs frequently carried piecework setups; rework never.

It would not require the imagination of an Edgar Allan Poe to see how these formal work routines might be modified to fit the perceived needs of machine operators. Possibilities for the development of "make-out angles" should be immediately apparent in a work situation characterized by (1) job repertoires that included piecework and daywork operations, by (2) minimum wage guarantees uniform for all work done, and by (3) separate payment computations by jobs and days worked. If, for instance, time formally clocked as daywork could be used to gain a "head start" on subsequent piecework operations, such a transferal might mean the difference between earning and not earning premiums on doubtful piecework jobs. Similarly, time on hopeless piecework jobs might be applied to more promising operations; and the otherwise "free time" gained on gravy jobs might be consumed in productive anticipation of formal receipt of ordinarily unrewarding piecework. Especially lush gravy jobs might even contribute extra time enough to convert stinkers into temporary money-makers. Realization of such possibilities in any given case would necessarily involve obtaining, without a work order, the following: (1) identification of future operations as listed in sequence on the schedule board inside the time cage; (2) jigs, blueprints, and cutting tools appropriate to the work contemplated; (3) stock to work on; (4) setup help and advice; (5) inspection service; (6) trouble-shooting assistance as needed. Obviously this sequence of accomplishments would call for the support of one or more service groups at each step. That the required assistance was actually provided with such regularity that it came to be taken for granted the writer discovered by observation and personal experience.

The following diary recording of a bit of interaction between the writer and a time checker may be indicative of the extent to which service group collaboration with the operators in perverting the formal system of work routine had become systematized.

When I came to punch off the rework, the time cage girl said, "You don't want to punch off rework yet, do you?" suggesting that I should get a start on the next job before punching off rework.

Even line foremen, who in regard to intergroup collusion preferred the role of silent accessory after the fact, became upset to the point of actual attempted interference with formal rules and regulations when the naïve neophyte failed to meet the expectations of his own informal system.

Art (foreman) was at the time cage when I punched off the daywork of re-reaming and on to the piecework of drilling. He came around to my machine shortly after. "Say," he said, "when you punch off daywork onto piecework, you ought to have your piecework already started. Run a few; then punch off the daywork, and you'll have a good start. You've got to chisel a little around here to make money."

Acceptance of such subversive practices did not extend, however, to groups in management other than local shop supervision. The writer was solemnly and repeatedly warned that time-study men, the true hatchet men of upper management, were disposed to bring chiselers to speedy justice.

Gus went on to say that a girl hand-mill operator had been fired a year ago when a time-study man caught her running one job while being punched in on another.

## NEW RULES AND NEW SYSTEMS

During the near-year that he spent in the shop the writer felt the impact of several attempts to rip out the wires of intergroup irregularities and enforce conformance to managerial designs of procedure. He coincidentally participated in an upholding of the maxim: *"Plus ça change plus c'est la même chose."*

Attempts to tighten controls came in a series of "new rules" or "new systems" promulgated by bulletin board edicts. How far the beginning of the series antedated the writer's arrival is not known. Old-timers spoke of a Golden Age enjoyed before the installation of the Booth System of production control; then operators "kept their own time," turning in their work orders as they saw fit and building "kitties" on "good jobs" to tide them over rainy days on "poor jobs."

The first new rule of the observation period went into effect less than two months after the writer was hired. It was designed to tighten control in the tool crib sector, where attendants had not only been passing out setups ahead of time but allowing operators or their setup men to enter the tool room to make the advance pickups themselves. One aim of the new rule was to curb an operator practice of keeping "main setups" at the machines instead of turning them in at the completion of operations.

A new crib ruling went into effect today. A memorandum by Bricker (superintendent) was posted on the side of the crib window. Those who check out tools and jigs must sign a slip in triplicate, keeping the pink one and turning it in with the tools in exchange for the white original, which would constitute proof that the tools had been returned. No new setups would be issued until the old ones had been turned in.

An optimistic perception of the new procedures was expressed by young Jonesy, a tool crib attendant and otherwise willing conniver with the operators:

"Tools are scattered all over the shop. This way we'll have them all in order in the crib, and the fellows can get them any time they need them."

But multiple-drill operator Hanks, old-timer on the line, drew upon his lengthy experience with managerial efficiency measures, and saw the situation differently:

Hanks commented unfavorably on the new ruling. He and the day man (his machine partner on the other shift) had been keeping the tools for their main setups at their bench or, rather, under it. This practice, according to Hanks, was to ensure their setting up promptly without inordinate waste of time, and to ensure their having all the tools needed. Hanks said that on a previous occasion he was told to turn in one of his main setups, which included over a dozen drills, reamers, taps, etc., of varying sizes. He did so, but when he needed this setup again, the crib man couldn't locate all the tools. He asked Hanks to come back in the crib and help him find them. Hanks refused. After several hours of futile search, Hanks was finally induced to "come back and find his tools." He did so on condition that it would not be on his own time. The foreman agreed to this.
"The same thing is going to happen again," predicted Hanks, "and I'm not going back there to find my tools they scatter all over, on my own time."

Though the operators went through the formality of an exchange of slips when they exchanged setups, the new procedures did not modify the practice of getting setups from the crib ahead of time. Appreciable effects of the new ruling included making more paper work for crib attendants at the same time that more work at assembling setups was thrust upon them. Jonesy's happy prediction did not materialize; the tools were not always in order. In the writer's experience subsequent events seemed more in line with Hank's gloomy forebodings.

Included in the new ruling was a stipulation that blueprints and gauges be turned in by the operators at the end of each shift, though set up paraphernalia other than prints and gauges was to be left at the machines as long as jobs were in operation. Calling for prints and gauges at the beginning of the shift consumed operator time, waiting at the crib window in the line that naturally formed, even when these items were located immediately. But they, like other equipment, could not always be readily found by the crib attendants:

Due to the new crib ruling he (Joe Mucha, the writer's machine partner on another shift) turned in the tap gauge. I spent 20 minutes trying to get it back again. The crib man could not find it, and claimed that Joe had not turned it in. Joe stayed after 3 o'clock to help me get it, countering the arguments of the crib with the slip he retained as evidence. Finally the gauge was located in the crib.

I started out one-half hour late on operation 55 on the pedestals, due to delay at the crib waiting to check out the print and gauge that Joe had just turned in.

Then, four months after the new crib ruling had been laid down, it was modified by another new order that canceled the stipulation regarding the turning in of blueprints and gauges and called for changes in the paper work of operator-crib attendant relations. These changes were featured by a new kind of work order, duplicates of which became involved in tool crib bookkeeping. The change reduced operator waste time at the start of shifts, but did not seem to lighten the burden of the crib attendants, as far as paper work irritations were concerned. In addition to the problem of finding tools for the impatient operators, they now had the problem of finding paper.

When I punched in on the rework and asked Walt (crib attendant) for a print, he fumed a bit as he sought a duplicate of my new-type yellow work order in a new file of his.

"I haven't been able to find more than one in five duplicates so far," he said, "and there's supposed to be a duplicate for everyone," Walt said tonight, when I presented him with a work order card for tools. "That makes the twelfth card I've had and no duplicate!"

The tool crib under the new system is supposed to have duplicate work orders in its file of all jobs given operators. These duplicates are to be put in the toolroom files as soon as they are put on the board; and the operators are to sign these duplicates when checking out setups.

The new system did operate to handicap operators in that they were not to receive new setups from the crib until they received the new yellow work orders from the time cage to check with the duplicates in the crib. However, setup men roamed at will in the toolroom, grinding tools and fixing jigs, and were able to help the operators by picking up setups ahead of time for them. Their detailed knowledge of the various setups made it possible for them to assemble the necessary tools without the use of setup cards.

"This is a good job," I said to McCann (now setup man). "I wish I could get it set up ahead of time, but I guess it's no use trying. I can't get the setup now from the toolroom until I get the new work order from the time girls."

McCann thought a moment. "Maybe I can get the jig and tools out of the crib for you."

McCann did get the jig and tools, and I got a half hour's head start on the job.

The writer had found Ted, a stock chaser, and his truckers, George and Louie, willing connivers in the time-chiseling process. They moved up stock ahead of time, even after the new system made presentation of the new work order to the stock chaser a prerequisite to getting stock. At first the writer felt "stymied" by the new system, but later found that for all practical purposes the situation was unchanged.

I could not go ahead with the next order, also a load of connecting rods, because the new ruling makes presentation of a work order to the stock chaser necessary before materials can be moved up. So I was stymied and could do nothing the rest of the day.

About an hour before I was to punch off the connecting rods, I advised Ted that I would soon be needing another job. He immediately brought over a load of reservoir casings.

The new system also included complication of operator-inspector relations. Inspectors were now to "sign off" operators from completed jobs before new work orders could be issued at the time booth. The signing-off process included notation by the inspector of the time of operation completion, a double check on the time checker's punch-out. This added, of course, to the paper work of inspectors.

Drill man Hanks at first responded to this feature of the new system with an individualistic approach:

Hanks commented on the new system tonight. He thinks that its chief purpose is to keep the operators from getting ahead on an operation and starting the next job on saved time. He said the inspector checked him off a job tonight at 4:40 and he was not due to punch in on the next one until 6:10. He changed the time recorded by the inspector on his work slip to 6:10, and went ahead as usual. If he had not done so, there would have been a "gap" of one hour and 30 minutes unaccounted for in the records.

The writer found himself stymied at first, but soon discovered that the new obstacle could be overcome without engaging in such a hazardous practice as "forging."

It was ten o'clock when we were ready to punch off setup, and Johnny (setup man) asked Sam (inspector) to sign me off setup earlier, so that I could make out on setup.

"Punch me off at nine o'clock," I said, not expecting Sam to check me off earlier, and purposefully exaggerating Johnny's request.

Sam refused. "I can't do that! If I do that for you, I'll have to do it for everybody."

Sam seemed somewhat agitated in making the refusal. A few minutes later he said to Johnny, "Why did you ask me to do that when Hanks was standing there?" Hanks had been standing by my machine, watching us set up. "I can't take you off an hour back. Go find out when you punched in on this job in the first place."

Johnny consulted the time cage girl as to the time I punched on the job, later talked to Sam at Sam's bench while I was working, and came to me with the announcement that it was "fixed up" so that I made out on setup and was credited with starting production at 9:30. This gave me an hour and a half of gravy.

By the time the new system was a month old Sam was not only "doing it for everybody" but actually taking the initiative in conniving with operators:

When I punched off setup for the eight pieces, Sam asked me if I wanted him to take me off setup at an earlier time in order that I might make out on the setup. I refused this offer, as it wasn't worth the trouble for me to stop to figure out the time.

Instead of looking at the clock when an operator asks to be taken off setup, Sam usually asks the operator, "When do you want to be taken off?"

No sooner had the shop employees made their adjustments to this new system to settle down to normal informal routine than the big bombshell hit, a new pronunciamento that barred admittance to the toolroom to all save superintendents and toolroom employees. The rule seemed to be enforced.

On one occasion tonight Paul (setup man) asked Jonesy to let him into the crib; he was in a hurry about something. But Jonesy shook his head, and Paul had to wait at the crib window with the rest of us.

Johnny (another setup man) says that the new rule is going to be tough on the grinders and crib attendants, because the setup men and foremen have been doing much of the grinding, and have made it easier for them by coming in to help themselves to tools, jigs, etc.

Johnny says that the new rule suits him fine. Now he can just stand at the window and holler, and let the tool room employees do the work.

The line foremen seemed to take offense at the new "exclusion act" and threatened reprisals to the crib attendants.

At quitting time I noticed Gil (line foreman) talking to Walt at the crib window. Gil seemed very serious; Walt was waving his arms and otherwise gesturing in a manner indicating rejection of responsibility. I didn't catch any words, but gathered that Gil was voicing disapproval or warning, and after Gil left I said to Walt, "Looks like you're behind the eight-ball now!"

I noticed that Walt's hair was mussed, and he looked a little wild. He denied that he was in any trouble whatsoever; nor was he worried about anything whatsoever. "I'm just working here!" he exclaimed. "I just go by the cards and beyond that I've got no responsibility!" I was curious as to what Gil had told him, and asked Johnny later, on the way home. I had noticed that Johnny was standing nearby when Gil was talking to Walt. Johnny said that Gil was telling Walt that from now on the crib was going to be charged with every minute of tool delay to the operators—that if there was any waiting for tools, Gil was going to make out allowance cards charging these delays to the crib.

The boys seem very much disgusted with the slow service at the tool crib. They crowd around the window (always a crowd there) and either growl or wisecrack about the service.

It was at this time that Jonesy, erstwhile optimist and regarded by shop employees as the most efficient of the crib attendants, decided that he had had enough. He transferred to the quiet backroom retreat of tool grinding. But several days later, just ten days after the new rule had been promulgated, the sun began to break through the dark clouds of managerial efficiency.

While I was waiting for tools at the crib window tonight, I noted the jockey (turret-lathe man) dash into the tool crib through a door that was left ajar; he was followed soon after by Gil. Later, when the door was closed, Paul shook it, and shouted to the attendant, "Let me in!" He was admitted.

Steve (superintendent) called out, "Hey!" when he saw the jockey go into the crib. When the jockey came out, he spoke to him, and the jockey joshed him back. Steve did not seem to be particularly put out about it.

Soon the boys were going in and out of the crib again almost at will, and setup men were getting setups ahead of time for operators ignored by the crib attendants.

The management edict remained posted on the tool crib door. The fix was on again, and operators and their service group allies conducted business as usual for the remaining weeks of the writer's employment.

Roy's account ends here.

Here we see a common sequence of activity in the factory. Management imposes an incentive system. The workers do not respond as management theory anticipates. Therefore, management pronounces new rules in an effort to compel this response. Since the new rules upset established ways of doing things in the department, workers (and sometimes foremen too) seek to find safe channels for rule evasion. When management issues its pronouncements from on high without any understanding of the shop situation or consultation with shop people, somehow the workers seem always to be able to find effective means for evasion or sabotage. When management discovers that the problems still exist, management often responds by making a *new* set of new rules. This apparently can go on endlessly, with new rules leading to new methods of rule evasion, and those in turn leading to more new rules.

Some people are inclined to think of a factory as a place where management applies its "logics of efficiency" and workers respond with their nonlogical sentiments of resistance. Such a characterization hardly applies to this case. Here it seems that management is so preoccupied with its efforts to establish control over the workers that it loses sight of the presumed purpose of the organization. A casual visitor to the plant might indeed be surprised to learn that its purpose was *to get out production*. Certainly, if it had been possible to enforce some of the rules described by Roy, the result would have been a slowing down of production.

Furthermore, the workers, far from being mere passive resisters, show a lively use of intelligence and social ingenuity in devising their methods of rule evasion. However, it is not our aim to show that it is the worker and not management who behaves logically. We can make no progress if we think only in terms of logical and nonlogical behavior. We shall gain more understanding if we examine behavior in terms of the sets of human relations experienced by the behaving individuals.

# 8

# Intergroup Conflict

Under certain conditions the incentive system may give rise to an integrated intergroup cooperation in opposition to management, as we have already seen. In other situations we see the introduction of an incentive system leading to bitter intergroup conflicts among the workers. This does not mean that the intergroup conflict takes the place of worker-management or union-management conflict. Conflict may be waged simultaneously upon all fronts. In such a situation it will be impossible for union and management officers to resolve their own disagreements and establish an effective government over the plant community unless they can understand and cope with intergroup conflicts.

In this chapter, Leonard Sayles presents for us a case study of the introduction of incentives in a department where all workers had previously been on straight daywork.

## Sayles' Study

The department under study employed about two hundred men engaged in grinding bronze castings,[1] on a three-shift schedule. The grinding department performed three similar operations. Castings coming into the department from the foundry were first put through the so-called "rough" grinding machines. Next the castings were given a "finish" grind by two types of special machines. Some of the finish grinding equipment, particularly the older machines, were Bell grinders that had been purchased about a quarter of a century earlier. Recently the company had begun purchasing and installing new high-speed equipment, the Scott-Winston machines.

[1] The names as well as the description of the work performed are fictional in order to protect the identity of the company and the union involved. However, none of the other facts concerning the case have been altered.

67

Finally, some but not all of the castings were put through a battery of "fine" grinding machines for special orders.

Most of the machines required one or two operators depending on the load being processed, and in some instances one employee or two employees operated several machines. The bulk of the work force was concentrated in the finish grinding section. Although all

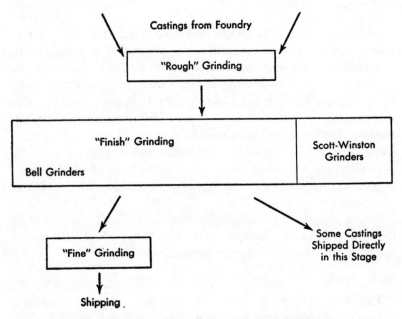

Fig. II. Machines and Work Flow in the Grinding Department

operations paid approximately the same wage, many of the older workers had gravitated to the Bell grinders. Some years before, these had paid a higher rate; the job was still more prestigeful and presumed to require somewhat greater skill than the other jobs in the department.

## THE STRUGGLE TO INTRODUCE INCENTIVES, 1947-1951

After the war the management decided that its costs in this particular department were not competitive. As a means of increasing productivity, the industrial engineers worked out a system whereby one operator could run several fine-grinding machines. When the union claimed this change in work method was a violation of the contract, and succeeded in proving its case through arbitration, the company turned to incentives.

The union resisted these just as vehemently as it had resisted the increased work loads and again the case went to arbitration and again the union was victorious. To spur acceptance by the fine grinders, the company officers threatened to remove the entire grinding operation to another plant if the union continued to refuse to negotiate an incentive plan. The pressure is described by an older employee of the department:

We didn't want the plan but there were meetings galore. The men didn't know what to do. The union couldn't assure them that the company wasn't bluffing about moving out of town if they didn't accept some plan. The union, of course, wanted to be sure they wouldn't be blamed for what happened. The labor relations director really scared us. He gave us a lot of facts about how the company was looking over new sites for their mill. Then they brought some new machines into the plant and didn't even unpack them—they said it would be easier to ship them the way they were. So we reasoned just like a lot of other fellows reasoned who had homes here in town that our jobs were important to us. The next thing we knew there was a provision in the contract that the company would develop incentives.

Thus the company was finally successful in introducing the first incentive plan in the grinding department. If employee memories are accurate, the fine grinders were relatively well satisfied for at least a year with the plan that was negotiated by their union. Then discontent appeared which, although focused on the incentive formula, appeared to have other causes.

It was even rumored that the union's international representative had lost his job by permitting the company to negotiate a clause in the 1947 contract that permitted them to put in incentive plans. Many members stated boldly that the union had sold out the membership on this particular issue:

We never wanted incentives in the first place in the grinding department. We took it to arbitration and won it. But then someone sold out. They must have because the next thing we knew there was the incentive plan in and the guys were running four and one-half machines—how we'll never know!

Another grinder summarized his fears concerning incentive plans:

Incentives may be all right now—we're not doing too badly under them, but, BOY, in a depression they're no good. Then you're just working yourself right out of a job, believe me. We never would have accepted them if it wasn't that they started putting them in during that recession.

## EFFECT ON THE FINE GRINDERS

This change of attitude toward the incentive plan was caused partially by jealousy on the part of other groups concerning their premium earnings.

The men in the rest of the place always think you are hungry. They're as jealous as anything of any money that we make. They think you're killing yourself to turn out all this stuff just because you are greedy.

As time went on, social exchanges between the fine grinders and the rest of the department diminished and they became almost a separate unit, although geographically attached to the department.

At the same time others in the department began to belittle the fine grinders. To be sure, these had once been highly desirable jobs because the work was lighter and cleaner than many of the earlier operations performed. Now, however, the work was devalued in the currency of worker attitudes, or as one finish grinder commented:

Since they put incentives in no one wants those fine grinding jobs any more. It's hard work and you don't get very much. Therefore, our policy is going to be to fight incentives every step of the way. We hope to be just like the guy who gets a rent increase from his landlord—we'll yell loud enough so that the next time the landlord thinks of making a rent increase he will be a little more careful.

This worker was voicing the fear that by 1949 had become a major concern of the department—that the company was contemplating the expansion of its incentive program to include the *entire* grinding work force.

## THREATS FROM THE NEW MACHINES

The company now announced that it hoped to develop a satisfactory incentive formula for production on the new Scott-Wintson machines in the near future, and opened many of these jobs to bid from the department. The lure of future high earnings attracted few of the older employees, who had no desire to work at an incentive pace. However, many relatively young employees saw these new jobs as a means of obtaining better shift schedules than their seniority would have entitled them to if they continued to work on the more favored jobs in grinding. The union finally gave some guarantees of protection against "bumping" in case of decreased employment in order to fill all the vacancies. The officers assured the men taking the Scott-Winston jobs that they would be in a separate promotional ladder and thus immune from displacement by Bell operators.

With the 1949 recession past and a strong market available, the company did not resist strongly union demands for a good rate on the job. Aside from the high demand for the company's products, production on the fine-grinding machines had outrun the production of the Bell machines. With the Bell grinders becoming a more critical bottleneck, management needed an assured high output in this middle group of machines. It was estimated that the Scott-Winstons were several times faster than the Bell grinders.

Thus, when union pressure combined with management eagerness to expand output produced a rate that seemed liberal to the men, production soared. Not only was the incentive rate an attractive one, but the younger men on these jobs were less likely to be concerned with the long-run repercussions of their output on job security. With output at a high level, union officials feared that when the trial period for the incentive plan expired the company might be reluctant to agree to a permanent adoption of the current formula.

## REPERCUSSIONS IN FINE GRINDING

There were two strong reactions to the increased output and concomitant increased earnings on the Scott-Winston machines. The men on the fine grinders, who had already been complaining that high earnings were impossible under their present rate, grew more restless when they observed what their colleagues were able to earn on neighboring machines. They were determined to restrict their production as a means of pressuring the company to loosen their own rate.

At this point an interesting incident took place that further illustrates the sensitive intergroup relationships that are affected by the operations of an incentive plan. The entire grinding department was working on a three-shift, round-the-clock basis. When the company officials observed that production on the fine-grinding machines was not sufficient to absorb the increasing output of the intermediate finish grind stage (stimulated by the new incentive plan on the Scott-Winstons) they informed the fine grinders through the union that they were contemplating introducing a fourth shift.[2] Heretofore many of the men had been enjoying a six-day workweek, at overtime rates, of course. The introduction of a fourth shift would obviate the need for any overtime work.

The first shift on the fine grinders was most concerned about this threat. While many of the men on later shifts held two jobs (in part explaining their preference for the later shift), the day shift people's earnings were restricted to their work in the grinding department itself. Several of these, therefore, determined to relax their slowdown somewhat as a compromise which they hoped would still encourage the company to restudy their rates without adding another shift. They thus increased their output about 15 per cent above their previous slowdown pace.

The third shift reacted violently to this, claiming an informal agreement had been violated, and then dropped its production about 5 per cent *below* the slowdown level! The second shift, finding itself pressured from both sides, from the night group to reduce its effort and from the day group to increase output, split down the middle and eventually began producing at a rate about 5 per cent *above* the previous (slowdown) level.

## BELL GRINDERS TAKE THE OFFENSIVE

The more profound repercussions of the Scott-Winston incentive plan, however, took place within the finish grinding group on the Bell machines. The feelings of these men were summarized by one of their leaders.

[2] The fourth shift in a round-the-clock operation is designed to fill in the shifts that are unworked in a normal 168-hour week by a three-shift operation. Three shifts can only cover 120 hours, assuming a 40-hour week for each employee, leaving 48 hours "uncovered"—available either for an additional shift or as overtime.

The company is putting the squeeze on us. First, they put an incentive on the fine-grinding machines, then they put it on the guys who work next to us. They know they'll have us then—pulling on one side and pushing on the other!

Then another incident rocked the entire department. Some of the men on the old finish grinders, the Bell machines, half jokingly and in part seriously, threatened to bump some of the younger men employed on the Scott-Winston machines who were reputedly making $20 to $30 a week in incentive earnings. The legality of such a move was very much in question, at least under the existing interpretation of the seniority rules in the department, considering the assurances given the men who had taken the Scott-Winston jobs. Still the threat had some force behind it. No one could remember exactly how the agreement had been worded. Further, one of the most forceful Bell operators was active in the union and might, it was feared, push through a changed interpretation of the rules. At this point one of the youngest men on the Scott-Winston machines, an operator on the third shift, was reputed to have said:

If they think they are going to start that kind of thing, we'll make this job so that no one wants it. Let's see if they want it after we get done with it.

This pronouncement was followed by a substantial increase in output on the third shift of the Scott-Winstons—to make good the threat. There followed a series of charges and countercharges, grievances and meetings. A group of men on old finish grinders submitted this grievance:

In the past we tried to go on these Scott-Winston machines. We were informed that we could not demote ourselves. Now, due to the fact of added machinery and of an incentive plan, all grinding machines are paying the same amount. Therefore, we maintain that we have the right to "bump" as per the department seniority agreement. . . .

We request our body of grievance men to study this terrible state. A few individuals have cast very derogatory remarks about our union and one had the nerve to say that we'll either work on these machines ourselves or ruin the jobs forever for the older men who think they can get these jobs. We leave this entire matter in your hands.

## EFFECT ON MANAGEMENT

At the same time two other grievances were submitted to the bargaining committee from other men in the department, countering the charges of the men on the old finish grinders. These were signed primarily by the men currently employed on the new machines. While the grievances in form were directed at management, it was apparent that the problem could only be settled by an internal union decision. Management itself was powerless to act. As the skills were transferable, management was willing to place any of the men on the disputed jobs.

The supervisor in the department made his own position more difficult by telling the Bell grinders that their jobs could not exist in a few years when the Scott-Winstons "really got going." He had hoped to stimulate the Bell grinders to increase their own output, but only aggravated the tense intradepartmental feud which later prevented management from securing acceptance of overtime work.

## REACTION BY THE ROUGH GRINDERS

The men on the rough-grinding machines were in a peculiar dilemma now. The company had recently announced its intention of applying an incentive to their jobs also, as soon as practicable. A production record on the finish grinding machines that indicated the current incentive formula for those machines was an overly loose rate might encourage the company to tighten its standards when it came to applying incentives to rough grinding. To that extent they were not sympathetic to the men on the Scott-Winston machines, who threw caution to the winds and produced "for today only"—for the immediate financial rewards involved (and perhaps as well to discourage other men in the department from coveting their jobs). At the same time the rough grinders recognized that, were their own incentive plan to prove equally attractive, their jobs also might be threatened by men from the old finish (Bell) grinders bumping to achieve more favorable weekly earnings. They resented this prospect particularly because they had always borne the brunt of the heaviest operations in the department at an hourly rate that was no greater than that paid the finish grinders. The chance to better their position was not altogether ignored. They were fearful that if they sided with the old finish grinders they might sacrifice future opportunities. It is interesting to note that rough grinders who felt themselves in the middle of this dispute signed several grievances that were self-contradictory. Caught in crosspressures, they responded by moving in two opposing directions at the same time!

## REACTION TO THE UNION

Accusations flew that various union officers based on their own occupational interest were split on the legitimacy of the grievances. The department steward, a Bell grinder, resigned because he said "all the men in the department aren't behind me." No union official was seen as neutral, as trying to do the right thing. The groups competed for the favor of the leadership group. A department meeting was dominated by the older finish grinders, who passed a motion that would give them the right to take these lucrative positions on the Scott-Winstons. However, the bargaining committee of the union refused to recognize this decision.

The same committee ignored all the grievances that had been filed, hoping that the men would eventually settle the dispute among themselves. This would avoid a difficult political decision. The union leaders, like the management, would have been satisfied with any decision the department itself could agree on.

## A DEPARTMENT DIVIDED

All these grievances and countergrievances, meetings and threats had had their effect on departmental unity. The coexistence of two incentive plans and men working on similar machines on a non-incentive basis were destructive of the informal organization that normally governed the workers' affairs.

The best example of this is an incident that took place early in 1951. The company, anxious to expand output, offered to schedule a regular sixth day of work for the entire department. Management had made this offer only after substantial pressure from the union. This reflected what had been a serious inequity in the eyes of the rank and file. The grinding department was the only unit in the plant that had not been working six days a week, because of its fourth shift. Union leaders had implied that they could not be responsible if a walkout took place in the grinding department, unless substantially more overtime was granted.

The only barrier to implementing the company's proposal was agreement *within* the department on a new work schedule to facilitate the additional day of work, the major problem being that everyone could not have his day of rest within the weekend period (with four shifts operating).

Under normal circumstances the men themselves, through their own informal organization, would have arrived at some arrangement to schedule days off. Now they were unable to do so. The turmoil was so great that when the company called for a vote on the plan for implementing the overtime agreement, the proposal was defeated. This was catastrophic to the hopes of most of the men who wanted an extra day of work to catch up with the steadily rising cost of living. When some weeks later the company offered men in the department overtime work at a lower hourly rate in another part of the plant, a majority of the men accepted. Here they had no voice in the selection of their day off, the work was harder, less well paid and much more inconvenient than would have been their assignment in their own department.

## ANALYSIS OF THE CASE

What had been at the early stages a union-management problem was now an intergroup crisis. The division within the work group presented an unmanageable problem to the union leadership. This situation might seem to present certain advantages to management. On the other hand, the story clearly indicates that the department was out of control from a management standpoint also.

The introduction of incentives, coupled with technological change, gave rise to the intergroup conflict. That conflict in turn presented union and management with certain difficult administrative problems and had serious adverse effects upon worker attitudes toward each other, toward the union, and toward management.

To understand how such intergroup conflicts arise, we need only review the history of the department. Almost since its establishment in 1920 the elite of the department had been the operators of the Bell finish grinders. The fine-grinding operation was relatively new in the department, and the rough-grinding job was unpleasant, dirty, and heavy. Now, however, the Bell grinders could not claim the best jobs in the department, the men on the Scott-Winston machines were displacing them, almost overnight.

Not only were they losing their status position in the department, but they were falling behind in relative earnings.[3]

In addition, more than status was involved. The very jobs of these finish grinders were endangered by the company's experimentation with the Scott-Winston machine. As one of the grinders observed:

What's the use of kidding ourselves? Those guys can produce so much more than we can it isn't funny. Don't you think the company knows that? How much longer do you thing they're going to leave our old machines around? They're just junk.

While the incentive plan on the fine grinders was a threat to their nicely fixed production levels, the supreme threat was, of course, the production on the Scott-Winston machines, which could produce identical work in a fraction of the time that their own required.

The old finish grinders had fought valiantly against the changes, particularly against any departmental acceptance of incentive plans. Forgetting that the acceptance had been figuratively at gun point, they now jeered at the employees who worked under incentives for "killing themselves in the hunger over more money."

Even while jeering, many of the Bell operators sought a means by which they could assume title over the lucrative jobs on which some were killing themselves. Both activities served to deepen the internal split within the department.

Some of these differences among the various machine groups had existed prior to the introduction of incentives. For example, there were certainly real status distinctions based on seniority and job. One old-timer described the relations existing between the Bell machine men and the rough grinders:

Those guys over there feel they're a little different than us. One friend of mine worked over there with them one day and they didn't even talk to him, just ignored him.

But until recently the department had been content to let the men on the old finish grinders, the most senior employees, play a

---

[3] For a more complete analysis of the effect of incentive plans on worker evaluations of these jobs and on job evaluation see Sayles, "Worker Values in Job Evaluation," *Personnel*, Vol ᵛᵛ No. 4 (January 1954), pp. 266-274.

leadership role not only in the union but in department affairs as well. In departmental meetings the active participants were always the men from the old finish grinders. The stewards similarly were always elected from this group as was every chief steward except the current incumbent. Their leadership position was abetted by their geographic position in the department—their machines were exactly in the center of the work floor. Many of the other men had resented their easy jobs, some of their airs of superiority, and all their advantages. Nevertheless, their leadership had never been challenged. The other groups felt small and insignificant by comparison.

After all, they had the easy jobs and we had what they figured were pretty tough jobs. They stuck together a lot and we never talked very much. They always looked at us as men who were taking a job that they would never have taken.

The decline in the leadership position of the old finish grinders was most evident in the six-day question. Here they found it impossible to crystallize agreement on any new schedule that would permit the department to accept the company's offer. As the controversy progressed, the men on the rough grinders for the first time began to participate in the department affairs, perhaps due to the power vacuum created by the decline of the Bell operators.

The operations of the incentive plan had created a new vested interest group, the Scott-Winston machine men, who had something important to lose in the continued leadership of the Bell grinders. This stimulus to activity caused them to unite with the rough grinders to block any adjustments in the seniority system.

The Bell grinders, who had been committed to resisting incentives at all cost, were not able to shift their ground fast enough to avoid the economic pressures that now threatened the existence of their jobs. The other groups gained at the same time, not just economic power, but political power within the union structure.

## CONCLUSION

This case illustrates the human problems that can result from the introduction of incentives in a department. In this case, for example, the prestige and relative attractiveness (to the workers involved) of two operations, the Bell grinding and fine grinding, decreased substantially during the period under study. They became increasingly separated from the rest of the department. On the other hand, the men operating the Scott-Winston machines were rewarded with increased status and power in the department, primarily at the expense of the Bell operators.

The changes that are the resultants of incentive plans, changes in quantities produced and relative earnings, can upset established social relationships. (Only with the knowledge of these informal group problems can management understand the operations of incentive plans.)

We need not place any particular value on this disruption and declare it "bad" or "good" to observe that the administrative skills of both management and union may be taxed to their limits. Here, for example, both management and the union were troubled by their inability to gain acceptance for a new work schedule incorporating a sixth day of work.

The workers' reactions to incentive systems are often pictured as irrational, emotional, and more specifically, noneconomic. While the distorted economic man theory, with its concentration on automatic adjustments to economic stimuli, has been discredited, the workers we observe operating under incentive plans are not unaware of their economic interests. Just as Roy shows that workers select jobs with the loosest rates upon which to concentrate their productive efforts and hold back on stinkers, an examination of an entire department will show *groups* of workers attempting to adjust themselves to the total environment for maximum personal gain.

The maximum gain, as perceived by employees, does not duplicate the image retained by the industrial engineer—a worker striving ever harder to beat the standard and thus earn additional bonus credits. On the contrary, the work group's definition of maximization is much more sophisticated, taking into account many variables besides immediate effort and bonus income. Maximum gain involves long-run job security (a highly economic variable), possibilities of adjustments or changes in the rate systems themselves, the effort cost of additional incentive earnings, and potential future effort costs.

Job security itself is not a single simple variable. One's job security can be affected by the amount of available work (and the speed with which it is processed), relative efficiency of competing processes and plants, susceptibility of the job to bumping by other employees during a period of economic decline, etc.

All these are viewed in relative terms: how have other workers fared in these matters, compared to oneself? And the comparisons that are made most easily involve work groups nearest one's own—particularly in the same or adjacent departments.[4] As we consider the impact of an incentive, we must look beyond the group for which it is designed and examine its relations with other groups in the social system of the factory.

Only after we observe the total situation, as seen by the participants, can we assess the economic as compared to the uneconomic motivation for their activities.

[4] A recent study of plant level collective bargaining concludes that some of the most important policy differences within the union, which in turn affect union elections, involve differences between face-to-face or adjoining work groups: Leonard R. Sayles and George Strauss, *The Local Union* (New York: Harper & Brothers, 1953), pp. 134-135.

# 9

# Problems for Union and Management

The grinders' case presented a problem for union as well as management. That is not unique. An incentive problem in one department may affect relations in various areas of the plant. The union is necessarily involved in any disequilibrium in the social system. These incentive disturbances often involve pressures directed simultaneously against union and management officials. Such pressures are difficult to cope with. A decision in favor of one group may antagonize another. Thus the adjustment of one disturbance may only give rise to another. As long as we deal with piece rates, the problems of "inequities" are always with us.

Below we present a sampling of cases to illustrate the various dimensions of these problems:

## WORK-FLOW DISTURBANCES

In our first case, Conrad M. Arensberg[1] shows how behavior in the plant reflects customary patterns of behavior in the community. This will be especially true in small-town plants where the workers associate outside of work.

In collecting case materials on industrial strife, I undertook not long ago to interpret the causes of a paper-mill strike. I had access to both union and management records, and I had the opportunity to interview those concerned, both on and off the job. The strike, it turned out, had been called by the paper-machine crew. The fact seemed strange to management, because the immediate cause of the strike, an incentive scheme introduced into the cutting-room, did not officially affect this crew in the least as it involved a totally different department. To management trained like many sociologists to keep community and industry apart in their minds, it seemed incomprehensible that men in no way connected during working hours with the crucial department should feel themselves aggrieved.

[1] "Industry and the Community," in S. C. Hoslett, *Human Factors in Management*, pp. 289-290. (New York: Harper & Brothers, 1947).

Yet it was easy enough to understand. On investigation one could show that the company's incentive scheme had effects far beyond the formal industrial relationships prescribed by the company's organization chart. The two sets of workers were bound by ties of kinship and by traditional patterns of age and occupational prestige, entirely outside the factory. The company's engineers had done far more than merely provide a better output in a single working department. They had, in fact, reversed the customary patterns of authority; they had set juniors and inferiors to hurrying up their seniors and superiors. The machine-room men had struck against the disturbance of their community.

The incident is a small one, but it illustrates that the relationship between community and industry is a matter of influences within a continuum in the lives of the persons working and living together. And it proves that it is social behavior, not geography or production, that defines the continuum. To separate one set of events of social behavior from another is merely to distort the reality.

When the incentive upsets behavior patterns that have existed in community as well as in plant, then the problem is doubly difficult. A disturbance within the plant system is quite enough by itself to present problems to union and management.

Leonard Sayles[2] presents these comments upon such work-flow disturbances:

When management introduces an attractive incentive plan that is successful in promoting increased production, some groups of workers feel that their interests are hurt. These are often the men on day-rated jobs who are just *above* or just *below* the incentive workers in the line of production. If the men on incentive speed up significantly, more material must be handled to supply them or in the finishing stages following their production operation. The day worker laments:

"Those guys get paid for every little bit extra, but we've got to handle all that increased production at the same old hourly wage rate."

In one case, for example, a day worker group became so incensed that they attempted to pressure their union leaders into "inducing" the incentive workers to cut down on production. This presumably would alleviate their sense of injustice.

Day worker groups can respond in other ways as well. In many instances they may demand an incentive plan of their own. Often they believe they should be included in the incentive plan that has affected their work loads, particularly if this is a group bonus system. However, management may not always be aware of this demand or at least may not be in a position to bargain effectively with the union. There are situations in which

[2] This case and the following ones are from "The Impact of Incentives on Inter-group Work Relations," *Personnel*, Vol. XXVIII, No. 6, (May 1952).

the present participants in a group incentive plan have no desire to broaden the base of the plan and include adjacent work groups. They believe, often mistakenly, that the inclusion of more workers diminishes their own share of the incentive and they encourage their officers to block any attempts at widening the group.

## INCENTIVE WORKER VS. DAYWORKER

While some inequities may affect only small groups in the plant, others have a plant-wide impact. In most plants having incentives, the piece rates cover only a part of the work force. In effect, management's pay policies divide the workers into two parts, dayworkers and incentive workers. This division does not exist only on paper. Workers respond to it and shape their behavior in terms of it.

All the cases that follow in this chapter are presented by Leonard Sayles.

### Leonard Sayles' Cases

Most personnel administrators are familiar with the feelings that separate dayworkers and incentive workers. Often there is a distinct differential between the average earnings of these two groups that favors the incentive workers in the plant. Union officials are constantly in a position of having to justify such differences. The problem becomes an especially acute one for the union during negotiations when the decision must be made: how much of a wage increase should we ask? How much means, in fact, how much should we give one group and not give another; for a majority of union leaders recognize that management has limited resources, just as the union has limited bargaining power.

Many dayworkers refuse to believe that the pieceworker actually earns all his extra wages. Although they themselves may be unwilling, or at least not anxious, to accept an incentive plan for their own job, they look at the incentive earnings of others as pure gravy. In turn they may expect the union to get them additional hourly benefits to compensate for these incentive earnings.

In one recent case in a medium-sized plant the union was able to work out a negotiation formula with management that apparently satisfied both dayworkers and incentive workers. The wage increase afforded the dayworkers somewhat greater benefits, presumably because of an existing inequity between these two large groups. All went well until the question of retroactive pay came into the picture. Management was willing to grant as an effective date for the wage increase the contract expiration date. A strike and the delay imposed by the Wage Stabilization Board finally resulted in a sizable pie to be divided among the membership. The union then discovered that the incentive workers were not satisfied with the wage settlement; they felt that the least that could be done would be for the day workers to consent to an equal sharing of all back pay.

The union meeting at which this proposal was discussed provides considerable insight into the feelings of these two groups toward one another. Several dayworkers got up to say:

These high-paid pieceworkers never offered to split their wages with a dayworker before, and so why should we split our wage increase?

In most of these negotiations we dayworkers have always taken a beating and we're certainly not going to give up any money that's coming to us now.

A former union president who was an incentive worker replied:

As far back as I can remember, and I've participated in a lot of negotiations, the union always went out of its way to see that the dayworker got a better break because the union realized that the dayworker didn't share in the incentive bonus.

A maintenance man shouted him down:

Sure, the union officers always have good intentions, but they don't mean a damn. The dayworker still has always been underpaid in this plant.

He was answered by another rank-and-file member who worked in an incentive job:

Maybe they're paid a little less because they do a little less work!

A long argument raged as to what group outworked the other until finally the president had to call an end to the debate.

After talking with the members one had the feeling that their attitude toward the wage increase itself would be conditioned by the outcome of this dispute between incentive workers and dayworkers. Thus, how workers interpreted the value of management's wage concession was related to the relative earnings of the two groups.

Differences within the rank-and-file group over incentives are not restricted to negotiations. But these are the most striking examples of intergroup problems resulting from the existence of different types of wage payment systems in the same plant. During the contract period itself, union officers have a multitude of decisions requiring them to *choose between* various work groups. Many of these do not directly involve grievances against management although indirectly plant morale and in turn productivity may be affected. In these cases union leaders are faced with the problem of deciding whether or not one group should be placated at the expense of another.

### PROMOTION FOR LESS MONEY?

Relative earnings among various jobs are important to management and workers alike when it comes to promotions. Theoretically, the jobs in the plant are arranged in a number of promotional ladders, with higher pay for each step up on any given ladder. Promotions then provide rewards for ability—or at least for long and adequate service. This enables management to fill the higher positions. But then the incentive system comes in, and we must ask: when is a promotion not a promotion?

The men in the stock cleaning room of a large manufacturing plant had a lucrative incentive plan. When an opening occurred for the job of inspector in that same department, the company was hard pressed to find candidates who would accept, although departmental seniority prevailed. Not only were the daywork inspectors bitter that their higher rated job paid *less* than the cleaners', but the men on cleaning rebelled whenever their union officials asked them to "promote" according to seniority.

### SHIFT VS. SHIFT

Various shifts on an incentive job closely compare their daily earnings records. As one worker from a shift "on the high side" expressed it:

Oh! you know they [the men on the other shift] always think you're hungry, that's all. They're jealous of anything. They think you're killing yourself to turn out all this stuff.

The case of department Z in a large mill is a good example of the type of disagreements that occur among shift crews. Three shifts had

been turning out about the same quantity until this incident occurred, as described by one of the men in the department:

On the first shift we put out a little bit more. In fact one day we unex-
pectedly hit 225. Well, then, the third shift got really sore—they figured
we were trying to break the line. So they cut their production even lower
than it had been the next day. In fact they got really mad and started
producing so little that the company began to complain.

It was rumored among the workers that management purposely
had inflated the first shift's production record in order to cause
trouble and break an informal production limit set by the men.
Internal jealousies magnified the third shift's reaction. In time social
pressure forced the first shift to reduce its production in line with
the other shifts. The level reached was lower than it had been
before the incident, for the men had grown increasingly antago-
nistic toward the company over the "mistake," and the intershift
differences this had generated. The rumor may have been false, but
the effect was substantial.

Internal conflicts among shifts resulting from a comparison of
earnings can have just the opposite effect, at least temporarily. A
feud between night and day shifts caused the night shift to *increase*
its daily output, in a casting department. This increase was a means
of expressing contempt for the day shift. Since earnings and, of
course, production are recorded by management, this group thought
it could embarrass the day shift by a substantial increase in its earnings and production. Management obviously benefited by this dispute.

Such benefits, however, are usually short-lived, for the instability
of such situations, leads eventually to an unpleasant aftermath. In
this case, for example, resentment built up until the shifts subtly
began sabotaging each other's efforts.

## LOOSE RATES AND UNION SOLIDARITY

We are accustomed to thinking of a loose rate as a problem for
management. In the field of intergroup relations, however, such a
rate can present just as severe a problem for the union. Union officers would be glad to have all rates equally loose, but this ideal
state seems never to arrive.

The same holds true for individual departments. When a loose rate appears in one section of the shop it is not unusual for men in other parts of the plant to begin to worry about what will happen when their jobs are studied for new incentive plans. They reason as did the men in department Y:

Those guys over there are killing the job. The union beat its brains out to get the company to give in a little on the incentive, and now the men are going to show it up so when the company gets around to putting an incentive on this job, it'll really be a tight one.

This rank-and-file logic as to the company's reaction to high earnings in one department working under a given incentive plan may or may not be correct. More important was the response of these dayworkers in their union.

Union officers were told in no uncertain terms that they had better "get those guys in department Y to cut down on their production." The argument that they were jeopardizing potential incentive earnings in other parts of the plant was bolstered, because indeed the union had struggled with the company to attain this particular rate for the job.

One situation was a classic example of interdepartmental differences. There had actually been a wildcat strike. The men had obtained union support to force the company to improve a particular incentive plan. When management consented to a compromise proposal and the men went back to work, production and earnings soared in the department that had walked out first. Shortly after, one could hear murmurings throughout the plant.

And to think we walked out for those guys. Look what they're earning now!

You can be sure it'll never happen again. They're working the rest of us to death.

Production in that department felt these pressures.

We found another loose-rate problem in department X, which was assembling and welding large steel containers for the armed forces. The work was considered of relatively low skill, and the department contained some of the lowest rated jobs in the plant. However, there was an urgent demand for the product, and management was much concerned when it could not get more than five or six units out of the department in an eight-hour day.

The union president urged management to offer the department an incentive rate. Management agreed, but somewhat reluctantly, since the group operation presented especial difficulties from a time-study standpoint.

As the time sudies proceeded, the union president himself spent a good deal of time in the department. Being a welder, he considered himself qualified to pass judgment upon time-study estimates. He also thought he was on good terms with the workers in the department, so that they would talk to him freely and frankly. On the basis of these observations and conversations, the president became convinced that eight units a day would be about the maximum possible production for an eight-hour day. After considerable argument with time-study men and production management, the president finally persuaded management to offer a rate figured in terms of maximum production of eight units.

No sooner had the rate been established than the workers began to do the impossible. Perhaps it was because they were short-service employees not yet used to the ways of restriction of output or perhaps it was because the defense order was considered a temporary run. Whatever the reasons, the workers cut loose. Within a few days production was up to twelve units, and it leveled off at sixteen per day.

Presumably the Defense Department was happy with this outcome, but all hell broke loose within the plant.

Long-service employees were bristling that young men who had been in the plant for less than a year were earning substantially more than they. One worker, a former union officer, summed up their sentiments:

Can you imagine how I feel walking into a bar and getting my check cashed next to some youngster who has only been in the plant a few months? He maybe gets thirty dollars more than I do and I've been around here for 15 years.

Throughout the plant there were demands that all incentive rates be renegotiated. At the time the company was attempting to establish a new system that would provide better cost control. For many months their efforts to gain union acceptance were fruitless; the men refused to cooperate in the new program.

Of course, there were also rank-and-file pressures on union officers to permit the older men to leave their regular jobs and bump some of the young men with the exceptional earnings. In fact, the union faced a whole series of internal squabbles on seniority questions related to such moves as men competed with one another for the right to move into that department. This in turn threatened the company with the loss of many experienced workers who were requesting transfers from other departments.

The union president now occupied a most awkward position. He had gone out on a limb to get an incentive for this department, and his beneficiaries had chopped the limb right off. Workers in other departments thought he had been played for a sucker and demanded that he go right back and get that rate cut. But who ever heard of a union demanding that management cut a rate?

Finally, the president and his grievance committee went to management with demands that management loosen certain tight rates in other parts of the plant. Management responded with a demand that it be allowed to cut the rate in department X. When management agreed to loosen certain of the tight rates, the union committeeman found no difficulty at all in agreeing to the rate cut.

This decision was greeted with indignation in department X. The workers protested loudly that the union—and particularly the union president—had sold them out.

Several months later the plant was shut down by an unexpected month-long strike. The issues presumably concerned a general wage increase under a contract reopening clause. However, the conflicts within the union may well have been a factor in precipitating the strike and building up the bitter feelings that accompanied it. The desirability of a general wage increase seemed to be the only point on which the various factions of the union could agree.

In an election of officers several months after the strike, the union president was defeated. In the earlier period he had seemed to be highly popular with the members. Was the department X case his downfall? Such an overturn cannot be accounted for by any single factor. No doubt many factors influenced the election. However, can it be only a coincidence that the man who defeated the president had once worked in department X and had remained close to the workers there?

# 10

# Group Dynamics and Intergroup Relations[1]

This is the story of an experiment that failed because it succeeded too well.

The Hovey and Beard Company manufactured wooden toys of various kinds: wooden animals, pull toys, and the like. One part of the manufacturing process involved spraying paint on the partially assembled toys and hanging them on moving hooks which carried them through a drying oven. This operation, staffed entirely by girls, was plagued by absenteeism, turnover, and low morale.

A consultant, working with the foreman in charge, "solved" the problem. But the changes that were made in order to solve it had such repercussions in other parts of the plant that the company abandoned the new procedures, despite their obvious benefits to production in that local area.

### THE PROBLEM

Let us look briefly at the painting operation in which the problem occurred.

The toys were cut, sanded, and partially assembled in the wood room. Then they were dipped into shellac, following which they were painted. The toys were predominantly two-colored; a few were made in more than two colors. Each color required an additional trip through the paint room.

Shortly before the troubles began, the painting operation had been reengineered so that the eight girls who did the painting sat in a line by an endless chain of hooks. These hooks were in continuous motion, past the line of girls and into a long horizontal oven. Each girl sat at her own painting booth so designed as to carry away fumes

[1] This chapter was written by George Strauss, based upon information furnished him by the consultant in the story, Alex Bavelas. The consultant also reviewed and revised the chapter.

and to backstop excess paint. The girl would take a toy from the tray beside her, position it in a jig inside the painting cubicle, spray on the color according to a pattern, then release the toy and hang it on the hook passing by. The rate at which the hooks moved had been calculated by the engineers so that each girl, when fully trained, would be able to hang a painted toy on each hook before it passed beyond her reach.

The girls working in the paint room were on a group bonus plan. Since the operation was new to them, they were receiving a learning bonus which decreased by regular amounts each month. The learning bonus was scheduled to vanish in six months, by which time it was expected that they would be on their own—that is, able to meet the standard and to earn a group bonus when they exceeded it.

By the second month of the training period trouble had developed. The girls learned more slowly than had been anticipated, and it began to look as though their production would stabilize far below what was planned for. Many of the hooks were going by empty. The girls complained that they were going by too fast, and that the time-study man had set the rates wrong. A few girls quit and had to be replaced with new girls, which further aggravated the learning problem. The team spirit that the management had expected to develop automatically through the group bonus was not in evidence except as an expression of what the engineers called "resistance." One girl whom the group regarded as its leader (and the management regarded as the ringleader) was outspoken in making the various complaints of the group to the foreman. The complaints had all the variety customary in such instances of generalized frustration: the job was a messy one, the hooks moved too fast, the incentive pay was not being correctly calculated, and anyway it was too hot working so close to the drying oven.

## INTRODUCING THE NEW APPROACH

The consultant who was brought into this picture worked entirely with and through the foreman. After many conversations with him, the foreman felt that the first step should be to get the girls together for a general discussion of the working conditions—something, incidentally, which was far from his mind originally and which in his own words would only have been "begging for trouble." He took this step with some hesitation, but he took it on his own volition.

The first meeting, held immediately after the shift was over at four o'clock in the afternoon, was attended by all eight girls. They voiced the same complaints again: the hooks went by too fast, the job was too dirty, the room was hot and poorly ventilated. For some reason it was this last item that they complained of most. The foreman promised to discuss the problem of ventilation and temperature with the engineers, and he scheduled a second meeting to report back to the girls. In the next few days the foreman had several talks with the engineers, and it seemed that the girls' cynical predictions about what the engineers would say were going to be borne out. They and the superintendent felt that this was really a trumped-up complaint, and that the expense of any effective corrective measure would be prohibitively high. (They were thinking of some form of air conditioning.)

The foreman came to the second meeting with some apprehensions. The girls, however, did not seem to be much put out, perhaps because they had a proposal of their own to make. They felt that if several large fans were set up so as to circulate the air around their feet, they would be much more comfortable. After some discussion the foreman agreed that the idea might be tried out. (Immediately after the meeting, he confided to the consultant that he probably shouldn't have committed himself to this expense on his own initiative; also, he felt that the fans wouldn't help much anyway.) The foreman and the consultant discussed the question of the fans with the superintendent, and three large propeller-type fans were purchased. The decision was reached without much difficulty, since it seemed that the fans could be used elsewhere after their expected failure to provide relief in the paint room.

The fans were brought in. The girls were jubilant. For several days the fans were moved about in various positions until they were placed to the satisfaction of the group. Whatever the actual efficiency of these fans, one thing was clear: the girls were completely satisfied with the results, and relations between them and the foreman improved visibly.

The foreman, after this encouraging episode, decided that further meetings might also be profitable. He asked the girls if they would like to meet and discuss other aspects of the work situation. The girls were eager to do this.[2] The meeting was held, and the discussion quickly centered on the speed of the hooks. The girls maintained that the time-study men had set them at an unreasonably fast speed and that they would never be able to reach the goal of filling enough of them to make a bonus.

The turning point of the discussion came when the group's leader frankly explained that the point wasn't that they couldn't work fast enough to keep up with the hooks, but that they couldn't work at that pace all day long. The foreman explored the point. The girls were unanimous in their opinion that they could keep up with the belt for short periods if they wanted to. But they didn't want to because if they showed that they could do this for short periods they would be expected to do it all day long. The meeting ended with an unprecedented request: "Let us adjust the speed of the belt faster or slower depending on how we feel." The foreman, understandably startled, agreed to discuss this with the superintendent and the engineers.

The engineers' reaction naturally was that the girls' suggestion was heresy. Only after several meetings was it granted grudgingly that there was in reality some latitude within which variations in the speed of the hooks would not affect the finished product. After considerable argument and many dire prophecies by the engineers, it was agreed to try out the girls' idea.

With great misgivings, the foreman had a control with a dial marked "low, medium, fast" installed at the booth of the group leader; she could now adjust the speed of the belt anywhere between the lower and upper limits that the engineers had set. The girls were delighted, and spent many lunch hours deciding how the speed of the belt should be varied from hour to hour throughout the day.

Within a week the pattern had settled down to one in which the first half hour of the shift was run on what the girls called medium speed (a dial setting slightly above the point marked "medium"). The next two and one-half hours were run at high speed; the half hour before lunch and the half hour after lunch were run at low

[2] These subsequent meetings were effective largely because of the reduced tension and the good will engendered by the original discussions.

speed. The rest of the afternoon was run at high speed with the exception of the last forty-five minutes of the shift, which was run at medium.

In view of the girls' reports of satisfaction and ease in their work, it is interesting to note that the constant speed at which the engineers had originally set the belt was slightly below medium on the dial of the control that had been given the girls. The average speed at which the girls were running the belt was on the high side of the dial. Few if any empty hooks entered the oven, and inspection showed no increase of rejects from the paint room.

Production increased, and within three weeks (some two months before the scheduled ending of the learning bonus) the girls were operating at 30 to 50 per cent above the level that had been expected under the original arrangement. Naturally the girls' earnings were correspondingly higher than anticipated. They were collecting their base pay, a considerable piece-rate bonus, and the learning bonus which, it will be remembered, had been set to decrease with time and not as a function of current productivity. (This arrangement, which had been selected by the management in order to prevent being taken advantage of by the girls during the learning period, now became a real embarrassment.)

The girls were earning more now than many skilled workers in other parts of the plant. Management was besieged by demands that this inequity be taken care of. With growing irritation between superintendent and foreman, engineers and foreman, superintendent and engineers, the situation came to a head when the superintendent without consultation arbitrarily revoked the learning bonus and returned the painting operation to its original status: the hooks moved again at their constant, time-studied designated speed, production dropped again, and within a month all but two of the eight girls had quit. The foreman himself stayed on for several months, but, feeling aggrieved, then left for another job.

## ANALYSIS OF SUCCESS AND FAILURE

It is not difficult to understand why installing the fans and permitting the speed of the hooks to be controlled by them should have affected the girls the way it did. No normal person is happy in a situation which he cannot control to some extent. The fans may not have actually changed the heat or the humidity, but they were a visible and daily reminder that worker ideas were given consideration.

About the speed of the hooks an additional observation may be made. The idea that efficient work results from proceeding at a constant rate derives certainly from the operations of machines and not from the characteristic operation of human beings. If anything is clear about human performance it is that it is characterized by changes of pace. Some production operations by their nature permit little variation in this respect, but even when the possibility exists it is not readily perceived by many engineers as a source of increased efficiency. From the operator's point of view, to be paced unvaryingly by a machine which he may not even shut down with impunity may be psychologically uncomfortable. In such a situation the only avenue left for the expression of any independence is that of complaint: the machine or its master, the engineer, must be shown to be wrong. Also, there appear to be inherent and unconscious defensive mechanisms which operate against the threat of being "stretched out."

Control over the speed of the hooks in this situation not only allowed changes of pace which were in themselves restful and refreshing, but also allowed the operator the natural enjoyment of operating at top speed without fear that he might be compelled to stay there. Of course, the manner in which the change was instituted was significant. The opportunity to exercise initiative, the gratification of being listened to seriously, helped to bring about changes in the emotional overtones of the situation which were in themselves favorable to increased effort.

In the light of all this it is not surprising that the situation fell apart so completely when the management retrogressed. And the management's action, while it may not have been wise, was certainly an understandable response to what had become an uncomfortable situation. Along with improved production in the paint room had come a host of embarrassments. The extra production in the paint room had created a pile-up in front and a vacuum behind, and both results were unwelcome to the adjoining departments. The wage structure of the plant had been shaken. The prestige of the engineers had suffered, and some of the prerogatives of management were apparently being taken over by employees.

It is clear from this instance that *local* improvements can often be obtained by the methods described here; but it is also clear that they may not lead to benefits for the enterprise as a whole. Changes in one part of an integrated organization may require widespread changes elsewhere, and the cost of such readjustments may far outbalance the benefits received in the local situation.

The changes made in the paint room implied over-all managerial attitude and philosophy that were not in fact present. This being the case, there was no conceptual or philosophic resource for dealing with the eventual implications of what had been done in the paint room. The management neither expected nor was ready to make the kind of changes that seemed necessary. It would have been far better if the consultant had done with the relevant management group what he had done with the foreman in the initial discussions, so that there would have been some shared understanding of the long-range implications of the moves. In a real sense, the superintendent was justified in feeling that the foreman and the consultant between them had put him on the spot. True, his assent to the changes had been secured, but the consultant had not been sufficiently concerned with his genuine understanding of the possible consequences.

The factory is a social system, made up of mutually dependent parts. A drastic change in one part of the system—even a change that is viewed as highly successful within that part—may give rise to conflict reactions from other parts of the system. It may then be dangerous for management to try a new approach in one small part of the system unless it is prepared to extend this approach to the whole organization.

Can the group methods that have been so successfully applied in small groups and single departments be applied on a factory-wide scale? We shall seek to answer that question in subsequent chapters.

# PART III

## THE PLANT-WIDE SOCIAL SYSTEM

# 11

# Pattern for Industrial Peace[1]

The reactions of the individual to the incentive system depend on his relations with his fellow workers. We have seen how an attractive incentive offer to one group of workers may create intergroup problems in the plant. Everything that we have done so far suggests that we are dealing with the factory as a system of mutually dependent parts where a change in one part can affect others throughout the system. If this is so, then we need to look at incentives in this broad plant-wide context.

The Inland Steel Container Company case to be discussed here involves individual and group incentives of conventional types. Here we see dramatic changes in worker attitudes toward incentives and in their productivity that can only be explained through examining developments within this broad social system.

The productivity record can best be represented by tons per man-hour produced in the plant. Before 1944 no such figures were compiled. If we use the 1944 record as a base figure of 100 per cent, we get the following table:

| Date | Productivity |
|------|-------------|
| 1944 | 100 |
| 1945 | 107 |
| 1946 | 105 |
| 1947 | 125 |
| 1948 | 143 |
| 1949 | 128 |

Here we note small fluctuations from 1944 through 1946. Then there is a sharp rise of almost 20 per cent in 1947. The following year there is a still further rise of more than 14 per cent. The 1949 figures represent a drop, but in the opinion of management and

[1] This chapter is based upon William Foote Whyte, *Pattern for Industrial Peace* (New York: Harper & Brothers, 1951).

union officials alike they represent changes in the types of orders that were running through the plant at this time rather than changes in the level of worker effort. The striking rise of productivity from 1946 through 1948 is, then, what we have to explain.

The changing situation can also be represented through union grievances directed at the incentive system. Here the Air Hose case can symbolize for us, as it did for the workers in the plant, all the bitterness they felt toward incentives and time study—and toward management in general.

The case involved a change in rates for two jobs on one punch press that blanked out steel covers for pails manufactured on the pail lines.

Some months, or perhaps even years, earlier there had been difficulty with this press, as the steel sheets stuck to the machine and failed to drop off automatically onto the inclined plane that took them to the next operation. To remedy this defect, a rubber air hose was attached to blow down on the covers from above. No one would say who had attached the hose except that everyone agreed that it was a worker and not a member of management.

This change had been in effect for some time and apparently known about and accepted by one or more foremen when it was noticed by a time-study man. The time-study man called in the engineering department. An engineer arranged to attach a metal hose in such a position that it would blow air up from the base of the machine.

After this change had been made, the time-study department restudied the jobs and cut the rate 9 cents per thousand pieces on one job and 11 cents per thousand on another. On November 11, 1946, the union steward lodged a grievance charging that management had had no right to cut these rates. He commented later, "They held us up on that just as if they had stuck a gun at us." Other workers and union officers greeted the change with equal bitterness.

Within two weeks the grievance had gone through three steps in the procedure, but at the fourth step the union's international representative was to come in. Since the union was then in process of changing its international representative in this area, it was some months before the fourth step discussion was held. In the meantime the negotiations of 1947 took place, and the union brought up this case as an example of its problems under the incentive system. Following conclusion of the negotiations in the spring of 1947, the Air Hose case finally reached discussion at the fourth step of the grievance procedure. At this time the burning issue of a few months earlier was settled amicably in less than two minutes' time.

How do we explain such a striking change? We shall not find our answers through an examination of technical aspects of the incentive system. There were no such changes of sufficient magnitude to account for either the sharp rise in productivity between 1946 and 1948 or for the shift in worker and union attitude toward the Air Hose case. It is only through examining *changes in human relations* that we can account for the changes in productivity and in attitudes toward incentives. The incentive system is part of the social system of the factory. As other parts of the social system are changed, the impact of the incentive upon people will correspondingly change. Our task is to examine the changes in worker-management and union-management relations and also the changes taking place within management and within the union, to see how these results were brought about.

### THE INCENTIVE UNDER CONFLICT CONDITIONS

In the years up through 1946 the incentive was a focal point of conflict in a bitter struggle between union and management. Management was plagued by a flood of grievances and by sporadic slowdowns and wildcat strikes. Production was disorganized. Turnover in management ranks was high, as one man after another tried in vain to cope with the conflict.

This is not the place for a detailed story of that conflict.[2] However, we can cite one incentive issue that grew out of the conflict and served to intensify the bitter feelings. In 1942 the union was demanding a 10-cent an hour wage increase. Since even in those prosperous times the plant was operating at a loss, management was determined to grant no increase. When it appeared that a strike was inevitable, the factory manager changed his position. He felt that at least the maintenance workers and others who received no incentive pay were entitled to 10 cents an hour and therefore he

[2] See William Foote Whyte, *op. cit.*, for the detailed story.

offered to add 10 cents an hour to the base rates in the plant. The contract was settled on this basis and it was only later that the incentive workers discovered that there had been no change in incentive rates. Thus their guaranteed minimum pay was higher, but their earnings remained the same for the same amount of production.

It is not clear whether the union leaders were fooled on this point. President Lucius Love said that he knew the incentive workers were not going to get anything, but he thought that management thereby had bargained itself into such an impossible position that it would have to give the incentive workers a raise in the near future. However that may be, it is clear that the incentive workers did not understand what was happening. When they discovered that they were receiving nothing, their resentment was intense. This built up pressures among the workers that led to sitdowns and slowdowns in department after department.

In 1944 a new top management took over the Chicago plant. John Gossett became vice-president and Robert Novy came in as general factories manager.

They came to Chicago from successful experience in operating the Jersey City plant of Inland Steel Container Company. They had known that the Chicago plant was having its troubles but they were amazed at the extent of the disorganization and demoralization they found when they began work there. The foremen all seemed on the verge of quitting. The union, with its slowdowns and stoppages and department and plant-wide meetings seemed to be in control of the factory. Even in the period of wartime prosperity, the plant was losing money. John Gossett decided that the first job was to stiffen the back of management. He would stop the wildcat strikes by refusing to discuss any issues until the men were back at work. He promised to back the foremen in discipline and urged them to regain the upper hand in their departments. He would be willing to meet with union officers on the basis of written grievances that claimed management had violated the contract, but he would refuse to have anything to do with discussion meetings such as had sprung up throughout the plant under his predecessors.

John Gossett took his stand on his first day in the factory. He was in his office discussing the situation with the retiring president when his secretary announced that a delegation from the union was waiting to talk with him. He told her to tell them that he would not see them. She said that they would simply sit in his office and wait for him. Thereupon he stepped into the outer office where President Lucius Love and three others waited for him. Love moved forward and extended his hand. Gossett put his hands behind his back and leaned against his secretary's desk.

"What is your business here?" he asked curtly.

"We want to discuss the general situation," Love explained.

"There is nothing to discuss," Gossett said.

Love cast about for a different approach. He started to say that there were many problems in the plant that needed attention, but Gossett cut him off by saying that grievance meetings were set up for that purpose.

Love tried again. The plant was in war production, its products were vitally needed. "Mr. Gossett," he said, "aren't you patriotic?"

"Is that a subject for negotiation?" Gossett countered.

Still the union men tried to argue, but Gossett would have no more of it. Furthermore, he said, "This is the last time I will ever see you in this office unless I call a meeting myself."

That was all. The men went out, stunned and boiling mad.

This instance made Gossett immediately the symbol of all the hatred over all the years that the workers had borne toward management. One man put it this way, in the next union meeting, "I'd like to take a rope and put it on Mr. Gossett's neck and hang him out of the second-story window of his office. I'd let him hang there, and I wouldn't even let a fly touch him until he agreed to respect our union officers."

There was an even more explosive aspect of the respect problem. By refusing to shake Love's hand, Gossett meant simply that he did not recognize the right of the union to have a meeting with him in this place at this time. But Love suspected that the man was prejudiced against Negroes.

Love's next encounter with Gossett added fuel to the flames. They met to discuss several third step grievances. The arguments grew bitter and at one point Gossett said to Love, "I know all about you. You're out to make a reputation for yourself. Well, I'm going to see that you don't do it here."

"I know all about you too," Love replied, "and I'll see to it that you don't stay here long."

As Love said later, "I thought to myself: Is that man really going to keep me from making my reputation?" The challenge made it even more of a personal issue to Lucius Love. All union-management relations in the plant revolved around the struggle between Gossett and Love.

Now, for every management move the union found a counter-move. For example, when John Gossett insisted that all grievances must be presented in writing, the union officers countered by writing up grievance after grievance and swamping the management with these written reports. For months, according to Love, at least half the grievances discussed in any meeting were of no importance to the union except as they were introduced in order to make trouble for management. Grievance meetings went on for hours, day after day, and still it seemed impossible to keep up with the flood of new grievances.

When Gossett threatened to fire employees who participated in slowdowns, Love countered by abandoning slowdowns and insti-tuting breakdowns. While the machines were not particularly deli-cate instruments, it was easy for an experienced worker to tamper with them so that they would break down. Since the departments were large and the foremen could not be everywhere at once, it was easy to do the trick without being observed.

Through late 1944 and the first part of 1945, tension steadily built up. The explosion came in August over a management disciplinary action. Several workers were suspended when, on in-structions from the union officers, they refused to follow manage-ment orders involving a change in their working schedule. When management sought to replace these men, other workers in the plant refused to accept the substitutions and were thereupon also suspended. The process went on from August 27 until September 12, by which time management had discharged fifty-three employees (about one-tenth of the work force) and was then forced to close the plant. The plant was closed for nine weeks while the case was argued before an arbitrator. His decision confirmed management's right to discipline employees for insubordination, but on the grounds that the discipline had not been properly carried out he ordered that the discharged employees must be brought back to work. Thus neither side won a clear victory and the war went on.

The plant operated for less than three months after this case when it again was closed by the steel industry strike on January 21, 1946. The industry strike lasted only three weeks, but here the union and management people were determined to resolve their differences once and for all and the strike dragged on for 191 days. The situation came to look so hopeless to management that the top officials began exploring the possibilities of closing the Chicago plant permanently and moving the machinery to some other location.

While people were relieved to go back to work after a long strike, no one was satisfied with the outcome. The management people recognized that the bitterness was still with them. The union leaders felt that they had lost important ground in the strike. They had got a wage increase in line with the prevailing industry pattern, to be sure, but they felt that certain contract changes strengthened the power of management against the union. The most important of these in their eyes involved the arbitration of incentive rates. Up to this time it had been possible for the union to take grievances concerning incentive rates for settlement by an impartial arbitrator. The new clause provided that grievances on incentive rates were not subject to arbitration. This meant that the workers could discuss such grievances with management, but management would have the final say in the matter.

To the workers and union officers this meant that management could cut rates in any way that it wished, and the union would be powerless to defend itself on this point. Management, of course, insisted that it had no intention of cutting rates, but to the union officers the Air Hose case represented exactly the sort of rate cutting they had feared. It was for this reason that the Air Hose case became a symbol of all the union-management problems that grew out of the incentive system.

### THE BEGINNING OF CHANGE

While the struggle went on, the middle management people and the foremen felt under extreme pressure from top management and from the union. The foremen had received written instructions that they were to listen carefully to any complaint raised by individual worker or steward, but there was no indication from top management that they were to consult the steward about any actions they took. They took this to mean that it would be dangerous to make any approach to the steward. Consequently, most of them took up a defensive position and stood the harassment of the union as best they could. Al Short, the general production supervisor, and Joe Kluck, the personnel manager, had been explicitly forbidden to meet with any union officers except to discuss formal grievances raised by the union. Thus the whole of management was organized to defend itself against the union.

The first tentative feeler in the direction of cooperation was made by Kluck and Short. By now they had despaired of reaching any peace with the union through following the policies of John Gossett. They were also under such constant nervous tension with the union-management struggle that the prospect of losing their jobs through violating orders was no serious threat. So one day Short and Kluck called in Lucius Love to begin talk about their mutual problems. Short began by displaying the pipe that he had been smoking at the last grievance meeting. There was a piece broken off its end, and he explained that he had bitten the piece off in anger in the midst of a union-management argument over grievances. He felt that this could not go on. Perhaps they might see whether they and Love could begin to find some basis for agreement.

Love welcomed the approach, and the two parties began to discuss their problems at this level. Several years later no one could remember any agreements reached here, but both sides agreed that this had been the beginning of a change.

### INCENTIVES FOR BARRELS

Following the end of the 1946 strike, management had introduced some far-reaching technological changes in the barrel department. This gave management the right to institute new incentive rates throughout the barrel department. At the same time management introduced a new procedure for the control of down time —time when the machines were not operating. The previous arrangement had been that the first 15 minutes of down time were absorbed by the workers but, if the down time extended for more than 15 minutes, management gave them hourly rate credit for the total period. This, of course, had put an incentive on lengthening the down-time periods. Even if the workers could have got the machine back into action in 5 or 10 minutes, they naturally preferred to string out the time to over 15 minutes so as not to absorb any of it themselves. The new 5-minute down-time feature required that the first 5 minutes of any down time should be absorbed by the workers but beyond that they were to get their regular hourly rates for additional time. This was expected to be an incentive to get the machines back into operation in a hurry.

Management sought to introduce the new rates and regulations in November 1946. The union charged that the rates were too tight. The arguments went on back and forth for nearly three months, in all of which time the workers were holding down production—and losing money themselves—in order to put pressure upon management.

Finally, on February 2, 1947, management called a meeting to give its final decision regarding the barrel department problems. John Gossett announced that there would be absolutely no change in the incentive rates. However, he did make certain concessions. Two men were to be added to each line so as to avoid production bottlenecks and there were to be several minor changes in job classification whereby people at several positions received a few cents more per hour.

Ed Snyder, foreman of the barrel department, was given the task of selling this decision to the union president, Lucius Love, who also worked in the barrel department. This proved to be a wise decision. In spite of the conflict going on all around them, the two men had got on reasonably well together. In fact Snyder had made a practice of consulting Love regarding various changes in the barrel department even though he was afraid this would not be approved by top management.

When the rates had first been announced in November, Snyder himself was not convinced that they were fair. Now, with the addition of men on the lines and changes in classifications, he was satisfied and prepared to sell the decision to Love. Love was by no means enthusiastic, but he was convinced that John Gossett would not change his mind and therefore he agreed to take the proposition to the men in the department.

After a long and heated discussion, the men agreed to give the new rates a try providing management would take action to correct some bugs in the lines. (The men had been aware of these bugs for some time, but had raised no complaints. The strategy was to loosen up the rates first, if possible, and then get the bugs eliminated.)

Love now reported back to Snyder and then union president and foreman walked back and forth along the lines while Love pointed out the mechanical problems the men had been discussing. Snyder felt that the claims were reasonable and agreed that he would try to get some action on them. When he first went to his boss, Al Short, he got the answer, "Oh, they're always bellyaching." Later Snyder made another try and this time was able to persuade Short to look into the matter. Now Short and Kluck got together and went over the lines with Love. Short and Kluck discussed the matter and then agreed to do what they could to carry through all the changes proposed by Love.

This decision put the two middle management officials in an awkward position. It was necessary to call in the engineering department to eliminate the bugs on the production lines, and Short did not have the authority to call in the engineers. For this purpose he had to go to his boss, Bob Novy, and in going to Novy he had to admit that he had violated John Gossett's orders and had been conferring with the union outside of the grievance procedure.

Novy listened to the story with some surprise. He considered the matter for a moment and then commented that he had noticed an easing of tension throughout the plant. He promised to send in the engineers. He told Short to go ahead with his meetings with Love but to be very cautious, for Novy was not inclined to trust the union leaders. Short in turn asked that Novy not notify John Gossett regarding this violation of his orders. Novy agreed that he would keep it to himself as long as he could.

Thus the changes were made in the barrel department and at last productivity began to rise.

### TELLING THE BOSS OFF

The story of the barrel department changes shows that within management there was considerable resistance to John Gossett in this period. The management people felt that Gossett was laying down the law to them just as he was to the union. No adjustment with the union was possible while management was divided against itself.

Al Short took the bit in his teeth. He went in to tell Bob Novy that he was ready to explode against the big boss, and he wanted Novy to make an appointment so that Short could tell Gossett just what he thought of him. Short didn't care whether he was fired then and there; he had to get his feelings off his chest. Novy listened sympathetically, agreed to make the appointment, but said that he wanted to talk to his boss first.

Novy then went in to see Gossett and laid it on the line. He told Gossett bluntly that the morale of the management organization was very low, that Gossett's autocratic approach had the members of management up in arms against him, that if Gossett did not change his ways even more serious problems could be expected.

Perhaps this was the turning point in the whole case. The big boss does not expect such a challenge from a subordinate and the natural tendency in such a situation is to defend himself and somehow take his resentment out against the subordinate who brings in the complaints. Had Gossett reacted in this way, no constructive solution of the industrial relations problems would have been possible. But, instead of fighting back, he recognized that the intense feeling manifested toward him was evidence of the serious problems in which he had become involved. If the situation was so explosive, then measures had to be taken quickly to drain off the pressure and make the necessary adjustments. When Bob Novy told John Gossett that there were many other members of management waiting to tell him off, Gossett responded that they should be given their turn at once. For the rest of the day, Gossett listened to Al Short and various others. Not once did he argue and when each finished Gossett thanked him for his full expression of feeling.

From this point on, John Gossett was a different man in the plant. He began more and more to consult with his subordinates. He seemed to take an active interest in their problems. He walked through the plant more and stopped to chat casually with the management people. The pressure was eased within management.

The management organization was preparing itself for the resolution of the union-management problems.

The change was recognized by the union also. As Love describes it:

So Mr. Gossett finally began to give some to the union and that was the time I had been waiting for. I knew things couldn't go on like this forever. If we kept on fighting, we just would kill each other off. I was hoping to see the day when we could live like people, so when Mr. Gossett began to give a little, I gave some too. That was easy to do then because half of the grievances we had in there didn't mean a thing and was just put in to make things hard for management.

### BARGAINING FOR COOPERATION

The parties were now preparing for the 1947 negotiations. While some improvements had been noted on both sides, it was obvious that if the two parties could not settle their negotiations without a strike, these first tentative gains in cooperation would be lost to the new conflict. The chances of a peaceful settlement appeared slim. Even though the union had had a long strike the year before, the local officers were anticipating a strike again, and the local had raised $3000 from its membership of 600 to prepare for the strike. A strike seemed indeed inevitable, for the union officers were determined to win back the right to arbitrate incentive grievances and the management people were equally determined not to relinquish the point that they had won the year before.

A new international representative, Lawrence G. (Jake) Shafer, entered the situation at this tense point. Since the new man felt there was a chance of reaching a settlement, Love and his fellow committee members were willing to let Shafer take control in making the effort.

In the first five negotiation meetings, the parties skirted about the incentive rate arbitration issue in order to make progress in other areas. Agreements were coming at certain points, but the key issue could not be avoided indefinitely, and so at last in the sixth meeting the incentive argument began. It was opened up by the lawyer for the company in this way:

KAUFMAN: All right. "The arbitration provisions of Section 2 shall not apply to the determination of wages, wage rates, or job classifications."

Now, that is one that I believe we are going to have to insist on. I don't know how familiar you are with the history of our problems in this plant, and I can imagine, without knowing, what the union has said about it. If the union wants to explain why it wants that change, maybe we had better hear from them first on it. I want to tell you at the outset that has been in there several years, I think, and we think that that provision is what has enabled us to beat several programs—when I say programs I am not mentioning a program that Lucius or Don or Ernie [local union negotiators] or anybody else is involved in—several concerted efforts which were pretty clearly slowdowns.

Is that a fair statement of our position, Bob?

NOVY: That is putting it very mildly.

KAUFMAN: I am a mild fellow.

SHAFER: I am interested in Mr. Novy's statement. You say, "That is putting it very mildly."

NOVY: That is right. We have had not several but a good many conditions here which, because of the inability of people to recognize at the time they were put in whether or not rates were fair, became slowdowns in an attempt by that means to force management to revise or change the existing conditions in relation to those rates, and it was not a healthy condition from either side. Everybody lost by it and since that time, in many cases, after the rates were in for a period of time, I am sure that the people found that they were not as unfair as they originally thought they were because they made out very amply on those rates.

We have no reason or method behind setting the rates other than setting them up fairly and equitably for everybody concerned on the basis of the way rates have always been set in this plant.

Gossett, Novy, and Kaufman went on to state that employee earnings in this plant were "substantially the highest in our industry."

Shafer replied simply, "I am very happy to hear that."

When management demanded to know how the union had been hurt by the clause prohibiting arbitration of wage rates, the union brought up the Air Hose case. John Gossett here kept insisting that the earnings of the worker on these particular jobs had increased and therefore it was not right to say that the rate had been cut. The union did not challenge the increased earnings point but argued that the man was putting out more effort for his pay and therefore the rate had been cut.

After the local committee had argued this case, Shafer came in with this concluding statement: "In the final analysis, the important factor in the making of a wage agreement, whether we are kidding ourselves or whether we like it or not, it is based on production."

Then he went on to state the issue in this way:

Certainly this organization of ours, the Steelworkers Union, is as interested in production as management because we are well aware of what it means . . . but certainly we can't be in the position of saying, "Now, here is a method we are going to introduce but any factor that may arise from this in no way whatsoever shall be arbitrated."

I am sorry, gentlemen, I just can't go along with you on that basis.

At this point the disagreement still seemed impossible to resolve.

As meeting followed meeting, the parties were able to reach agreement on one point after another until finally only the arbitration issue blocked settlement. Somehow, in the course of negotiation, the interpersonal atmosphere began to change so that the men were beginning to understand and trust one another. How this happened cannot be retold here,[3] for we are simply concerned with showing that with changes in human relations come changes in reactions to incentive systems.

### REACHING AGREEMENT

What has been said should not lead us to the conclusion that reaching agreement depends entirely upon the personal adjustment among the parties. In this case there was no difficulty in reaching agreement on a wage increase because management was prepared to offer and the union to accept an increase which fitted in with the industry pattern that had been developing quite outside of this case. Furthermore, the avoidance of a strike still depended upon finding a solution to the deadlocked issue of rate arbitration. As late as the ninth negotiation meeting, even though we read in the record impressive tributes from one side of the table to the other, we still find the union prepared to strike if management does not concede arbitration and we find management prepared to stand a strike rather than yield.

While we recognize that a good understanding among the negotiating parties does not guarantee settlement, it nevertheless seems to create an atmosphere in which the settlement of difficult issues becomes easier to achieve. Such was the case here.

[3] See *Ibid.* for full account.

In the middle of the tenth meeting the deadlock suddenly gave way, and in the eleventh and final meeting agreement was reached. Management held firm in its refusal to arbitrate new incentive rates. The union won a new provision applying to changes in old rates. Management could change a rate only if there had been a change in the content of the job. The union was free to raise a grievance claiming that no significant change in job content had been made. Such a grievance could be carried to arbitration. If the arbitrator then ruled in favor of the union, the previous rate would be retroactively reinstated. It seemed to the union negotiators that this clause would cover any new case resembling the Air Hose case and therefore they felt they had won substantial assurance against rate cutting. Also, in connection with new rates, the union won from management an assurance that every effort would be made to set them in line with existing rates on similar jobs—even where an industrial engineer might consider those rates to be on the loose side.

### CONSOLIDATING THE GAINS

The signing of the contract seemed to promise a new era in union-management relations and yet many people naturally had their fingers crossed. They recognized that the real measure of the change would be made in the day-to-day handling of problems within the plant. And the most important first step was to come in the fourth step grievance meeting that followed the signing of the contract. This marked Shafer's first appearance on grievance cases. He came in with the union committee to deal with an accumulation of twenty-two cases that had piled up over a period of months.

Shafer opened the meeting by announcing that, in addition to the grievances the union had one problem in the barrel department that was not strictly a grievance. Instead of taking a legalistic position and refusing to discuss a nongrievance problem, the management people invited the committee to take this one up first.

There followed a brief discussion of a series of incidents that indicated to the union people certain deficiencies in the foreman's handling of his men. John Gossett accepted the criticisms without argument and promised to act to clear them up. Shafer responded by expressing appreciation of the position taken by management and proposing that the union work together with management to increase productivity in the plant. This offer was, of course, welcomed.

The celebrated Air Hose case reached its final settlement here. Novy reviewed the figures. The job, he explained, came up infrequently. Management had records of running the job only twice in 1945, before the new rate, and three times in 1946, and five times in 1947. The average earnings on the job were 86 cents in 1945 and (not counting straight-time pay increases) $1.19 in 1946 and $1.20 in 1947—an increase of 33 to 34 cents per hour.

A union negotiator said that if he could see the earnings record in the time-study department he would withdraw the grievance. Shafer added, "That's for sure, it will be withdrawn."

So the case was cleared, with ridiculous ease. In two minutes these men disposed of an argument that had been going on for over a year. Why did the hard problem suddenly become so easy? Was it the introduction of the earnings figures that made the difference? No. They had been aired in earlier stages of the grievance procedure, but they had made no difference then.

We can understand this case only if we view it *symbolically*. Before the adjustment of relationships, the Air Hose case had been one of the key symbols of the conflict. For the workers and union leaders the case had symbolized the hatred and distrust they bore toward management. It was evident to them that management was unfair and ruthless. So long as they continued to believe that management was unfair and ruthless the case could have no other meaning to them, no matter what logical arguments were brought against them. But as soon as relations were reorganized so that the hatred and distrust were beginning to be dissipated there was no longer an emotional need to hold onto that symbol of conflict. It then became possible to treat the case in terms of facts and figures, and by that time it was hardly worth bothering about.

The other grievances were settled with equal ease, with adjustments being made on both sides. Twenty-two grievances—enough to occupy several long meetings in earlier years—were now settled in little more than an hour. When the men around the table had built up confidence in each other, the thorny issues of earlier years seemed easy to handle.

## TYING IN TIME STUDY

Though the workers through their union had won some assurance of protection against the activities of the time-study man, they still regarded his presence in the department as a threat to the stable situation they had achieved. Management recognized this problem by making a change in the relations of the time-study men to production management and to the union. In an earlier period the time-study man had been completely free to move about the plant and to make such observations and studies as he had been directed to undertake by his supervisor. He might come into a department without any explanation or warning to the foreman or to any of the workers. Management now established a new procedure whereby the time-study man was not to enter any production department without written authorization from the general factories manager or the general production supervisor. Furthermore, before he made any observations of workers, he was to present his authorization to the foreman and discuss plans with him. The foreman then was to call in the union steward so that the three men could discuss the steps to be taken. Only after this had been done was the time-study man free to go out on the factory floor, and he was always accompanied by the foreman and steward who explained to the workers what he was planning to do.

Furthermore, in the earlier period the time-study man had established the new rate without necessarily consulting the foreman. The rate was discussed with the union only when a grievance was raised against it. Under the new procedure the time-study man submitted his proposed rate to the departmental foreman for approval. In case of disagreement between the two, the decision was made higher up in production management. Finally, before the rate was to be put into effect, it was announced to the union steward and he was allowed to check the figures that had gone into the decision. Management did not ask the union's permission to institute a new rate, but by involving the union in the discussion at this point the management was in a position to decide whether to insist that the rate was fair in case of disagreement and invite a grievance or to reexamine the situation and see whether a change should be made.

These changes were greeted with enthusiasm on all sides. The time-study man does not have frequent enough contact with the workers in any single department to reach any sort of personal adjustment with them; it is therefore unrealistic to expect that he personally be able to win any degree of acceptance for himself or his function if he operates alone. Since the foreman is in constant touch with his men, it is only sensible to tie the time study in through the foreman channels. As the foreman and the steward work increasingly closer together, the time-study man finds his road toward acceptance in the department through working with both men. Finally the change in procedure in establishing new rates eliminates a not uncommon situation where even the foreman feels that the rate established is unfair but is powerless to do anything about it. Furthermore, the informal discussion between steward and foreman regarding the proposed rate allows management to reassess its position before the issue has been sharply drawn. It is much easier for management to make a change at this point, if a change seems desirable, than is the case when both parties have taken a firm position.

These new interpersonal procedures in the handling of time study—together with a great change in the over-all relationship—almost completely eliminated grievances on incentive rates. In fact, in a short time the total number of grievances of all types dropped almost to zero.

### GETTING ACTION THROUGH THE UNION

In the conflict period, management had sought to maintain a firm defensive position toward the union. Contacts with the union were strictly limited to grievances. Thus, in almost every case where the two parties came together they were discussing a union challenge to a management decision. In such a situation it is natural for the management people to find each contact unpleasant.

Now the management approach changed at the top level and at lower levels all down the line. Management was calling upon the union for help and advice on all sorts of problems of mutual concern.

This was done in particular problems, such as a temporary refusal of receiving department workers to accept overtime work. It was also done on large-scale and complex problems, such as that involved in a reorganization of the work of the maintenance department. There management, plagued by high costs, initiated a series of discussions with Shafer and top local union officials and with departmental union officials that led to changes within the department that not only improved efficiency but also eliminated trouble spots in union-management relations.

Union and management together evolved a joint approach to their mutual problems. Either union or management took the initiative in bringing a problem in for discussion. If the initial discussion took place at the top level, lower levels of union and management were then involved in discussing the problem before action was taken.

We can take an incentive problem to show how this new approach worked. The case involved the assignment of jobs in the punch press department. That department handled a number of jobs, each of which had its own incentive rate. As we might expect, some rates were looser than others and some jobs required more physical effort than others. Since the jobs were similar and all the workers had the skill to perform all of them, the question of choice of jobs had no clear-cut answer. The custom had grown up that each day workers could have the choice of jobs available according to their seniority ranking in the department. If each job had lasted an equal length of time, then the choice of jobs would have been relatively simple, for the workers had similar ideas as to the relative desirability of the various jobs. However, the schedule might call for job A, the most desirable job, to run for about two hours, while job E, which was not nearly so desirable, would run all day long. Would the top seniority man choose A and take his chances on getting perhaps a much less desirable job than E when his first job ran out? Or would he play safe and pick job E? Sometimes he would do one and sometimes the other. This meant that the worker next in seniority did not know what job he would have until the first man had made his pick, and the third man did not know until the second man had made his, and so on down the line. This also meant that the foreman had an impossible task in planning the work. He had to take home each night a list of the jobs to be run the next day and make up his job assignments on the basis of his guesses as to what each worker would choose. If he guessed wrong, then the schedule was turned upside down and the department was thrown into a state of confusion. Production time was lost, and there were arguments between foreman and workers, foreman and steward, and among workers as to who had a right to what. The low seniority people were particularly annoyed, for they felt they never got a chance at a good job unless it was to run for just a short time.

Columbus Gary, vice-president and chairman of the grievance committee (and later president), found that he was spending part of every day trying to straighten out confusion and conflict in the punch press department. He called the steward aside to work out a new procedure for job assignment. The two men then went to plant management to make this proposal. The plant manager checked with the foreman, who agreed. Then Gary called a departmental union meeting which he conducted with the aid of the steward.

The proposed new procedure involved three main points:

1. All jobs in the department were to be ranked according to their relative desirability, leaving entirely out of consideration different running times of particular jobs on particular days.
2. This fixed ranking was to be determined in discussion and vote by the members of the department themselves.
3. Workers were to be assigned to these jobs corresponding to their ranking on the seniority roster. This meant that the top seniority man would always get the top ranking job, but he would have to take his chances that sometimes it would only be for a short run. He would thus do better on the average than lower seniority people, but they would sometimes get a chance to do jobs that paid well because of their long duration on a particular day.

The workers agreed to the proposal and then went about determining job rankings. In most cases there was little disagreement that job X was better than job Y, and in a short time all the jobs of the department had been ranked. This ranking was accepted by popular vote and submitted to the foreman as a guide to job assignment.

The results were gratifying on all sides. The work went forward without interruption, and the foreman no longer had to worry over job assignment after working hours. Troublesome arguments

between foreman and steward and among the workers were eliminated.

For our purposes, the substance of the agreement is not important.
Its significance lies in the social process that led to agreement. Here
we see a proposal initiated by the union and worked out with several
levels of management. But we also see a general plan carried through
to specific implementation by means of involving the rank-and-file
workers in the department.

We do not mean to suggest that every decision in union-management relations should involve such active participation on the part
of the rank and file. That would lead to chaos. However, it is one
of the secrets of the successful relationship evolved here that it is
not only a top level agreement; the rank and file is actively involved
wherever the opportunity offers itself.

### INTERPLANT COMPETITION

As worker and union-management relations changed so that holding back production was no longer a desirable goal, management
did not rest idle on the production front. In the same subsidiary
there were two other container plants making some of the same
products with the same sorts of production lines. In the period of
conflict production at the Chicago plant was always lower than at
Jersey City or New Orleans. As Chicago's production rate began to
rise, management saw to it that workers and union officers were
constantly informed about the standing of their production lines,
department or plant, in relation to the other two plants. When the
Chicago barrel department first surpassed the production record
made in one of the other two plants, the occasion was celebrated
with Coca-Cola and cigars all around. Management followed up
by hanging in the department a wooden plaque bearing the names
of the foreman and assistant foreman and each worker on the production line that had made the record, plus of course the amount
produced. As record followed record in department after department, each new achievement was symbolized in a similar manner.

In the space of a few months the Chicago plant moved up from
third into first place in its average production per man-hour and
won most of the records for individual runs in the various departments of the three plants.

Production rose so phenomenally that on some production lines the workers were turning out more units than the maximum capacity of the line as estimated by the engineers. This does not mean that the machines operated faster than the engineers thought possible. The increase came in the elimination of down time. All the engineering estimates called for a certain allowance for mechanical failures. The same workers who in the conflict period had developed great skill in encouraging the machines to break down now brought the same skill to bear in keeping them in running order.

Production was pouring out faster than ever before and yet the workers did not seem to feel under pressure. In fact, many of them said that they felt less tired at the end of the workday than they had in the conflict period when they had produced far less.

In the changing situation high production had now become a goal for workers as well as management. In the conflict period any attempt of management to stimulate interplant competition and to get the workers to take an interest in records made at other plants would have been scoffed at and bitterly resisted. Now, in the new context of human relations, these devices came to be looked upon as deserved and welcomed recognition for a job well done.

## CONCLUSIONS

In this case we have seen productivity rise spectacularly during a period when there were only minor changes in incentive rates. If the economic incentive remained more or less constant, something else must have made the difference. What was that something else?

It is our thesis that *changes in human relations* provided that something else which led workers to react in a new way to the incentive system. We have described some of those human relations changes. In our analysis in Part IV, we shall seek to show systematically how human relations changes described here, and to be observed in later cases in Part III brought about this changed reaction to incentives.

# 12

# Sharing Labor Cost Savings[1]

The difficulties observed in individual piece-rate systems are not a new discovery. They are familiar to factory production and engineering people.

Some have sought to meet this problem by making technical improvements in the time-study procedures. Others have sought a solution, as in the preceding chapter, in effecting basic improvements in worker-management and union-management relations. And finally there are those who have sought to devise new types of incentive which might encourage productivity without at the same time creating conflict within the factory. It is such an effort that we shall now examine.

Management is interested in the performance of the plant as a whole. It cannot be satisfied with successes in certain work groups that are counterbalanced by failures in others. Why, then, should we not develop an incentive that is based upon the performance of the plant as a whole? Such efforts are now becoming increasingly common. In some cases they have been marked by spectacular success. In other cases little if any improvement has been shown. If we are to assess the possibilities of this new approach to incentives, we must examine various cases in order to account for the results achieved.

Here we shall examine two cases occurring in plants of the Acme Manufacturing Company (the name of the company and other identifying features have been changed, but the essential facts are as discussed below).

In the Metropolis plant the new incentive plan was an im-

---

[1] The first case study is based upon William Foote Whyte, "Incentive for Productivity," *Applied Anthropology*, Vol. VII, No. 2 (Spring 1948).

The second case study is based upon a research report by Frank Miller and Friedrich Fuerstenberg.

mediate and impressive success although in the long run it did not bring all the gains that management had hoped for. Introduced later into the branch Valley plant, the incentive has been relatively unsuccessful from the standpoint of both workers and management.

The cases provide us with a natural comparison as the two plants produce the same lines of products: parts for the automotive and appliance industry. Each plant is divided into two main parts: a production department where the product is manufactured on automatic machinery and a larger finishing department where the final fabricating is accomplished. In addition there are of course smaller tool and die and maintenance departments. Workers in both plants are represented by the UAW-CIO. The main difference between the two is in size, with the Metropolis plant having about 1000 workers at the time of our research while the Valley plant had 500.

Let us first tell the story of each case and then seek to account for the differences in results.

### THE METROPOLIS CASE

The new incentive plan in the Metropolis plant was born in a period of economic crisis for the company. That crisis in turn grew out of years of difficulties with incentives and productivity.

When the UAW organized the plant in 1937, one of its first and strongest demands was for the elimination of the incentive system then in force. The company reluctantly conceded on this point, but insisted that instead the company should establish production standards for all the various operations and should be empowered to insist that these standards be met.

The following years were marked by almost unremitting strife over the production standards. Management estimates that 65 per cent of its grievance time was spent in arguing cases involving interpretation of standards. Management also encountered formidable resistance to the introduction of new machines or new methods of work. Furthermore, the engineers reported that even when it was possible to overcome this resistance and to introduce the new machine or more efficient method there would frequently be no increase in productivity. Instead, the workers would take advantage of the change in order to produce the same amount with less effort.

When war contracts came along, there was less pressure to keep costs down and finally in May 1944 production standards were abandoned. According to the company, this move was accompanied by a further drop in productivity.

In the fall of 1945, with the end of war production, management changed from a three-shift to a two-shift operation. When there had been three shifts, the workers had been paid for their 20-minute lunch period. Now management proposed to have the workers take 20 minutes of their own time so that the full eight hours would be devoted to production. This issue precipitated a strike. While the strike lasted only a little over a month, it generated considerable feeling on both sides and placed the company in a precarious economic position.

At this time the basic patents that had led to the rise of Acme had run out and the processes were now freely available to its competitors. Management estimated that efficiency in the plant was down to 60 per cent of what it had been in 1937. Competitors were operating more efficiently and paying lower wages. Finally some of the automobile manufacturers were beginning to make these particular parts for themselves.

In this crisis the president of the company resorted to a drastic measure. He called all the employees together and, after giving them the background of the economic problem, announced that the board of directors had authorized the closing of the fabricating division of the plant. Such a shutdown would have thrown 75 per cent of the workers out of their jobs and would have resulted in the dismissal of about the same proportion of supervisory employees and large numbers of office workers.

Having painted the grim picture, he now reported that there was just one chance to save the fabricating department. He put it this way:

I propose that we introduce an incentive system in the fabrication department. I propose that that system be worked out jointly between management and representatives of your own choosing.

Management followed up this speech by holding a referendum in the plant on the question as to whether the union and management should get together to work out such an incentive plan. Workers, office people, and supervisors all voted, and they voted, of course, to try to keep their jobs.

The union then held a meeting and ruled that the referendum had no force, since the union had not authorized it. However, in this desperate situation the union leaders did not feel that they could risk turning down management's offer. Several meetings were held between management and local union officials and a representative of the UAW office. The union officials expressed interest in profit-sharing arrangements, but management refused to consider such a course. When the union had nothing further to suggest, management came in with its Savings-Sharing Plan which had already been worked out except for a few details. After full discussions of this plan the union officials decided to give it their backing and it was approved at a membership meeting. The new plan went into effect on April 1, 1946. At the same time workers received the 18½ cents an hour increase which was, then, the industry-wide pattern.

*The Savings-Sharing Plan*

The Plan in essence calls for equal division between hourly rated employees and management of savings in labor costs. The standard against which the savings are computed is a 16-week period, October 1, 1945, to January 22, 1946. The company agreed to take this as a standard even though it had been arguing that costs were unduly high. In this period labor costs were 30 cents on the sales dollar. This figure was computed from the figures in three categories of production, each category having a somewhat different average figure. As these three categories vary in their proportion to the total production from month to month, the labor costs standard varies accordingly going a little above or a little below 30 cents on the dollar. However, for our purposes we can think of the figure as an even 30 cents.

To illustrate the operation of the Plan, let us assume that in a given month the Metropolis plant produced an even million dollars of products. The 30 cents on the sales dollar figure would then allow for an expenditure on labor of $300,000. Let us assume that in this case only $240,000 was actually spent, leaving a figure of $60,000 to be shared between labor and management.

Let us assume that the 1000 workers worked a total of 160,000 man-hours. If we divide this figure into the $30,000, which is labor's share of the savings, we get a figure of 18¾ cents.

All hourly rated employees—whether in production, fabricating, toolroom, or maintenance—share equally in the savings plan according to the number of hours worked. For example, a worker who in this hypothetical month had put in 160 hours would receive a bonus of $30.

The Plan was based on prices of the company's products in the base period (October-January 1945-46). This relationship was fixed so that price increases would not add to the workers' bonus nor would price decreases subtract from it.

## Inauguration of the Plan

The Plan was an immediate success, yielding 24 cents an hour bonus to the workers in its first month of operation. The workers, of course, responded happily to this bonus. The management people were enthusiastic not only at the initial achievement but also because they were convinced that much greater possibilities lay ahead. However, in this expectation they were disappointed. The average earnings for the first year under the Plan fell just slightly below the first month's figure of 24 cents. In succeeding months earnings fluctuated around this figure with no upward trend. Management estimates the productivity increase for the year at 68.4 per cent—a substantial gain indeed, but all attained in the first month.

Fruits of the Plan were not limited to productivity and earnings. Comparing the first year of the Plan's operation with the previous year, we find absenteeism down 43.9 per cent, labor turnover down 43.5 per cent, and time spent on grievances down 41 per cent.

While the effects of the Plan were apparently quite diffuse, we shall here concentrate upon the productivity problem. We shall try to answer two questions: Why did productivity jump so strikingly the first month? And why were no further gains achieved after the first month? To arrive at our answers, we shall have to examine the network of human relations into which the Plan was introduced.

*Management-Worker Relations*

In discussing the problems existing between workers and management before the introduction of the Plan, we should not overemphasize the severity of the conflict. There were sharp disagreements, to be sure, but there were also elements of stability in the relationship.

The foremen and the general foremen had all come up through the ranks. Throughout the conflict at least the people knew each other and knew what to expect from each other. Furthermore, even though they sometimes fought inside the plant, when they were outside they carried with them some identification with the company and the Metropolis plant. There was, for example, a bowling league of Acme people through every winter season. At the time of the strike in the fall of 1945 the bowling league consisted of fourteen teams on many of which workers and members of management bowled together. The works manager bowled on one of these teams and was quite a popular figure. The league carried on through the strike period. It seemed that the people were used to working and playing together and simply felt that sooner or later their differences would be resolved. The mingling of workers and management people on the same teams also suggests a deemphasis on the status distinctions that separate workers and management in many plants.

The Plan therefore had something to build upon. At the same time we heard on all sides that there was a much better feeling between workers and management than existed in the pre-Plan period.

*The Role of the Foremen*

The most marked change seems to have occurred in the role of the foremen. In the early period of union-management strife, the foremen occupied the uneasy position of "the man in the middle." They were under pressure from management to get out production and at the same time they were criticized for not handling workers skillfully. The foremen found now and then that their decisions were overruled in higher level union and management discussions. Furthermore, they were placed in the awkward position of learning about prospective changes in the plant from the union steward instead of from management.

Higher management had begun to work on the problem with some effect even before the institution of the Plan. The works manager and his general foreman made every effort to see to it that the foremen had information regarding changes at least as soon as such information went out to union officers and before such release in many cases. The works manager also conducted monthly meetings with all the foremen at which time there was an opportunity to discuss their problems. Such monthly meetings are not unusual in management, but here it was the spirit with which they were conducted that was significant. After a brief exposition on the company's plans, the works manager would say, "Let's have some gripes from the foremen." The foremen learned that such complaints were actually welcomed—and acted upon. The foremen interviewed in 1946-1947 said that a great improvement in the relations with higher management had been brought about.

The most marked change in the foreman's role involved his relations with workers, and this change was attributed directly to the Plan. For example, one foreman put it this way:

I'm more friendly with the people working for me now than I was before. Before the Plan came in, people didn't want to work and you had to keep after them all the time and that made the foreman a son-of-a-bitch. Now they have some interest in working so you don't have to push them so much.

The job is harder and easier than it was before. It's easier because you don't have to keep pushing people but it's harder because you've got to be on your toes to see that things keep moving. You've got to watch everything to see that when somebody runs out of a job you have the next thing lined up for them. If you don't do that they come after you and want to know why you can't organize the work right.

Eighteen months after the inauguration of the Plan the top union local officers reported that there had been a great improvement in foreman-worker relations and that now also foremen and union officers got along much better together.

## The Role of the Methods Engineer

There has been perhaps an equally significant change in the role of the methods engineer. In the early period he had been involved in the task of making time and motion studies in order to establish production standards and to restudy standards that had been challenged by the union. He was thus at the heart of the conflict.

With the inauguration of the Plan, time study was abandoned except for an occasional study made to provide a cost estimate on a new product. At this same time the chief methods man, who had been supervising the time studies, quit the company and other members of the department sought to adjust to their new functions.

Apparently the adjustment has been good. While all the methods men were graduate engineers, they had had unusually intimate contacts in the shop, some of them having actually worked in production or in the toolroom while going to school at night. Even the time-study label did not seem to have a permanent effect on the relationship. One former time-study man made this comment:

It's true that they didn't like the job that we were doing but in some cases they would make a distinction between the man and the job. I've had fellows say to me outside of work, maybe when we were bowling together, 'How does a fellow like you take a stinking job like that?' While there was a lot of friction around the job, it did get us out on the floor where we got acquainted with all the men.

In methods the engineering function shifted from an effort to control workers toward an effort to help them and the foremen get good production. The methods man would spend many hours of the working day in the shop observing the work and talking to workers and foremen about the methods being used and about possible improvements.

In the time-study period workers would rarely suggest an improvement in method to the industrial engineer. Eighteen months after the inauguration of the Plan, the engineers were saying that about forty-five suggestions a month were presented to them directly or indirectly by workers. When a worker came to them directly regarding a suggestion, they would consult with him on it and then try to develop a three-cornered discussion including the foreman so that he would not be by-passed. In other cases the foreman would present to the methods engineers an idea that had been brought to him by a worker. An easy informal relationship seems to have developed here. Such a relationship seems to be essential to the development of improved methods in the plant. Often the worker has an idea that is basically sound, but he lacks the opportunity or the detailed knowledge necessary to work it out. The foreman is in somewhat the same position. The methods engineer, who can get workers and foremen to look upon him as one who is there to help them to effect improvements, is in a position to tap a rich vein of practical knowledge.

Management here offers no direct financial reward for suggestions. The workers are encouraged to write their idea on a slip prepared for the purpose, and turn it in to the personnel department. Decisions on practicability are taken by the methods engineers, who may have been in on an earlier informal discussion with the worker. If the suggestion is accepted, it is put into effect in the shop and the name of the suggester appears in the house organ. The nature of the idea is not reported there, according to the methods man, because it has been found in the past that often several workers have thought about the same general idea, whereas only one has put it into writing. While there are no cash rewards for suggestions, the acceptable ones are recorded on the personnel records of workers and foreman so that they may be used as the basis of determining qualifications for advancement. Today, some years after the introduction of the Plan, there is a feeling on the part of some people in management and in the union officer group that individuals are not sufficiently rewarded for offering suggestions. We shall examine in a later chapter the possibilities and limitations involved in several methods of stimulating suggestions from the ranks.

The methods engineers also report a remarkable change in worker reactions to technological changes that have been introduced. Now they meet little resistance in this area. Part of this may be attributed to the effects of the Plan, for it is now possible for management people and union officers to say to the workers involved that everyone is sharing in the economic benefits resulting from this improvement. However, this is not the only explanation. Change here is made easier by the very way in which the engineers have learned to handle changes. Their informal relationship with the shop is a great help here. They build on this through consultation with workers, union officers, and foremen regarding the introduction of improvements well before a new machine is to be put into operation. They seek to modify their own plans in response to complaints and suggestions from those affected by the change.

## The Role of the Union

Turning to the field of union-management relations, we also find considerable improvement. But here we find the answer to the question as to why the Plan has not been even more successful. We shall examine attitudes and actions in relation to the Plan after we have looked at the structure of union-management relations.

It is evident that union-management relations at Acme have been settling down and fitting into a stable pattern. Grievances have become easier to handle and most of them are now worked out at the bottom level, with the steward reaching an agreement with the foreman. On many occasions the foreman takes the initiative on his departmental problems and then calls in the steward for support. At the top level in the plant the works manager and the personnel manager have been increasingly taking the initiative in union relations. When changes are to be made they avoid trouble by calling in the union and talking things over in advance. Many issues are settled in this manner before they become difficult.

When we turn to the Plan itself we find that the union officials have an ambivalent attitude toward it. They think it is a good plan, but they also think that it is not their plan. It is management's plan, which was sold to the workers and to the union leaders themselves. The Plan has proved so popular that, as one of the union officials said: "We'd have a hell of a time taking it away from people now even if we wanted to."

To understand the attitude of the union leadership we must review the manner in which the Plan was introduced. As one man put it:

The whole thing got off to a bad start. You might say that the company held a gun at our heads and then shoved the Plan down our throats. Of course, we got our 18½ cents raise and we got this besides, so really we didn't have anything to lose. But we were pushed into it.

The feeling that this was exclusively a management plan was strengthened when the first publicity releases came out seven months later. The union leaders claim that management had wanted to set up the Plan on an experimental basis, giving it six months' trial before any changes should be considered. Management asked that no press releases be sent out during that trial period. The union officials say they agreed to this on condition that when the company was ready to give out a press release the union would get together with them and the release would be a joint product. Then suddenly the union was surprised to find press releases and magazine stories appearing all over the country. The article in a national magazine was considered typical. A picture of the president appeared above the story and, while it did not say this outright, the story conveyed the impression to the union leaders that the real news angle here was that the management had outsmarted its union. Furthermore, the men objected to a quotation from the president calling this: "A Sugar Coated Incentive Plan." In view of the intense feeling of the workers against piece rates and standards, together with the firm policy of the UAW in opposition to incentive systems, management and the union in negotiations had made a great point of giving the Plan a name which would differentiate it from the ordinary incentive system. Now here was the president himself coming out to explain how he had tricked people into accepting his plan. (Actually the president made no such statement. The words "an incentive plan with a sugar-coated name" were those of the reporter. However, since the president's picture appeared at the head of the article, it was easy for the confusion to arise. Similarly, while management could not logically be held responsible for the general tenor of the article, the circumstances surrounding its release made it easy to identify the point of view with that of management.)

The union has had no real function in administration of the Plan, although some small details were originally negotiated between union and management. At first there were monthly meetings held by management and union to discuss the figures and clarify points of interpretation. But the Plan is simple in principle so that few such meetings of interpretation were needed and union and management have not met on these points for many months.

The bonus figures are announced to the workers each month. Before the public announcement is made, the union committee is called in and management presents the figures to the officers. However, since these figures are checked by an outside accounting firm once a year and no question has ever been raised as to their accuracy, such meetings are no more than a formality.

Following this meeting with the union committee, the works manager announces the figures and talks to the employees over the plant's public address system. He uses this opportunity to let the employees know the plans management is developing for the company, and this part of the talk appears to be welcome. The Savings-Sharing Plan report is the chief topic of his remarks. After he announces the bonus figures for the previous month and congratulates the workers upon their increased earnings, he goes on to assure them that they have not reached the ceiling, that much more can be earned. According to the union officers, this is in the nature of a pep talk given by the football coach to members of his team. It appears, however, that the talk fails to provide the inspiration that is intended. For this there seem to be two chief reasons: The impression is given that the only reason the workers are not earning more is that they are not putting out sufficient effort, whereas the workers observe that there are a number of times when they are slowed down in production by shortages of materials or interruptions in the flow of work provided by management. They do not like the implication that productivity depends upon themselves alone. Probably more important than this is the fact that when the workers have earned 25 cents an hour bonus for the previous month and the works manager announces that 35 cents would be entirely possible and urges them to go after it, it is management that is setting the goal. Neither the union organization nor individual workers have any role in setting the goal for group achievements.

It is important to note that the limited effectiveness of this talk is not due to any feelings against the man who makes it. All our evidence indicates that the works manager himself is exceedingly highly regarded by workers and union officers. He is, nevertheless, a member of management and is unable to gain acceptance for goals which workers and union have no part in shaping.

This background should explain why it is that the union officers take no active role in promoting the Plan. In general, they believe it is a good plan, but they do not feel that it is up to them to speak to workers about getting increased production. It is only in extreme cases where a worker is obviously shirking his job that union officers have felt they could intervene. In cases where workers are working steadily, but nevertheless far below capacity, the officers feel that it would be contrary to their role as union officers to urge greater productive efforts.

This neutral attitude toward the Plan is especially evident in the union newspaper, which, as a matter of policy, never prints any reference to the Plan. By contrast, the company's house organ makes frequent and enthusiastic reference to the Plan.

In commenting upon the technical aspects of the Plan, the union officers had a number of criticisms which pointed to details which, if changed, would have only a minor effect upon earnings or which referred to hypothetical events—what would happen under circumstances that have not yet been encountered. These criticisms seemed to be symptomatic of the lack of worker and union involvement in development of the Plan rather than pointing to any particular defects in it. The union officers did, however, raise one point that would have involved a substantial change in the impact of the Plan. They asked why the split on improvements should be 50-50. Why not 60-40 or 70-30 with the workers on the long end of the division?

Management argues that the improvement is not contributed entirely by the workers. A large part of the gain must be attributed to more efficient management and to technological changes introduced by management. Apparently management has been able to satisfy the union on this point, for we found that in 1954 the percentage division was no longer an issue.

On the whole, union officers seem to think that this is a good plan. They also look upon it as management's plan.

### Where Does the Improvement Come From?

Where does the productivity increase come from? A good part of this improvement must be due to the increasingly better integration of the organization that manifests itself also in the indices of absenteeism, turnover, and grievance time. Beyond that general background condition, let us examine three other factors.

1. *Are the workers working harder?* Here we have no measurements and can only rely upon impressions from brief observation backed up by comments from management and union officers. There seems to be general agreement that the workers are not working exceptionally hard. The pace of factory work seems rather relaxed.

On the other hand, there is general agreement that there is much less "goofing off" than there used to be. As the foremen report, it is no longer necessary for the foreman to check carefully to see that people are working. Management is encouraged to find that a union officer will reprimand a worker who is obviously and continually goofing off. Such a reprimand is so rare as to excite comment in terms of a specific incident. Nevertheless, in the days before the Plan no union officer would have thought of reprimanding a worker on these grounds. The particular instance here is not important except in so far as it points to a changed climate of public opinion in the plant. Good production has now become a good thing for everybody. Thus, even though there is no conscious union policy on the matter, a union officer will sometimes naturally let his feelings be known.

2. *Workers' and union suggestions.* It is not, of course, only harder work that increases productivity. Better methods of doing the job may add more products than could possibly be brought out with harder work. Here there have evidently been some gains. We find workers bringing suggestions for new methods to the foreman or to the methods man in considerably greater numbers than occurred before the Plan. We find them also telling the foreman now and then to check on certain aspects of his planning so that they can be sure there will be a steady flow of work in the department. On a higher level we find union officers taking a critical look at questions of managerial efficiency. At the time of our first visit to the plant, nine months after the introduction of the Plan, we found union officers complaining that management inefficiencies limited the workers' possibilities of making good bonuses. A year later they reported substantial improvements here. (Top management people were happy to have these inefficiencies brought to their attention and regarded this as a significant gain in the Plan.)

3. *Technological changes and improvements in managerial methods.* Of course, management is constantly seeking to improve its methods in operating the plant. The Plan seems to have provided an atmosphere in which needed changes can be more readily brought to management's attention, but we must assume that some of the improvements would have been brought about by management independently of the Plan.

In defending the 50-50 split management has pledged itself to invest a substantial part of its share of the savings in new and improved equipment. These technological changes have contributed greatly to the improved productivity in the plant. In fact, the changes have been so substantial as to raise the question whether the Plan now enables the workers to maintain a constant level of productivity with a gradually decreasing amount of effort.

Management has unquestionably gained through a lessening of resistance to technological change. In some cases management has sought to make the new machine more attractive by paying workers assigned to it higher rates than they previously received. This has probably been of some help, but more important seems to be the recognition that the fruits of the technological changes are shared by the workers generally and do not accrue solely to management's benefit.

While these points provide something of an answer to the increasing productivity in the plant, they do not explain why the productivity after reaching a new plane has remained constant from the early period on. We shall return to that question after examining the case of the Valley plant.

## THE VALLEY CASE

The incentive plan was introduced into the Valley plant under circumstances quite different from those prevailing in Metropolis. To appreciate these differences, we must first examine the historical and social background of the Valley plant.

The Valley is a chronically depressed coal mining area. At the end of World War II, Valley residents, seriously concerned about the employment prospects of returning veterans, contributed generously to a fund for attracting industry. In 1947 negotiations were completed between a committee of Valley residents and the company. Community funds were used to build a plant which was "given" to the company for operation under certain conditions. Especially important among these conditions was the employment of Valley residents. After a certain period of time and after the employment of a certain number of Valley residents, ownership of the plant would completely revert to the company.

A cadre of Metropolis management came out in 1947 to superintend the erection of the plant, installation of machinery, and so on. Maintenance crews were hired beginning in October 1948. Production began in April 1949. Among the key imports are: the plant manager, controller, personnel director, production manager, processing general foreman, and maintenance foreman. One general foreman (manufacturing), two assistant general foremen, and all line foremen have been recruited from Valley residents.

From 1948 to 1950 conditions in the Valley were favorable to highly selective labor recruitment. Attractive hourly wage rates, stability of employment, and attractive working conditions all made Valley plant employment extremely desirable. Even today the plant has a waiting list of would-be employees between five and ten times as large as the total plant work force.

As a result of this selectivity, the labor force in the plant has the following characteristics: over 90 per cent of the work force are high school graduates, over 90 per cent of them are veterans of World War II, and they are all males. As a result, they have an unusually well-educated group of young, but mature, male employees.

### From Coal Mine to Factory

Management attributes some of its industrial relations difficulties to the mining background of the workers and their families. The assumption is that workers carry with them into this new situation a stereotyped picture of the oppressive employer, growing out of the conflicts in the mines.

Somewhat to our surprise, we found the workers interpreting the mining background differently. They acknowledged that their present jobs were immeasurably better than the mines in working conditions and in economic security. However, in human relations, they looked back somewhat nostalgically to the mines.

One man said, "I don't think they know what it is to smile. In the mines they give you a pat on the back. Management here doesn't seem to believe in that." Another man contrasted local mine managers with Valley plant managers by saying, "Around here everybody knows everybody and talks to everybody. I don't know. It seems to me that the Metropolis people have a kind of big city complex. One of the things that bothers me is having foremen

watching me all the time . . . you can't work like that. . . . This
Christmas is the first the foreman ever said 'Merry Christmas' to
me. I've been here five years."

Although the greatest animus was shown toward Metropolis imports, locally recruited foremen also came in for their share of
criticism for maintaining social distance. Some men said that, although local supervisors were better *immediately* after promotion,
they gradually got to be like the others. It was felt that this behavior
was expected of foremen on the part of their superiors.

The plant manager was looked upon as a rather forbidding figure.
The union officers met with him only occasionally and then in some
crisis situation. The rank-and-file workers had no personal contacts
with him, but they sometimes observed him "patrolling" the plant
and looking at them and their work with what was interpreted as
an unfriendly and critical eye. Probably the lack of personal contact
is sufficient to explain the unfriendly sentiments here.

The personnel manager was seen as a more friendly figure. He
saw union officers at least weekly and generally in situations where
they were taking the initiative in bringing up problems and he was
seeking to adjust to them. He was also available to individual
workers.

Workers felt that generally the factory foremen gave them much
closer supervision than that prevailing in the mines. It seemed to
us significant that the foremen who supervised machine-regulated
processes did not provide as close supervision as the foremen con-
trolling hand operations, and attitudes toward the foremen were
more favorable where the supervision was less close.

It would be inaccurate to speak of a conflict between workers
and management at the Valley plant. However, the case must be
interpreted against the background of a definite cleavage between
Valley workers and the Metropolis management group.

*The Union Organization*

Union officials in the Valley locals are young, bright, and aggressive. The local itself is young—less than five years old—and there
is competition among the members for prestigeful leadership posts.
Although the UAW-CIO is a newcomer to the region, loyalty to a
strong union has been traditional to the area for at least two genera-

tions. Add to this the stereotype of Valley management as "stuckup outsiders," and the recipe for a strong militant local is completed.

The fact that the union is strong and well led does not mean that it is addicted to throwing its weight around. For one thing, members and union officers alike admit to a general satisfaction that the Valley plant offers employment terms superior to other alternatives available. Besides, in this area little alternative employment exists and unemployment often means emigration.

The realistic appraisal of their jobs as relatively good is reinforced by community pressures. Members admit that their friends and neighbors would disapprove of any overt conflict that threatened the continuation of the plant as a Valley employer. In fact, one leader remarked ruefully that "The miners will strike at the drop of a hat but they tell *us* to take it easy all the time."

Also, leaders are proud that they belong to a strong union with a tradition of responsibility in relations with management.

Both management and union officers agree that relatively few grievances are processed. Such disaffection as exists is expressed by latent or overt threats of strike action on the part of the union if grievances are not settled satisfactorily.

In the opinion of the personnel manager, this occurs more often in the Valley than in Metropolis, although the number of grievances is smaller. He attributes the cause of the strike threats to the miner tradition of militance.

It may also be that this is a function of lack of union sophistication. In some labor-management relationships, a union leadership which is chronically dissatisfied but unable to strike will clog the grievance machinery with a stream of grievances. This is not yet seen by Valley union leaders as a practical alternative to taking strong positions on a few issues.

### The Plan Is Introduced

Many Valley workers, including the union leadership, knew of the existence of the Metropolis Plan since the early days of the Valley plant. Occasional expressions of interest in the Plan were made to management in the pre-Plan period. Management, however, had to explain that it was not in a position to consider introduction of the Plan in the Valley because there was not yet time for the required period of cost experience. By the time of the 1953 negotiations (late summer) the company felt that the necessary experience had been accumulated and offered the Plan to the workers during contract negotiations. This was the Metropolis Plan in all except one respect. The base figure for the Valley was 26 cents on the sales dollar instead of the 30 cents established at Metropolis. However, the figures were arrived at in the same way: through analyzing the labor cost to dollar sales relationships for a base period prior to the introduction of the Plan.

Metropolis officials, as well as local managers participated in discussions of the Plan. A booklet outlining the logics of the Plan and including the figures for a sample month was given the committee. The favorable Metropolis experience was pointed out by management spokesmen. However, management people were also careful to point out that the Valley workers should not expect to equal the gain in earnings achieved at Metropolis. Here was a new plant which was already operating more efficiently than had the Metropolis plant at the time of the introduction of the Plan there, as the difference between 26 and 30 cents indicated. Still, it seemed reasonable to expect substantial bonus earnings.

The local union bargaining committee then called a special union meeting to discuss and vote upon the Plan. A majority of the workers attended and showed considerable interest in the discussion. Most of the job of explaining the Plan was undertaken by Metropolis union officials, who had been invited in for this occasion. They gave a highly favorable account of Metropolis experience with the Plan, although they too cautioned that the Valley should not expect quite so much. The Metropolis bonus figures were reported to have fluctuated between a low of 14 cents and a high of 39 cents per hour per month. Interestingly enough, no one mentioned the fact that Metropolis's first month figure was 24 cents. Our interviews showed that this figure was not known to any of the local union people or to any of the Valley management people except the controller.

At the end of this explanation meeting, the workers voted in the Plan by an overwhelming majority, and it went into effect on September 1, 1953.

During September a large chart, indicating productivity trends, was posted conspicuously at one end of the work floor. Based on local management's weekly estimates (official Plan calculations were made in Metropolis after the month was over), the chart indicated a steady rise in productivity.

Bargaining committee members were encouraged by their talks with managers during the month, although the managers refused to give *official* predictions. Four out of five committeemen responded to questions by fellow workers with guesses that their monthly bonus for September would be in the neighborhood of 16 cents per hour.

By mid-October the earnings figure for September was announced at 4.6 cents, the chart was removed from the plant wall, and the fat was in the fire.

### Management's View of What Happened

Management officials were, of course, disappointed at this lack of initial success. After all, they concluded, the men must not have worked appreciably harder in September than in preceding months.

The matter of the chart was seen as somewhat embarrassing by managers. They said that they hoped it would encourage the men. Naturally, it represented their best estimates, but they didn't have all the data needed to compute progress under the Plan. Only Metropolis had that, and then only after the month was over. They took the chart down because it had done more harm than good.

The matter of understanding how the Plan worked was not seen as crucial. Managers agreed that neither the work force nor the union committee understood the Plan very well. However, they indicated that workers or union officers in Metropolis didn't understand the Plan very well either. They said that the *important* understanding by Metropolis workers was the one that workers *could* make money under the Plan.

We asked how it happened that the union was given sole responsibility for explaining the Plan to the workers. Part of the explanation, as indicated above, was that the only thing people had to understand, *really,* was that if they worked harder they would make more money. Thus, it was not particularly necessary for a more sophisticated explanation to be given workers before the Plan took effect.

Also, "Right or wrong we don't take things direct to the people when we can go through the union. We take it that they are elected representatives of our people."

We also inquired whether, once the Plan had been explained and introduced, management had taken any steps to *promote* it. Were such media as booklets, pep talks, announcements, or posters used to stimulate interest and enthusiasm about the Plan? Were foremen instructed to take advantage of personal contacts with workers to remind them about the advantages and importance of increasing earnings by decreasing labor costs?

None of these channels of communication to workers was used as a conscious policy by top management. The foremen themselves reported to us that nobody had told them to "use the Plan with the men." Some of them reported that they had "done a little" of this, for the most part rather gingerly. Others said that they thought it might help the working of the Plan if they *had* done this, but they would be afraid to try to motivate men via the Plan until they, as foremen, understood it themselves.

So here was a Plan which will work only if people *believe* it will work and *want* it to work and, consequently, *change their behavior* to make it work. Yet, management did not take any steps to "sell" the Plan. Why was this?

Perhaps because in Metropolis no selling was done and yet the Plan had succeeded. In some respects the Metropolis problem of salesmanship was something like selling a life preserver to a drowning man—superfluous in the context in which it occurred.

After discovering that the Plan did not work *without* promotional effort, why did management not *then* promote the Plan? This is partly explained by the following view: "I give the men credit for being intelligent individuals like you and me. We've told them 'We're not going to give you any money in terms of flat increases, but here's a chance to make some if you work a little harder.' I think they ought to be able to get the idea without having us *persuade* them."

Implicit in this statement is the idea that it is undignified to manipulate workers' sentiments as though they were potential toothpaste buyers. It is true that a high-pressure sales campaign to workers is not likely to change their behavior drastically. This does not mean, however, that managers could not indicate, by changes in *their own inplant behavior,* that they were wholeheartedly interested in making the Plan succeed.

The basic hope of Valley managers was that the Plan would catch on as soon as the men were convinced that there was an attractive earnings potential there. The way in which that would become clear was "if we get a good month," meaning good earnings. Then the money-hungry drive would be allowed to take over and individuals would stretch themselves for the prize. Moreover, the less enthusiastic might be pressured by their fellows to cooperate in cutting labor costs. It was not made clear how the big month would come about.

Management did not seem seriously concerned with the notion that the first month's failure to provide big earnings made future success under the Plan a difficult and uphill climb. There seemed to be no clear strategy about management's role in helping the Plan to succeed. The seeds of success were felt to lie within the Plan itself.

*Workers' and Union Officials' View*

Both workers and union officials had perceptions quite opposite to those of management about the first month under the Plan. They felt strongly that the first month had shown a considerable increase in worker efforts.

We thought we would make a lot more than we did. I figured at least a dime because the men chipped in and they worked.

After the first month everybody was mad and disappointed.

(The only thing that keeps this view from being unanimous is the fact that certain people, who were both pessimistic and hostile to the Plan from the beginning, expected no earnings. Apparently everyone who was favorably or hopefully disposed toward the operation of the Plan was disappointed.)

Union bargaining committeemen, who had more or less promised high earnings the first month, were seriously embarrassed.

They, as well as workers, felt they had been misled by the chart. Frequent humorous comments were made by employees about how fast the chart disappeared. The "moral" of this incident was twofold. First, the chart "proved" they had worked harder. Second, the Plan must be complicated and the relation between efforts and earnings not direct. To some people it suggested that management either *was* trying to rig the results or, at least, *could* rig them, since the Plan was too complicated for workers to understand.

With the exception of the executive committee, which met regularly with the personnel manager, researchers got a general impression of apathy about the Plan in the fifth and sixth months of its operation. The over-all reaction breakdown is in two major parts:

First of all, it appeared to us that the majority of workers were favorable or *mildly* favorable toward the Plan. By this we mean they were hopeful that the Plan might still pay off, that they did not see much point in abandoning the Plan as long as it was paying *something* and nothing better was in sight. This majority indicated considerable disappointment with the results of the first month and the first quarter.

Some workers, especially high seniority men, were violently hostile to the Plan. Some said that they were opposed to all kinds of speed-up. Others stressed the fear that it might lead to layoffs. Still others did not make clear the basis of their opposition.

It seemed to researchers that although most union leaders and members were in favor of the Plan, those opposed to it (some of them strategically situated) were much more vocal and emotionally involved.

Thus the favorable balance of public opinion seemed quite precarious.

There is widespread and admitted lack of knowledge of the Plan on the part of rank-and-file workers and even of committeemen to whom management has made some explanation. The Plan *is* technically difficult to understand in terms of detail. Certainly in the eyes of the union there is no inevitable direct relationship between increased effort and immediate increase in earnings:

You just can't figure it. Sometimes the bonus goes down and people work harder and when people stop working, the bonus goes up.
We couldn't understand why productivity fluctuated so.

Given disappointing results in the first month, when workers felt there *was* genuine increase in effort, some suspicion toward management and toward the legitimacy of the Plan was inevitable. This was described to us in the following terms:

(a) Management will not let earnings get "too high."

(b) Management will see that earnings don't go so low that the Plan is abandoned.

(c) Whether or not management does rig earnings under the Plan—"they *could* if they wanted to"—and consequently the very complexity of the Plan means that workers and their representatives cannot control whether or not the Plan is being equitably administered.

There is another important aspect of lack of knowledge about the Plan. Some important ways of increasing earnings under the Plan are ignored or overlooked. First of all, suggestions which would increase a worker's efficiency without increasing his effort are not perceived as having much bearing. The cumulative effect of efficiency-improving suggestions has not been explained to the men as a likely source of increased earnings. It is interesting that, although logically this is one source of increased earnings under the Plan, local management disagrees about how *important* a source of bonus possibilities it is. Some management people think it is equally important to working harder. The majority tend to think it is less important. Some think it is of practically no importance.

Even less obvious as a source of possible earnings increases are suggestions which would not affect *worker* performance directly, but which would force *management* to increase efficiency in terms of layout, scheduling, and so on. Here, managers recognize that increasing management efficiency would boost Plan earnings, but most workers do not see this as relevant and *no* workers see this as something which workers can *influence*.

## METROPOLIS AND THE VALLEY: AN ANALYSIS

How do we explain the partial success in the Metropolis case and the disappointing results in the Valley?

The cases indicate, in the first place, that the relationship between worker effort and payoff under a plant-wide system is highly indirect. This does not seem to be due to any defect in the particular formula invented by the Acme management. We must recognize that productivity in a plant is a result of many factors, of which worker effort is only one. Under an individual piecework system, the worker often sees a direct relationship between his effort and his income. Under a plant-wide system, any given individual may feel that he

—and even his whole work group—worked harder and made less money.

The motivational problem under the plant-wide system is then quite different and more complex. Let us try to sharpen our ideas along this line through comparing the two cases.

In Metropolis, the Plan was born out of an economic crisis. The crisis presented not only new possibilities of making money, but also a real possibility of losing jobs. We have no direct evidence as to how this crisis affected the workers' response to the incentive. Presumably it had some direct effect, but perhaps, still more important, the crisis incentive made possible significant changes in foreman-worker, industrial engineer-worker, and union-management relations (on grievances). In these human relations changes, the works manager appears to have been a key figure. Even in the conflict period he enjoyed a fair degree of popularity and trust from the workers. Furthermore, he was close to many of them informally (at the bowling alleys, for example). Finally, the foremen and industrial engineers had had long experience here, most of them coming up from the ranks, so there was no sharp separation of workers from management. In other words, we might say that the social system had within it certain recuperative powers that enabled it to respond to treatment. The treatment of the plant-wide incentive released certain strengths already latent in the system.

In Metropolis, the initial success with the Plan assured its continued popularity. And this success also stabilized the changes in human relations that had taken place. The changes, however, did not involve the whole social system. We have noted that the union was largely left out of the changes. The officers had fewer grievances to process, but they developed no substitute for this grievance activity. They did not play any role in improving the efficiency of the plant, as has been the case in other situations we shall examine. Nor was any provision made for involving the individual worker with fellow workers on a group basis in this process of improvement.

In the Valley, the situation was different in important respects. In the first place, no crisis accompanied the introduction of the Plan. Management just presented it as if to say, "Here's a chance to make more money if you're interested and want to work harder."

The incentive was applied to a social system marked by a pronounced cleavage between Metropolis imported management and Valley workers. Management did not capitalize upon the incentive by taking action that would have narrowed the gap between these parts of the system. Whereas in Metropolis the works manager provided an integrating symbol, in the Valley he symbolized the separation of workers from management and the suspicion between them.

The first month's experience was crucial at the Valley plant. Given the fact that a plant-wide plan is complex, we may assume that the workers do not need to understand it intellectually. For it to work, however, they must believe that if they make an effort they will be rewarded. This belief can only be based upon experience. Perhaps if the Plan had paid off well for several months at the start and then had run into a lean period, the workers might have taken the disappointment without becoming disillusioned with the Plan. But here—perhaps for quite fortuitous reasons—the first month's payoff was far below expectations. To experience failure instead of success at the start seems to make a great deal of difference.

We should not overestimate the problem that may have been involved in working from a 26 cents instead of a 30 cents labor cost base. It can certainly be argued that it is only fair to base the standard on current performance, and 26 cents represented performance in the Valley plant. Furthermore, Valley people had been cautioned not to expect as much as had been gained at Metropolis, and our evidence indicates that they did not indeed have such high expectations. We recall that the union officers had been predicting around 16 cents for the first month. Actual earnings around that figure would have been greeted as gratifying evidence of success. The 4.6 cents payoff seemed, then, a flat failure.[2]

[2] In the first six months, the period covered by our research, the bonus fluctuated between zero and about 9 cents. Suddenly, in April 1954, the bonus jumped up to 17 cents. Since we were not carrying on our research at the time, we cannot undertake to explain this increase. It is, of course, entirely possible that the increase was due to a combination of circumstances *not* including increased worker effort. However, this outcome does cast some light on a prevalent management theory that "one big month" would really put over the plan and lead the workers to go to work with more enthusiastic efforts. The months immediately following April showed payoffs of about 9½ and 8 cents. At this writing, then, the Plan is probably looked upon more favorably by workers, but there is as yet no evidence that it generates the enthusiastic activity we see in other cases.

Perhaps if the first month had been a success, the difference between 26 cents and 30 cents would have been forgotten. When they were disappointed, the workers and union officers could tell themselves that they would have to do markedly better than Metropolis to make the same money. That made the prospect discouraging, indeed.

In the Valley we see none of the human relations changes that marked the limited success of the Plan in Metropolis. There is no point in talking about before-and-after comparisons, for we are describing essentially the same situation at both points in time.

Experience in these two cases suggests that the success of a plant-wide system depends upon the institution of human relations changes. On the negative side, the formula is: *no change in human relations, then no worker response to the plant-wide incentive.* The following chapters will explore what human relations changes seem to lead in that direction.

## NOTE ON RESEARCH METHODS

The discussion of the Metropolis case is based primarily upon Whyte's interviewing in that plant on December 5, 1946, and October 20-21, 1947. This is indeed a short time for such a study. However, he was aided by the full cooperation offered by both management and union officers. Interviews were held at the following levels: top management, works manager, personnel manager, general foreman, chief engineer, methods engineer, foreman, and union officers. In the time available, no sampling of rank-and-file opinions and experience could be sought.

In the spring of 1954, Leonard Sayles spent two days at the Metropolis plant, interviewing union and management officers. We have had the advantage of his research notes, but it has seemed best to concentrate in the Metropolis case upon the data on the earlier period.

Fuerstenberg and Miller studied the Valley plant during the period from January to March 1954. They spent a total of nine days consulting with management and union representatives at all levels of both organizations. Beginning with top management and union officials, they worked down through both hierarchies in parallel sequence. Management personnel interviewed included: plant manager, personnel manager, controller, production manager, general foremen, and about two-thirds of the line foremen. Their union counterparts included the local president, bargaining committee, executive board, and about two-thirds of the departmental stewards. In addition, they were able to interview a stratified sample of 12 per cent of the workers (45 individuals).

Management and union officials were interviewed both individually and in small groups. (Those interviewed as part of a group were later interviewed singly.) Workers were interviewed in groups of four or five, after being introduced to researchers by their union steward. The interviewers found these group discussions an effective means of establishing rapport quickly, reducing worker anxiety and resistance, and examining different sides of the same topic.

In both plants, the helpful cooperation of both management and union people was unstinted and should be acknowledged gratefully. This holds particularly true for the Valley plant, which made workers available for interviewing on company time. Since this was not an "action research" program, the company was thus remarkably generous in subsidizing general social research without hope of direct return.

# 13

# A Goal for Cooperation

In the midst of World War II the union leaders and the management of the Toronto factory of Lever Brothers carried through a program of reducing working hours from 48 to 40 while maintaining labor costs for the company and take-home pay for the workers.

The case is of special interest since it is the only one we have that involves not only a plant-wide incentive but a specific goal for the cooperative effort.

The magnitude of this achievement can be appreciated when we recognize that the parties here achieved without a strike what many unions and managements failed to accomplish in the postwar years in the United States after bitter and costly strikes. In the United States the unions sought to maintain weekly pay through working shorter hours at higher rates, and management sought to keep labor costs from increasing. In general, the outcome was a compromise in which management's costs increased and workers received more per hour but not enough more (in the first postwar contracts) to maintain wartime weekly earnings.

In effect, the Lever program achieved a 20 per cent increase in hourly rates for workers. Management also profited substantially, for the increased pay improved its position in the labor market without increasing its costs.

The case is noteworthy also because it took place in one plant of a giant, world-wide corporation. Most successful cooperation plans have developed in relatively small companies, although the Inland Steel Container Company case has already shown us the results that may be achieved at the plant level in a corporation of substantial size.

Finally, the case is of special interest because, a little over a year after the goal was achieved, the union's leaders, who had been in power for more than six years, were voted out of office. We must seek to determine whether there is any connection between this overturn and the cooperation program. Union leaders can hardly be expected to work for a plant-wide cooperative goal if, upon achieving it, they are voted out of office.

In order to explain the success of the cooperative program and the turnover of union officers, we shall need to tell the story of the case in detail. Here our account is based entirely upon the study by W. R. Dymond.[1] Since Dymond made his study from a different point of view and with a different purpose in mind, the data in the case are his but the interpretations are our own.

### BACKGROUND FOR COOPERATION (up to November 1943)

Lever management met a unionization drive in 1936-37 by sponsoring a company union. In 1940 the officers of the company union decided that they needed outside support in working out their adjustments with management, and they brought about affiliation with the United Packinghouse Workers CIO. In the meantime there had been a change in plant management, and a new management offered no opposition to this move. As soon as the workers had voted for CIO affiliation, management began to bargain for a contract. Differences were worked out satisfactorily, and the union was given a large measure of security. Those already in the union were not allowed to withdraw and new workers were required to join. This meant that the union at no time had to size up issues in terms of a fight for its existence.

The old company union officials were elected to office in the new CIO local. They remained in power continuously until after the end of the change in hours central to the case. In March 1944 the local shifted its affiliation to the International Chemical Workers Union AFL. The stability of its leadership and the high degree of autonomy enjoyed by the local are both significant factors in the success of cooperation in the case.

Cooperation did not begin in the Toronto plant with joint efforts to work out the change in hours from 48 to 40. A relatively

---

[1] Dymond's report was published in the *Canadian Journal of Economics and Political Science*, Vol. XIII, No. 1 (February 1947). The present chapter presents, with a few minor revisions, W. F. Whyte's article, "Union-Management Cooperation: Toronto Case," *Applied Anthropology*, Vol. VI, No. 3 (Summer 1947).

harmonious relationship had already been built up following union recognition in 1941. The union negotiating committee had met weekly with management until April 1943, when meetings were set at once every two weeks.

Management made no effort to limit the subjects brought up for discussion at the meetings. Anything that seemed to relate to worker job satisfaction could be discussed, whether or not it was covered in the contract. Out of such meetings grew joint union-management committees on the employee cafeteria and on job classification and evaluation.

Management and union had already got together on several occasions to call joint meetings of stewards and foremen to discuss the working out of cooperative relations on the shop level. Furthermore, beginning in February 1943, the union president was taken off his regular job for several months and paid jointly by union and management while he worked with shop stewards, educating them in the interpretation of the contract and in the adjustment of their union-management problems.

In response to these cooperative relations with management, the union agreed to assume some responsibility for discipline. A plan was worked out whereby the personnel manager and three members of the union executive committee were to interview chronic absentees. On one occasion the negotiating committee cooperated with management on a joint inspection of lockers to check thefts of soap. In January 1943 the union offered to cooperate with management in enforcing discipline upon manpower wastage, provided any penalties be first discussed with the negotiating committee.

While the union was cooperative in this period, there were limits to the cooperation. The negotiating committee ran into difficulty over suggestions it made which had the effect of displacing workers or enlarging job assignments. Consequently, in June 1943 the union asked a pledge from the company that no such changes be made without protecting the employees who were affected. At this time the union had no incentive for cutting company labor costs.

Management also was concerned with limiting the scope of joint activity. Here the now-familiar problem of management prerogatives was involved.

Lever Brothers has a long history of employee welfare activity.

Management felt that these activities should be kept separate from the union contract. That meant, in effect, that in some of its welfare activities management was still dealing directly with employees, without regard to union channels, although the union was free to suggest and criticize. The union held that all employee benefits should be covered in the contract.

As Dymond, author of the report of the case, reports:

This friction was brought out into the open in an interesting way. The company installed a "juke box" in the cafeteria so that the employees could enjoy music while they ate. One group of employees complained the music was not loud enough while others complained it was too loud. To forestall further employee bickering and dissatisfaction, the company removed the "juke box." The union executive thereupon lodged a grievance with the management and asked that the "juke box" be again installed. The management replied in effect that an amenity such as music in the cafeteria, which it had introduced on its own initiative, could be withdrawn at will. Furthermore, the union, under the contract, had no right to raise the issue of the "juke box" as a grievance.

Management (August 1943) then went on to make a statement of policy emphasizing that such benefits and welfare activities begun on the initiative of management must remain subject to unilateral decision by management.

A month later the union responded strongly on this point. It sent a letter to management and called a special meeting of the members to discuss the issue. The union's position was stated in the letter in this manner:

Your executives feel that they should examine the implications and dangers inherent in the whole system of handouts and must therefore question the good faith of any company instituting them. . . . The company claims the right to exercise sole and exclusive discretion as to the granting or changing or the discontinuance of any or all of them (working conditions or amenities not specifically mentioned in the agreement).

In the matter of mutual trust, the management has on many occasions proclaimed . . . their desire for teamwork and cooperation. This we accepted in good faith on the assumption that teamwork and cooperation implied equality. That is, the right to share in obligations and benefits accruing from the work of the group cooperating.

Next, in its October meeting with the negotiating committee, management reaffirmed its stand, stating that, while management had no intention of curtailing these benefits, unforeseen circumstances might necessitate such action, and that management was unwilling to tie its hands by including these matters in the agreement. The union continued to press this point, but made no headway.

The question of management prerogatives has been set forth here at length, for, in this case as in others, it appears to impose certain limitations upon joint union-management activity. The implications of the point will be discussed later.

### SETTING THE OBJECTIVES FOR COOPERATION (November 1943)

The union contract of 1941 had established a 45-hour week for day employees and 48 hours for shift workers. At that time only one-quarter of the employees were on 48 hours.

In view of the manpower shortage, the union had agreed in November 1942 to a general 48-hour week, with time-and-a-half pay only after 48 hours.

While the union had agreed to the general extension of this new shift of work, there was still in November 1943 considerable dissatisfaction among the workers on the question. Many were not convinced that the change was necessary in the interests of war production. The union therefore had already asked of management a pledge that hours would be reduced to 40 after the war. But management had not been willing to give such an unconditional pledge, feeling that the introduction of new machines would be necessary to ensure profitable operations on a 40-hour week.

A year after the general extension of the new hours, the union demanded in November 1943 that hours be cut from 48 to 40, with no reduction in take-home pay, claiming that the same output could be achieved on the reduced hours. The company rejected the demand.

There followed a period of almost five months spent, in effect, in searching for the type of social system that would make possible the reduction in hours. The search involved these events:

When the union continued to press its claim, management agreed to a meeting of the negotiating committee and stewards with the works manager and the production foremen. There, the union president says, the union presented concrete plans for manpower savings, but the company representatives dismissed them as impractical. The union members further got the impression that the management representatives considered them incapable of making constructive suggestions on efficiency. They responded by walking out of the meeting.

The union leaders then proposed that plans be worked out between the negotiating committee and management. Management was unwilling to make such plans a matter of bargaining and insisted instead that any committee must be advisory in nature.

To strengthen the pressure behind its position, the union leaders carried out a referendum among the members on the question of full cooperation with management to achieve the 40-hour week. The proposal was that a 40-hour week be instituted for a three months' probationary period with hours being lengthened again if necessary savings were not made. It was carried by a vote of 40 to 1.

With this backing, the leaders demanded once more that hours be changed and cost reductions be undertaken following the change. Management again replied (January 1944) that it was unwilling to shorten hours without a careful study of the possibility of making manpower savings. The union continued to press for action and finally drew from management a promise to work toward the establishment of the 40-hour week. Further discussion resulted in the setting up of a joint committee to study and act upon the problem of cost reduction.

Now, although there were a number of technical points on how the savings were to be computed so that both sides could determine when a necessary minimum of savings had been reached, enough had been accomplished to organize a system of cooperation under which it became possible to reach agreement on all questions.

Before the joint committee could get into action (March 1944), however, both union and management leaders had to launch an educational campaign in their own groups. The top union men had to give assurances as to the way changes were to be carried out. They promised that no one would be laid off in the process, that labor turnover would make room for workers whose jobs were eliminated. Any resulting demotions were to be carried through on a strict seniority basis. The leaders argued that, while some workers would lose with demotions and losses of pay, these sacrifices had to be borne if the majority were to benefit.

Management's educational problem was to prepare the foremen to be responsive to suggestions and proposals from union representatives. The works manager held "frequent meetings" to discuss the way in which this aspect of union-management relations was to be handled.

These assurances had their effect and the projected reduction of hours, even before any plan of savings could be worked out, made for marked changes in the labor force. In the first week of the December 1943 quarter, there were 693 hourly rated employees on the factory payroll. In March 1944 the number had dropped to 587. This meant simply that in this period management did not hire nearly so rapidly as employees left the plant. It proved possible to maintain output even with this reduction in the work force.

As Dymond observes, it was no coincidence that the work force could be reduced at this time. He claims that the employees saw the possibility of reaching the goal and therefore were willing to step up their individual efforts. It was also anticipated that there would be pressure from both management and union to get rid of inefficient or unwilling workers.

Since savings were to be figured from a starting point of November 13, this relatively painless process of staff reduction had accounted for a major part of the necessary savings by the time the joint committee went into action. Nevertheless, the joint committee did work out substantial changes throughout the factory. Dymond gives details but they will not be given here, since our main emphasis is upon the development of the cooperative social system that made the concrete results possible.

## BUILDING THE COOPERATIVE SYSTEM  (March-August 1944)

Regular personnel of the joint committee included the union president, two members of the negotiating committee, the works manager, and his assistant. In addition, as each department was discussed, appropriate shop stewards and foremen were brought in to sit with the committee. It was agreed that the joint committee should meet twice a week, with each meeting being devoted to the problems of a particular department.

But formal meetings were only one part of the evolving cooperative social system. On the basis of Dymond's data, we can construct the following picture of the sequence of interactions among the personnel of both union and management:

1. Steward interviews each worker in department, soliciting suggestions.

1a. Shift superintendent and foreman meet to discuss possible savings.

2. Steward calls meeting of all workers in department to discuss suggestions and agree on recommendations.

3. Steward reports to union members of joint committee.

3a. Shift superintendent and foreman report to management members of joint committee.

4. Steward and foreman take up plans in joint committee meeting.

5. Discussion leads to recommendations for management action.

6. Management carries out committee recommendations. Interaction down line of management hierarchy leads to changes at work level and at level of first-line supervision.

7. After a trial period, steward consults each worker in department to get reactions to new setup. (It is not stated whether this was followed by a departmental meeting, as in No. 2.)

8. Steward and foreman report reactions to changes to joint committee.

9. Committee then recommends new setup be given final approval. (In a few cases, modifications were introduced here.)

10. Management announces approval of new setup.

While this process of evolution and change was going on, the union agreed to support management in moving against workers who were not doing a fair day's work. The foreman reported such cases to the personnel department. The personnel department gave notice to the union. The shop steward then consulted every member in the department of the accused worker. If there was general agreement that the man was not pulling his load, then the steward agreed not to push a grievance in case the man was dismissed.

In order to facilitate the process of change, the union executives agreed that no grievance stemming out of this process should be channeled through the regular grievance machinery to management. Instead, a worker appealed to his steward, who took his case up with the union executive committee, where every effort was made to settle it without turning to management at all.

At the same time, management was impelled to make certain changes in its organization and procedures. In one case it was suggested that "the foreman would have to establish better relations with his men if efficiency was to be increased." In some parts of the factory the amount of supervision was reduced and more responsibility placed in the hands of the operators. Union representatives also demanded that certain foremen increase their efficiency in planning and organizing the flow of work.

When each department had been carefully gone over, management worked out its calculations of the cost savings achieved. These figures were then checked over by the union members of the joint committee. Figures soon showed that savings were large enough to make possible the shift from 48 to 40 hours. Foreman and steward in each department then jointly signed an agreement stating that the new manpower requirements were mutually acceptable and could be considered permanent. At last, when these agreements had been signed throughout the plant, management and union jointly submitted (August 28, 1944) to the regional War Labor Board a petition asking authorization for cutting hours to 40 and granting a 20 per cent hourly rate increase.

## SECURING GOVERNMENT APPROVAL (August 1944-January 1945)

But the process was not at an end. It still took four months to secure government approval for the changes jointly worked out by union and management.

A first petition to the regional Canadian War Labor Board was turned down on the grounds that the board had no authority, under the wage stabilization program, to grant such an increase in hourly rates. Then, on October 19, 1944, the case was appealed to the National War Labor Board, where it was dismissed on the same grounds. At this point advisers to the board pointed out to union and management a legal loophole in the stabilization program. Management might pay bonuses directly related to increased productivity. Therefore, union and management submitted a new petition (December 13), proposing a 20 per cent production bonus to be paid upon reduction of hours. This was approved on December 27, and the 40-hour week with, in effect, a 20 per cent hourly rate increase went into effect on January 1, 1945.

This long delay, with the consequent uncertainty, was a severe strain upon the union. The union members had made considerable sacrifices in increasing job assignments and accepting certain demotions, and they had received no concrete rewards in return until January 1, 1945. If the government would not accept the new plan, there would certainly be hell to pay. Each time the government turned down the joint petition there was a stormy union meeting, but each time the union leaders managed to ride out the storm and keep up some degree of trust that the plan would eventually win out. The government's favorable decision made the position of the leaders secure—temporarily.

## DECLINE OF THE UNION LEADERSHIP

Apparently joint union-management activity had been allowed to lapse while matters were in the hands of the government. On January 24 the union leaders requested that the joint committee, dormant since August, be reactivated. Management signified its agreement but said that it was then engaged in formulating proposals to put before the committee. This resulted in some delay. Then management asked the union to submit names for its representatives on the joint committee. The president and any two members of the negotiating committee were chosen. No further action was taken until March 16, 1945, when the union reported that the members had approved the establishment of a permanent Joint Union-Management Advisory Committee. "The union further intimated that they should be given the opportunity of earning the right to sickness and accident pay by the same means as had been used to achieve the 40-hour week."

Management's reply (April 6) was a turning point in this new series of developments. Management expressed appreciation of the spirit of the union, but stated that it did not think it practical to extend the procedure resulting in the 40-hour week to other matters. Furthermore, the company was then undertaking a building program and planning to install more efficient equipment so that "we have no basis of estimating the new efficiency level that must be established and against which any incentive must be calculated." Management said that it would welcome the formation of such a committee "operating at the outset with no other incentive than the mutual satisfaction, encouragement and education that such a committee would undoubtedly impart." Finally, management added, it "would be willing to have as an item on the agenda of such a committee discussion of various forms of incentive bonus schemes."

While this last point left the door officially open for the reactivation of the committee, no further action was taken by union or management. The joint activity of the change from 48 to 40 hours therefore died even before the plan received governmental approval, and nothing new succeeded it.

Then, at last, in the spring of 1946, approximately a year after the union abandoned its efforts to revive the joint committee, an election was held and the union officers who had spearheaded the cooperation movement were nearly all voted out of office.

## WHY DID THEY LOSE THE ELECTION?

Dymond writes that, "according to the statements of the former president, members of the executive (board) personnel manager of the company, and the present president of the union," this overturn "was in no sense directly connected with union-management cooperation." By this he seems to mean that the new leaders are not hostile to management. He offers no explanation for the defeat of the old except that "the members appeared to feel that the old executives had been in office too long and were assuming more power than was desirable."

Both of these statements must be carefully scrutinized. The argument over tenure of office can certainly cut either way, according to the circumstances. If the workers are satisfied with their situation, then they can say, "We need good, experienced men in office." It is only when they are dissatisfied with developments that a cry for new blood will carry much force. We must therefore ask why they were dissatisfied.

We should be able to answer that question by examining the claim that the overturn was not connected with union-management cooperation. For that purpose, let us briefly review the rise and fall of the system of cooperation:

Preliminary period, November 1941-November 1943: Here relations seemed to be on a much more harmonious basis than in the average factory. The union was secure. Management was willing to discuss many problems not covered in the contract. Some joint activity (cafeteria, job evaluation) developed. But management also showed a concern with defending its "prerogatives." Management met the negotiating committee once a week and then once every two weeks.

Negotiating the basis for an interactive, cooperative system, November 1943-March 1944: Here the union pushed for the 48-40 plan. Its needs were twofold: (1) to break the general problem down into manageable parts and (2) to develop a social system capable of handling the parts and then fitting them into the whole. These needs were met through the institution of union-management meetings, which, presumably, continued to be held every two weeks.

Developing the interactive, cooperative system, March 1944-August 1944: Here we note a tremendous increase in frequency of interaction and the development of new channels integrating union and management in the actual, joint exploration of the savings possible under the proposed new hours. The sequences of interaction enumerated in minute detail in ten steps above indicate how communication was stimulated from the top down and from the bottom up both in the union and in the management structure. And finally channels of communication were tied together at the top in the joint committee meetings. Its twice-a-week frequency of meetings represented a quadrupling of the former frequency of the meetings of top union and top management officers.

While decisions of the joint committee necessitated some difficult readjustments at the work level, the social system provided for active consultation with workers both before and after changes. Dymond's observation corroborates the point when he says that, while the men who lost status and pay in the change were naturally dissatisfied, there were no serious accusations that favoritism had entered into decisions on job changes. The developed interactive (social) system seems to have functioned so effectively as to compensate for the readjustments that were made.

Furthermore, most of the changes were originated for management by the union. Dymond notes that when management representatives had changes in mind, they preferred to sit back and draw the union representatives into making specific proposals.

Thus the period in question illustrates for us not only greatly increased interaction between all levels, but also an increase of origination of action moving upward in the union structure and onto the management organization.

Disintegration of the (social) achieved interactive system; August 1944 on: Meetings of managers and union officers dropped away when their first and early particular purpose had been achieved, even before the plan was passed by the government. Union efforts to reestablish joint activity met no real response from management, and no action was taken.

This meant a sharp decline in frequency of interaction between top union and top management, the destruction of some of the former channels of interaction up and down the union structure, and a drastic reduction in the frequency with which origination of action passed up the union structure to management. The equilibrium of the newly developed social system was destroyed.

Human relations research has shown us time and time again that when drastic changes in human relations take place, important changes in the sentiments of the people also occur. This certainly was a drastic change. It is inconceivable that such a change could have no bearing upon sentiments within the union and therefore upon the vote that turned former union leaders out of office. Let us see if we can now go a step further in explaining this event.

## WHAT HAPPENED IN THE UNION?

When management responded to the union's request to continue the joint committee, the union executives decided that they could not go along on any plan of meetings "with no other incentive than mutual satisfaction, encouragement, and education." A cooperative system cannot subsist on interaction alone. There must be some symbols around which interaction can be organized, some issue or purpose for the interactions. The 48- to 40-hour change project provided such common symbols and a common purpose. Management's response in this case did not provide scope for any common symbols or purpose to which both sides might point their activity.

While management agreed to discuss bonus scheme possibilities, it was hesitant about getting involved in such discussion in view of the technological changes it had in mind. No doubt there were conversations which fortified the union leaders in the opinion that management was not really prepared to go ahead. The union president made this statement:

Our interpretation . . . is simply that, while some of the employers are willing to go a long way in improving conditions for the workers, there is no indication of any desire by employers to admit labor to partnership in industry, or in other words this employer stated if we (he) install more efficient machinery and work out more efficient methods, whatever profits accrue belong solely to us (him) and will be disposed as we (he) see (s) fit without reference to any committee.

Thus the union officials were blocked. Responding to communication from below up the line of union hierarchy, they had been successful in originating action for management with a high frequency, and they had also been successful in originating new activity down the line calling for new responses from the union members. But now, when they were blocked from originating further for management, they also could not respond further to union members, as they had responded to them before, because such responses necessarily involved originating for management.

No doubt some communication was still channeled up through the grievance procedure, but a social (interactive, cooperative) system that has been geared to such intense activity apparently could not maintain its equilibrium simply through the routine handling of grievances. If, when upward communication was damped, the union leaders continued trying to originate for the workers with something approximating the old frequency, we should expect the worker reaction that they were assuming too much power.

This interpretation is further substantiated by Dymond's report (in a letter to W. F. Whyte) upon events taking place in the union between January 1945, when the 40-hour week went into effect, and mid-1946, when the leaders were voted out of office.

Dymond writes that the union leaders succeeded in legislating a radically new type of seniority system "which was little understood by the membership." Then the leaders sought to persuade the members to change the affiliation of the local from the International Chemical Workers Union, AFL, to District 50 of the United Mine workers. In this they were unsuccessful, which means, of course, that the union leaders had lost their hold on the membership well before they were voted out of office.

We do not know the nature of the new seniority system, nor do we know the background of the attempted shift in affiliation. But, for purposes of this analysis, it does not seem necessary to have such information. In both cases it is clear that the origination of action was from the top down, with little or no participation of the members in formulating decisions. Furthermore, these were not simply two instances of such origination of action. In order to carry through a new seniority system and attempt to change union affiliation, it must have been necessary for the union leaders to try to originate action for the members many times and over an extended period of time. And these events could not be balanced by frequent origination of action up the line from the members, for the union leaders were not able to originate for management with the former frequency.

While there is much documentation still needed to clarify the change in political power within the union, the general lines of explanation seem clear. The breakdown of the union-management cooperative social (interactive) system led directly to overturn within the union.

### COULD THE OVERTURN HAVE BEEN AVOIDED?

Would it have been possible for the old officers to have maintained themselves in control? We might say that they could have helped their cause if they had refrained from trying to put over the new seniority system and the change in affiliation. However, men who have been accustomed to originating action cannot stop and remain idle. Being unable to originate as before for management, it was natural for them to turn more to originating for the members. Furthermore, leaders can remain leaders only by continuing to originate action for their followers. The problem was that they could no longer respond to the rank and file as before, since they could not get management into action.

In asking whether the overturn could have been avoided, we must examine the position taken by management. Given this position, it is difficult to see any action that the union leaders could have taken.

If management had wished to maintain these union leaders in control, management would have had to support the social system that had developed out of the 48- to 40-hour change plan. To do so would have meant setting up a new objective and, through joint meetings, working toward that objective.

Certainly management could not have agreed to turn over to the union all labor cost savings achieved through new machines and new processes. On the other hand, Dymond notes that management was privately committed to "the principle of gains-sharing." It simply did not have the formula to determine the shares.

However, this might well have been no obstacle to a continuation of the achieved social (interactive) system. Management had not known how the 48-to-40 plan could be worked out, but the problems were solved through the elaborate process that built the social system. No doubt there were many difficult issues to be met in the introduction of new machinery, but management did not need to have the answers in advance. It was only necessary to accept the principle of gains sharing openly and invite the union to begin discussions to work out the problems. This would have maintained the equilibrium of the social system and would have protected the position of the old union leadership.

Why did management refuse to take this action? If management wished to help maintain the current leaders in control (and we need not necessarily assume that this was the case), management simply failed to recognize that there was a necessary connection between the cessation of the cooperative program and the overturn of the leaders.

Furthermore, the prospect of cost savings through new machines may have made cooperation with the union seem less important to management. Beyond that we can only speculate, for we do not know whether the cooperative program gave rise to any problems within the management organization which might make management reluctant to continue along such lines.

The problem of new machines may have been difficult, but that in itself seems hardly sufficient to account for management's attitude. Probably of more diagnostic value is management's continuing concern over its prerogatives. We have noted the importance of this issue in the period before the 48-to-40 change plan. Apparently nothing more was heard of prerogatives while this plan was in process of being worked out. But then in the 1946 union agreement management felt it necessary to insert a long paragraph defining its prerogatives.

This period of active cooperation had brought far-reaching changes in management's relations with labor. Apparently management had not been able to adjust itself to these changes in terms of permanent policy. Its sentiments here seemed to grow out of problems of status.

Management had not changed in its desire to cooperate with the union, but it failed to recognize that cooperation requires the building of a continuously operating social system, and that a system once achieved comes to depend upon the continuation of the cooperative process. Cooperation must be continuous. It cannot be stopped at one point and then be picked up when a new opportunity happens along. A gap in time between cooperative efforts may destroy the system of human relations necessary to achieve cooperation.

# 14

## The Scanlon Plan[1]

The most spectacular and certainly the best publicized plant-wide incentive plan is that which goes under the name of the Scanlon Plan. The new approach to productivity and industrial relations that bears the name of Joseph Scanlon, formerly of the United Steelworkers of America and now a lecturer at the Massachusetts Institute of Technology, has been reported upon in *Life* and *Fortune*. The plan has attracted the enthusiastic interest of many management and union people.

Popular interest is just beginning to be followed up by the sort of research that would provide us with systematic knowledge of how the plan functions in action and of the conditions leading to its success or failure. This, then, cannot be a finished research report. It is simply an attempt to piece together the fragments of information we now have, to place them in perspective of human relations theory, and thus attempt an explanation of the spectacular results that are achieved in some cases.

The Scanlon Plan consists of two basic parts: (1) a social process whereby suggestions for productivity improvements can be made and carried out; (2) a formula for sharing the fruits of productivity improvements on a plant-wide basis.

### THE INCENTIVE BONUS PLAN

Scanlon and his associates argue that there is really no such thing as the Scanlon Plan in the sense of a universal formula that is

[1] This chapter is based primarily on the following: George P. Shultz, "Worker Participation on Production Problems," *Personnel,* November 1951; George P. Shultz and Robert P. Crisara, "The Lapointe Machine Tool Company and United Steelworkers of America," National Planning Asso., November 1952; Russell W. Davenport, "A Case History of Union-Management Cooperation," in Paul Pigors and Charles Myers, *Readings in Personnel Administration* (New York: McGraw-Hill Book Company, 1952), p. 461. Parts of this chapter, especially the section on suggestion plans, are based on a manuscript by Savies and Strauss.

applied to every plant. They point out that the sharing formula must be devised to fit the particular operating conditions of the plant in question. They also argue that the formula by itself produces no results. It is the reorganized activity of people that pays off. In view of what we learned from examining the Metropolis and Valley plant cases of Acme Manufacturing Company, that point hardly needs further emphasis.

The Scanlon Plan objective is to devise a formula which will most adequately reflect the productive efforts of workers and management people as a whole. It may help us to concentrate on one example, the Lapointe Machine Tool Company, in illustrating one possible formula.

As in the Acme case, the formula is based upon a ratio of labor costs to sales value of products produced. There are, however, some important differences between the LaPointe formula and that used at Acme:

1. The first contrast, and perhaps the most important of all, involves the amount of union involvement in the plan in the two plants. At Acme the plan was presented to the union pretty much in finished form by management. Since the Plan has remained unchanged from the beginning, there has been no real opportunity for the union to participate in its development or evolution. At Lapointe the Plan grew out of the initiative of the local union president and his committee, who sought out Joseph Scanlon and persuaded him to meet with them and management to propose a new cooperative approach. The possibility of reexamining and even changing the formula from time to time provides a further field for union involvement even in this narrow area involving the financial formula.

2. While both formulas are based upon past experience, in the Lapointe case management argued that labor costs over the months preceding the introduction of the Plan in 1947 were unduly inflated by World War II conditions. Management proposed and the union, a local of the United Steelworkers of America, accepted as a base a ratio of labor costs to sales value 3 percentage points below that which had existed in the base period. In Acme the base figure was utilized without change.

3. "For each 1 per cent of increase in productive efficiency as re-

flected in production value, a 1 per cent participating bonus will be paid to each employee working under the Plan."[2] Thus 100 per cent of the labor cost improvement is paid out to participating members, instead of 50 per cent as in the Acme case. Management expects to make its gains through spreading its overhead over increased production.

4. In Lapointe all employees of the company, with the exception of top management, share in the bonus. This means that foremen, superintendents, engineers, and other managerial people have a recognized part in the Plan. At Acme management from the foreman level up is covered by its own profit-sharing plan. At LaPointe the top executives share in a bonus system of their own, based on sales.

5. The bonus is paid in terms of a percentage of the participants' regular pay. If the bonus is 20 per cent for a given month and the production worker's regular earnings in that month were $400, he would receive an $80 bonus. Similarly, the engineer who had a salary of $600 for that month would receive $120. Under the Acme plan, a flat number of cents per hour is paid out to workers according to the number of hours worked regardless of their level of pay.

6. The many Lapointe workers who had been on piece rates were guaranteed their regular hourly rate plus their average incentive earnings prior to the time that the Plan went into effect. In other words, the company was gambling that these men would produce at least as much as they had under piecework even after the direct individual incentive was withdrawn. Since Acme did not have piecework, there is no corresponding provision in the Acme situation.

7. The Plan at Lapointe provides for possible changes in the ratio of labor costs to production value. The agreement envisages several possible conditions that may make such a change desirable. Management might introduce substantial technological improvements that would lower labor costs "without any increase in productive efficiency on the part of the participants." Increases in wage rates might justify a change. Increases or decreases in sales prices would affect the ratio. A major change in the product mix might affect the ratio, and so on. The agreement makes no attempt to

[2] Shultz and Crisara, *op. cit.*, p. 71.

anticipate all such possible conditions. It simply opens up possibilities for union and management to negotiate a new ratio. Three such changes were negotiated in the first four and a half years of the Plan's existence. On the other hand, Shultz reports that there have been some major technological changes without a change in the ratio.[3]

In contrast, the Acme formula does not change when management introduces technological improvements. This must be borne in mind in connection with the sharing formulae in the two cases, since Acme shares with participants only 50 per cent of the improvements but contributes technologically to this improvement without changing the base for calculations.

8. The Lapointe Plan establishes a reserve fund to meet fluctuations in labor costs. This was not included in the original plan, but the machine tool industry is naturally subject to wide fluctuations in its volume of business. A month when business was down might show not only no bonus to be paid, but might reveal an actual deficit. The union agreed in negotiations with management that it would only be fair to meet such deficits out of a reserve fund. It was therefore agreed upon that one-half of the first 15 per cent of any bonus earned in any month should be set aside as a reserve. Any unused portion of this reserve by November of the given year should be paid out in December and a new reserve fund established. Acme provides for no such reserve fund, but we note that the payment is made on a quarterly basis so that a deficit in one month may be canceled out by surpluses in the other one or two.

## SUGGESTION PLAN: OLD STYLE

The system for developing and implementing suggestions is one of the basic parts of the Scanlon Plan. In order to see the significance of the Scanlon approach to suggestions, it may help us first to examine suggestion systems as they are generally applied in industry today.

Years ago there were probably many foremen and other management people who took the attitude toward workers represented in the statement, "You're paid to work. I do the thinking around here." No doubt such attitudes still exist in industry even though few

[3] Letter to W. F. Whyte.

people would give them such blunt expression. However, it is coming to be more and more realized that workers do think about their jobs, that they are capable of making suggestions that would lead to improvements in efficiency. In fact, many management people are convinced that there is a veritable gold mine in these ideas. The problem is to develop a plan that will systematically bring these ideas to management's attention.

Suggestion plans exist in many companies. They generally operate in this manner: The individual who has an idea tears off an entry form from the stack conveniently located in his department above a suggestion box. He writes his suggestion on this slip of paper and either signs his name or identifies himself by his clock number. He then drops his entry into the box. These slips are collected periodically from various departments and studied by a suggestion committee appointed by management. Departmental management is consulted before committee decisions are made.

For every idea accepted a cash award is made. For cases where no cash savings can be shown, the accepted suggestion draws a nominal award of perhaps $5 or $10. Where a savings in labor costs can be shown, management makes an effort to estimate the amount that can be saved in six months or a year and pays the employee some predetermined percentage of this figure. In some cases these payoffs are substantial. The top award in some companies may run into several thousand dollars.

Where such plans are well administered (within their own logics) and where the company is really prepared to offer substantial rewards for valuable suggestions, there is no doubt that such systems provide management with practical ideas worth far more than the costs of administering the suggestion plan. In other words, if such a suggestion plan were withdrawn—and no alternatives presented—management would lose and at least some employees would lose an opportunity of supplementing their earnings and expressing their ingenuity. Nevertheless, we find that many such suggestion plans are made little use of by employees, and even in the cases of the best of such plans we suspect that they do not begin to tap the storehouse of ideas actually possessed by workers, let alone those ideas that workers and management people together could develop if they devised more effective ways of stimulating such ideas.

There seem to be important limitations actually inherent in suggestion plans as commonly practiced. Often management only pays what workers regard as ridiculously small amounts for valuable suggestions. Even if we assume that management is prepared to pay generously for suggestions, there are other stumbling blocks, which are discussed below.

1. The traditional suggestion plan puts its emphasis upon the contribution of the *individual*. He is offered an individual reward for his individual idea. In many cases a cost-saving idea will involve the readjustment of jobs and people in the department. Such changes may be looked upon by other people as a threat to their position and security. Thus the individual who makes such a suggestion may win money and yet stir up the resentment of fellow workers. Under such conditions many people would rather keep their suggestions to themselves.

2. *Foreman-worker relations.* Many foremen look upon a successful suggestion submitted by a worker in their departments as a reflection upon their own competence. They fear that higher management might say, "Why didn't the foreman think of that himself?" Many workers recognize this and fear that the foreman will retaliate against them if they submit suggestions. Even when the worker prefers to withhold his name in the contest, the foreman is likely to have a pretty good idea as to which of his men might be putting in suggestions.

This problem can be met to some extent if management takes pains to give the foreman recognition for suggestions coming out of his department. For example, management is advised to have the foremen present the awards and with a maximum of fanfare and publicity, especially if the award is a substantial one. However, even these measures may not eliminate worker fear of retaliation if no other changes are made in the foreman-worker relations.

3. *Problems in the ownership of ideas.* The standard suggestion approach assumes that a good idea is devised by a single individual —though sometimes two individuals may sign their names to a suggestion. This assumption is contrary to experience and to research observations. We saw in examining Donald Roy's experience that the workers in his department had many production ideas that were unknown to management. No doubt some of these ideas were

developed full blown by a single individual, but even in those cases the ideas had been shared with the rest of the shop. Some of these ideas had been around for a long time, so that it would be quite impossible to determine who had invented them. There were also, of course, ideas originated by one individual but modified and improved upon by one or more others. This same observation can be made in many other factory situations.

Now suppose some individualist decides to take one of these ideas and put it in the suggestion box. Then we hear from fellow workers, "It was really my idea, but that bastard stole it from me and cashed in on it," and similar expressions of resentment. Thus the individual incentive on suggestions may stimulate conflict within a department.

4. *Complex ideas and human relations.* We generally find that the most valuable ideas for the improvement of efficiency are not those limited to one machine or to one productive operation. Such ideas may involve changes in the relations of machines to each other, in the relations of worker to worker and of workers to management people. In such a situation the individual worker is not in a position to see all parts of the problem that are necessary to the working out of a practical plan. The individual may have the initial idea but a group process may be required before the idea can be put into practical form. This calls for consultation among a number of people. However, the individual suggestion award discourages such consultations. The emphasis is upon individual ownership of the idea, and many people naturally fear to talk their idea over with other people lest they lose some claim on its ownership.

5. *Paper communication vs. social interaction.* The standard suggestion system is a depersonalized operation. It is only at the point of making the awards, especially in some of the larger cases, that a personal element enters in. The communication of the suggestion is in writing and the suggestion committee studies these written documents. Furthermore, many workers who have good ideas find it difficult to express them in writing. The writing requirement thus serves as a barrier to communication.

We once heard a personnel man say that he considered the suggestion plan "the most valuable form of communication between workers and management." This sort of paper communication may pay off in dollars saved, but it is one of the elementary observations of social research that if we wish to change the attitudes or behavior of people we will find that face-to-face interaction has far more powerful effects than written communication.

## SUGGESTION PLAN: SCANLON STYLE

The Scanlon suggestion plan is a marked contrast to traditional systems.

In the first place, there is no individual payoff. This means that the Scanlon approach relies on a completely different type of motivation. The individual is expected to contribute his ideas for the benefit of everyone. He is rewarded, of course, but in a less tangible way. We assume that where the system works the individual must receive a good deal of recognition from fellow workers, union officers, and management. Since he does not stand to gain on an individual financial basis, he is not caught between a desire to benefit himself and the possible adverse reactions of his work group.

Furthermore, the Scanlon suggestion system is not left to the initiative of isolated individuals. A definite structure is set up for the discovery, development, and implementation of suggestions. The structure operates through union and management. In every department a union production committeeman is appointed or elected. This committeeman and the foreman constitute the production committee of the department. They meet together at least once a month to discuss possible suggestions for improvement. This suggestion activity is separate from grievance handling, but the grievance committeeman is invited to sit in on discussions if he cares to do so. The production committeeman may also call in one or two employees from the department in connection with problems with which they are particularly familiar.

Above the departmental production committee level there is an administration or screening committee composed of three management and three union representatives. It is hoped that many suggestions brought by the production committeemen to the foremen can be put into effect within the department without further discussion. However, there will necessarily be other suggestions which require higher level consideration. These are referred to the screening committee. There will also be suggestions that originate at the screening committee level, since they involve interdepartmental problems.

Each departmental production committee is expected to keep minutes of its meetings, giving details on the suggestions made and on the action taken with them. These minutes are transmitted to the screening committee as a means of keeping that group informed about all developments.

According to the formal program, the screening committee is not a decision-making body. It simply presents recommendations to management. The fact is, of course, that higher management officers sit on this committee, so we can assume that a recommendation from the committee will receive most serious consideration.

The bare outline of the Scanlon Plan calls for suggestions to be put in written form by the production committeemen and for certain regularly scheduled meetings. This formal approach, of course, represents only the minimum foundation of the plan. Insofar as such an approach is successful, it must be supplemented by a good deal of informal discussion between production committeemen and workers, committeemen and foremen, committeemen and screening committee members, and so on. Even if suggestions are written, we assume that at least at the departmental level many items are discussed without being put into writing. Nor should the discussions be limited to those who hold formal offices in the cooperative program. The formal structure described above simply provides the channels through which suggestions are processed. These channels are supposed to provide a means for involving everyone—worker or management—in the cooperative system. If the cooperation is limited to the official functionaries, we cannot expect the results that have been achieved in some cases.

Just how do people become involved in this cooperative system? Some cases may tell the story better than any general discussion can.

1. *Eliminating resistance to change.* This example comes from a printing plant:

One of the pressroom employees pointed out that waste paper was now being crumpled up and thrown in a basket in preparation for salvage. Everyone conceded that, if this paper could be salvaged in flat form, its value would be much higher. Management had been aware of this possible saving but had been unable to enlist the cooperation of the employees in keeping the stock flat. A committee member pointed out the reason for the lack of cooperation: workers felt the foreman was trying to check on them to see how much paper they wasted. Consequently, through various subterfuges they made it impossible for him to police his system. With the suggestion and impetus coming from the employees themselves, however, there was no trouble in getting the waste paper placed in flat form on pallets located at appropriate places in the pressroom.[4]

Here it is not the idea that is new, but the way of carrying out the idea. The idea in itself was fairly obvious, but relations between management and workers within the department were such that it could not be carried out. When the cooperative program got under way it became possible for workers to bring about the changed behavior.

2. *Improving management plans.* This case involves the installation of conveyor systems in the printing plant before and after the development of the cooperative program.

Before the cooperative program began, management introduced a conveyor system into one of the departments in the traditional management manner. The planning department developed the plan without assistance of other groups. The conveyor system was explained to the superintendent and foreman involved, and a blueprint was placed on a bulletin board of the department. However, no explanations were given to the employees and they had no opportunity to express their thoughts and feelings on the matter.

The new conveyor system immediately ran into trouble. Instead of pitching in to help out in this situation, the employees were delighted with the apparent failure of the change. Production dropped below previous average figures and remained down for ten months, until management decided to junk the system.

Shultz describes the second conveyor case in this manner:

In contrast to this experience is the installation of a conveyor system after the plan had been in operation for two months. As in the former case the Planning Department had an idea for the rearrangement of the machines and the use of a conveyor to facilitate certain transport problems. In this case a blueprint was made and posted on the bulletin board, but the employees stated that they could not read the blueprint and that, therefore, they could make very few, if any, suggestions about the proposed

4 Shultz, *op. cit.*, p. 6.

plan. Consequently, a small-scale model or templet of what the layout would look like under the new plan was placed at a central location in the department. The employees still, however, made practically no suggestions about the new plan.

One afternoon a member of the planning group happened to be in the department and started discussing the proposed layout with a few of the employees. After he had criticized the proposal in a number of respects, a great many comments were made both by the foreman and by the employees. These comments were gathered together and a Production Committee meeting was held attended by the Industrial Engineer responsible for the proposals. At this meeting the employees and the foreman joined together in strenuous criticism of the conveyor part of the plan. After about two and one half hours' discussion, the Production Committee agreed that the rearrangement of the machines would be beneficial but wanted the engineer to reconsider several aspects of the conveyor system.

About a week later, another meeting was held and the Production Committee agreed to a modified version of the conveyor system, with the understanding that it would be installed in such a manner that they could make changes fairly easily. Subsequently, the Production Committee did make several important changes, especially in the manning of the new system. The drastic revision in the department layout and the revised conveyor system are now accepted as an improvement by the workers and the foremen concerned and the productivity of the department has been increased by about 20 per cent.[5]

Here we see that management has not abandoned its customary managerial function of planning for technological and process changes. The difference is that management now consults the people who are most directly involved in the changes. This has two effects. On the one hand, it reduces or eliminates resistance to the change. On the other hand, it makes possible the modification of the plan so that it will be more efficient in its technical as well as in its social sense.

3. *Joint discussion of complex problems.* Shultz presents this case again from the printing plant:

The long-term problem in the Press Room was loss of work to outside manufacturers who, because of their superior equipment, could presumably turn out the work more cheaply. One of the chief losses was the approximately two million workbooks a year contracted for by an outside press. With their own bread and butter at stake, the Press-Room Committee investigated the relative cost of doing the work at the plant as against

[5] *Ibid.,* pp. 7-8.

sending it outside. They found that the outside price was $15.90 per hundred for a particular order and that the Planning Department figured the cost of doing this job in the plant was $21.55 per hundred, a differential of $5.65 for each 100 workbooks. Then the Production Committee showed management how the plant costs could be brought down to $17.65 per hundred. This tremendous saving was the result of two factors: (1) the elimination of unnecessary operations, and (2) reductions in the estimated time requirement on the operations that were performed. By further investigation into other books of this type, the Production Committee found that certain administrative costs that were properly incurred by the company were not allocated to outside work. Finally it was found that the reduction of inplant overhead cost per unit resulting from the possible increased volume was not being considered. When all these factors were taken into consideration, it was found that a specific 50,000 workbook order could be produced at the plant for 50¢ per hundred cheaper than it could be printed outside—a figure 28 per cent under management's original cost estimate.[6]

Russell Davenport presents another illustration:

One of the greatest advantages of this kind of collective bargaining from the worker's point of view, is the knowledge that it gives him of the business. When a slump is coming, he knows it. He even is given a chance to combat it, in the sense that if he can devise a cheaper way of turning out his product, perhaps the company will be able to take business from somebody else. In a number of instances the Lapointe workers have actually done this, the most spectacular example being that of an order from a big automotive concern in December, 1948. The workers had been pressing management to accept orders even at the break-even point so as to tide over a bad period. Mr. Prindiville, who sometimes sits in on the screening-committee meetings, had given in to the pressure some months previously to the extent of taking an order from this firm for 100 broaches at $83 per broach. But Lapointe had lost 10 per cent on the deal, and Mr. Prindiville now put his foot down. If this business was to be taken again the price would have to be raised. In view of new competition, it meant that Lapointe almost certainly would not get the business—and at a time when work was scarce.

The gloomy gathering that listened to Mr. Prindiville's pronouncement was then electrified by a question from Jimmie McQuade, skilled grinder and one of the most outspoken members of the screening committee. "Who says we can't make those broaches at that price for a profit?" Mr. McQuade wanted to know, "If you'd give the men in the shop the chance to go over the blueprints before production starts, and to help plan the job, there are lots of ways of cutting costs without cutting quality." The idea

---

[6] *Ibid.*, p. 8.

grew, and the next day the suggestion ran around the shop like wildfire. The order was taken at the old price, this time with a *profit* of 10 per cent —a total gain in efficiency of 20 per cent.[7]

In these cases we see that the workers and union representatives are not simply concerned with problems of improving a particular machine. They become involved with management in problems that go to the heart of the business: the relationships among productivity, costs, prices, and profit. The cost situation presents a goal for them to shoot at. If people did not know what the cost problems were, they would have no particular motivation for developing such complicated plans for improvement. Now, the costs and the company's competitive position provide the goals around which the cooperative activity is organized. Apparently this searching inquiry into the cost situation can be initiated on the union's side by a challenge such as that made by the grinder to the company president or it can be initiated when management asks for union help in examining possibilities for reducing costs on a particular order.

4. *Teamwork on technical improvements.* Here let us turn to two cases presented by Shultz and Crisara from Lapointe:

Start—grind—stop—wait—"mike." And start all over again. That is the way to grind round broaches. Start the machine, grind off a little stock, press the stop button, wait for the machine to coast to a stop, then "mike" the broach. Learn to set up and operate the machine, read blueprints, dress the abrasive wheel, get the "feel" of micrometers. These skills are required of a cylindrical grinder.

Where was the problem? Production and quality were good. The foreman was satisfied. The company was satisfied. But a worker thought the job could be done better. For him there was too long a wait between pressing the stop button and being able to "mike" the broach. He had a vague idea that applying some kind of electrical brake on the machine would make it stop faster and therefore speed up production. His foreman liked the idea. But together they were unable to go any further with it.

They suggested it to management, but were told that it would cost $1,200 to buy a speed control, and that the present speed reducer which cost $450 would have to be scrapped. This was considered too expensive.

But neither the worker nor the foreman gave up. In a chat with an electrician they got further information and, in a few days, what seemed to be a practical solution. The results, as told by the electrician, were:

"This didn't require a major change in the machine, because we found a way of supplying a source of d.c. current directly to the motor windings

7 Davenport, *op. cit.*, p. 473.

and using a shot of d.c. current as a brake. The time saving is so great that, after we put it on the first one, they applied it to seventeen other machines. They tell me this saves one hour a day per machine. It cost only $1.25 for the fuse block, about $14.00 for a relay, plus a couple of hours for the maintenance man to install."[8]

In the above case it was a worker who took the initiative on the suggestion, but the plan finally carried out was a joint product of worker, foreman, and electrician. In the following case we see the foreman taking the initiative in this cooperative activity. He describes it in this way himself:

I was in engineering today and they gave me a blueprint of a job coming into the department about two months from now. There are some tough problems on it. I gave a copy to the operators who will be working on the job and asked them to look it over, suggest methods and tools. You'd be surprised at the number of things they can suggest that you'd probably never think of. Then, when the job comes in, I'm ready for it and so are the operators. Besides, doing it that way lets the operator know he is important. And he is important.[9]

5. *Real vs. paper control.* Shultz presents this case again from the printing plant:

One of the departmental Production Committee's most vigorously-pressed suggestions concerned the scheduling of jobs. Workers complained that they often set up their equipment as scheduled, only to find that the particular paper needed for that job was not yet on hand. Though paper for other jobs was apparently available, they could not make a switch since setup time was generally great. This complaint involved people outside the department, however, so the Production Committee could do little about it themselves. They passed it on to the top Screening Committee, a group which included the company president.

The head of the scheduling department, of course, felt particularly concerned with this complaint, and so he did some "homework" in preparation for the meeting. For each job, the worker turns in to the scheduling department a time slip on which is tabulated the total elapsed hours in terms of "running time," "delays," and so on. The department head examined the file of these slips thoroughly and found that there was actually very little delay due to "insufficient paper." When the question came up in the meeting, he triumphantly produced these "facts" and discounted the complaint as of minor importance. This disclosure was greeted with an embarrassed silence. After a long half-minute, one of the workers spoke

---

[8] Shultz and Crisara, *op. cit.*, pp. 49-50.
[9] *Ibid.*, p. 57.

up: "Those time slips are way off. We fill them out. We were told by the foreman that he would get in trouble if we showed that delay time, so we usually added it to the running time. We've been doing it that way for years. We had no idea you were using the slips as a basis for planning."

Further discussion brought out that the schedulers were using the time slips, not just as a check on coordination between paper storage and production departments, but also as a basis for calculating the running times on different types of jobs. Now, with a newly reliable source of information, the scheduling department is able to work much more effectively.[10]

This case illustrates a problem that is general in management in many plants. Management establishes control systems for two purposes: (1) to plan production efficiently and (2) to evaluate the performance of various individuals and units of the plant. From the standpoint of foremen and workers there is a possible conflict between these two objectives. To protect themselves from the impact of higher management evaluations, workers and foremen often seeks to present a picture of operations that looks good or at least looks stable. If they can eliminate large fluctuations from the record, they will be subjected to less pressure from above. The records they fill out, therefore, are often a combination of facts and fiction in such proportions that no one outside the department can know which is which. If management uses these records to plan its production and work-flow scheduling, these plans are built upon the shaky foundation of semifictional information.

Really effective control depends upon the availability of accurate information. In a conflict situation the workers, and even foremen, see to it that higher management is supplied with highly misleading information. People at low levels in management may realize that the information is misleading, but they are in no position to do anything about it. For the nature of the information provided depends in part upon the functioning of the social system. When more cooperative relations are established, it becomes possible to strip away the fictions and provide more accurate information. The fictions can be eliminated only when they no longer serve a function for the people who have created them. When workers and foremen no longer have such a need to protect themselves from higher management, it becomes possible to achieve a degree of management control of the production process that has not hitherto existed.

10 Shultz, *op. cit.,* pp. 8-9.

6. *Involving the total organization.* What happens under the Scanlon suggestion plan when there is no payoff? This occurred 16 times in 58 months at Lapointe.

The first three months brought bonuses of 24.5, 20.1, and 12.6 per cent. Then followed three no-bonus months, one with 4.7 per cent, and then two more barren months. How did the people meet the crisis? Shultz and Crisara tell the story in this way:

What happened later on when production dipped and there were no bonuses? The cause was simple and well-understood (though not excused) by everyone. They had "worked themselves out of a job." Management did not anticipate the effect on production of the new arrangement and consequently the backlog of business that had looked big was shortly dissipated. What should the parties have done? It might have been possible to maintain bonus figures in the period that followed by means of heavy layoffs. On the other hand, why should a few men earn bonuses while others earned nothing? And what about the delays and training costs involved in the future when the expected business developed? After considerable discussion of the reasons for the problem and the prospects for the months to follow, union and management agreed that the work force should be held together. This meant no bonus during the lean period. In the meantime management concentrated on the job of increasing sales. While some orders for standard equipment got them back to a small bonus in June, the bulk of the job-lot type of business typical of Lapointe could not be put directly into the shop; it had to go through the engineering department first. With July vacations coming up, another crisis appeared in the offing. But even before they were propositioned about it, the engineers decided to postpone their vacations in order to process the work. With this added pay roll and relatively little production, July figures looked bad; however, by September production was rolling again.[11]

The story is interesting from two points of view. It shows that people are willing to accept reversals without losing faith in the plan, providing they are thoroughly and personally involved in carrying it out. Under these circumstances, the information provided will be accepted and acted upon. A mere management handout of information, however accurate, would not suffice to maintain confidence.

Here we also see the importance of involving the total organization in the plan. After all, it is the total organization that accomplishes the results that lead to the payoff. If the engineers in this

[11] *Op. cit.*, pp. 36-37.

case had not been involved in the plan and had gone off on vacation at the customary time, it is likely that the whole cooperative program would have died at this point.

### NEW VS. OLD SUGGESTION PLANS

Let us review the suggestions discussed in the preceding examples. Could any of them have been provided management through the functioning of a traditional individual reward suggestion system?

Only in the first case is it reasonable to conceive of this happening. A worker might well have put in a suggestion that costs could be cut if wastepaper were piled flat instead of crumpled up. However, the idea was not the problem in this case at all. The problem was to get the people to accept and put the idea into effect. Under the individual suggestion plan, such a suggestion regarding the handling of wastepaper might have been made, and yet that in and of itself would have done no good.

We should also note that some of these problems involved not a single suggestion, but a combination of many. The emphasis here is not upon a specific suggestion, but rather upon the solution of a problem.

Perhaps the closest example to the type of suggestion that could come up through an individual plan is that which was involved in the electric brake case. We note that the worker had a germ of an idea but was not able to carry it out without the help of foreman and electrician. If this had happened under an individual plan, would the suggestion have actually been developed? Perhaps the worker would fear that if he took the suggestion up with the foreman, the foreman might take credit away from him. And if the electrician was called in on the suggestion, it would then become a real problem as to whose suggestion it was. The electrician could certainly claim ownership of the suggestion. Under such circumstances the worker might feel that it would be foolish to consult the electrician at all. Thus, the idea would probably have been stillborn.

The Scanlon approach seems to bring forward the type of suggestion that is available through other suggestion plans, but it also seems to tap a field that is totally outside the reach of such plans. We noted earlier that some of the most valuable suggestions involved changes in the relations of machines to each other, of men to machines, of workers to supervisors, and so on. It is exceedingly unlikely that the individual worker will have enough knowledge and experience to be able to present that kind of suggestion. Such a suggestion is traditionally thought of as in the realm of management planning; but we have seen in the case of the conveyor that when changes of this nature are made, without any involvement on the part of workers and supervisors, all sorts of dislocations develop. We can therefore conclude that the Scanlon approach taps a reservoir of ideas that would not be reached with the traditional approach at all. Perhaps reservoir is not a good simile because it assumes that the ideas just lie there waiting to be tapped. The cases described clearly indicate that for the most important suggestions this is not the case. People contribute much more in the way of valuable suggestions when they are stimulated to shoot for new goals by a social system that makes such activity possible.

We also see a contrast in the actual number of suggestions and particularly in the number of acceptable suggestions made. In the first four and a half years of the Scanlon Plan's existence in the Lapointe plant, 1506 suggestions were made. During this period the plant grew from 294 employees to 1085. If we average the quarterly figures of the number of employees on the payroll, we get a figure of just under 500 employees as an average for this 4½-year period. That means that the average employee submitted about three suggestions within this period. Of course, there were some who submitted no suggestions and some who submitted many more than three. However, Shultz and Crisara point out that new employees have fitted into the system and are contributing suggestions at a surprisingly rapid rate. For the final 12-month period recorded by them (October 1951-September 1952) there were 637 suggestions, of which 178 came from people who had never previously made a suggestion. Twenty-eight per cent, then, of the total volume came from these first-time people.

Even more impressive, however, is the proportion of suggestions that have been accepted and put into practice. Specialists on individual suggestion plans warn management that it should be prepared to find that a large proportion of the suggestions will be impractical. One expert states, "On an average 75 out of every 100 suggestions are turned down."[12] He then goes on to advise management as to how it should deal with these turned down suggestions.

Shultz and Crisara report that 80 per cent of these 1506 suggestions made at Lapointe have been accepted and put into operation. Another 5 per cent were still under consideration and only 15 per cent had been rejected.

How can we explain this striking contrast between 75 per cent rejected and 80 per cent accepted? On the basis of the data given we cannot be sure of the answer, but an examination of the suggestion-making process in the two cases gives us our best clues. We have noted that the Scanlon suggestion program involves a good deal of informal discussion among workers and between workers and management people. It is probably at this stage that impractical suggestions are weeded out. The man who has an idea checks with other workers and perhaps tries to get advice from management people. At this point he may either get the help he needs to put his suggestion in practical form or else he may decide that it is not worth submitting. In the case of the individual suggestion plan, on the other hand, the employee is not likely to have the benefit of this consultation. He feels he had better keep the idea to himself in order to retain possession of it. Under these circumstances it is natural that a large proportion of the suggestions coming up in such a program will be impractical.

## RESULTS ACHIEVED

Our story has already indicated some of the results achieved under this cooperative approach. Using the LaPointe case as an example, we can summarize them in this way:

1. *The growth of cooperation.* The union was organized at Lapointe in late 1944. Toward the end of the first year of its existence there was an 11-week strike. During the next several years, relations between the parties improved, but there was still a good deal of difficulty over some grievances. With the institution of the cooperative program at the end of 1947, worker-management and union-management relations changed markedly in the direction of

[12] Herman W. Seinwerth, "Suggestion Plans—The Value to the Personnel Relations Program," reprinted in Paul Pigors and Charles Myers *op. cit.*, p. 459.

cooperation. Shultz and Crisara report that grievances have practically disappeared.

2. *Strengthening of the company's competitive position.* The company not only has grown on a scale that might have been impossible without the cooperative program, it has improved its competitive position in a most impressive manner.

3. *Elimination of output restriction.* On the basis of previous studies, we have been accustomed to assuming that restriction of output exists anywhere and everywhere. Apparently in some of these Scanlon cases it has been well-nigh eliminated. The union president cites an example of a grinder at Lapointe who had been averaging $76.40 a week on his incentive rate. In four days after the Plan was instituted, he turned in enough work so that it would have amounted to $184 under the preexisting incentive plan. This is only a single example and is certainly not enough to allow us to assume that no restriction remains at all. However, it does suggest that the tight ceiling on production has been eliminated. With no more individual incentive rates there is no longer any threat of rate cutting, and the worker can contribute to the goal of the total organization without incurring the enmity of fellow workers.

4. *The payoff to workers.* What are workers getting out of it? The most tangible results are shown in the bonuses paid over the four and a half years reported by Shultz and Crisara. Between December 1947 and September 1952 the bonus has ranged between 0 and a high of 52.1 per cent. Sixteen of these 58 months showed no bonus and 20 showed 20 per cent or over.

## HOW WERE THE GAINS WON?

We shall need a good deal more research before we reach a full understanding of the spectacular results gained in some Scanlon Plan plants—and also of the failures encountered in other attempts, for there have been failures and we can learn from them too. The following analysis must be considered tentative.

1. *A new management approach.* Success of an activity such as is involved in the Scanlon Plan requires a veritable revolution in management's conception of its functions and in its behavior in relation to workers and union representatives. The management preoccupied with protecting its prerogatives had best not consider

the Scanlon Plan at all. The following illustration is presented by Shultz:

> Not too long ago, a group of about eight workers and their union business agent came to see Scanlon. They were worried people. Their company owned five plants, and the one they worked in was the oldest, the least efficient. As one of them put it, "We've seen these other plants and we know that we're the worst. If business gets bad, we're sure to go." The president of their company had made a number of widely-quoted speeches emphasizing the need for giving workers a "sense of participation." These particular workers thought that they had something to contribute, and they had heard that Scanlon talked about "participation," too. Would he help them?
>
> Well, he might, but what did they have to contribute? Were they just talking or could they be more specific? Raising this question was like opening the floodgates. The rest of the morning was spent listening to them discuss the mistakes that management made, the unnecessary waste of materials, the possible improvements in methods. The stories were detailed and convincing. Surely they would startle and inspire any company president who talked about participation. They did not inspire this one, though they may have startled him. He stated, in effect, that it was his job to manage this business and that he was paid well to do just that. He was sure the foremen would be glad to get these suggestions, but neither he nor the foremen could discuss them further. After all, he could not give up his management prerogatives.[13]

It is fashionable for management people to say that participation on the part of workers is important. But often they give themselves away by saying that the worker "must be made to feel he is participating." This synthetic sense of participation they seek to provide perhaps by distributing financial statements to workers and in other ways telling them how the business is getting along. But real participation involves changes in the behavior and activity of people. It involves getting workers to initiate changes in the behavior of management people. If management is unwilling to make any significant changes, then it is futile to start on such a program.

2. *Reciprocity in initiating action.* We have noted that in order for the cooperation program to succeed, management people must be willing to respond to action initiated by workers and union representatives. As we look over the cases above, it becomes evident that this initiation is not one-sided. We see cases where management

---

[13] *Op. cit.*, pp. 3-4.

has called upon union officers and workers to take action in solving management problems. If management simply sat back and waited for union people to come up with ideas, the cooperative program would soon peter out. Management is expected to take the initiative in the solution of manufacturing problems, but in these cooperative cases management learns to take the initiative in a different way. Instead of simply initiating through giving out orders, management makes clear to the participants in the program the real problems of production that management faces. In this way management enlists skill, understanding, and intelligence that otherwise are little utilized.

3. *Ability of management to make changes.* The program requires not only a receptivity on the part of management people, but also an ability to make changes. The two do not necessarily go together. We have fragmentary information on one case where the Scanlon Plan has failed to achieve the sort of spectacular results noted at Lapointe and in some other cases. The union's international representative gives this explanation of the situation: He points out that the company manufactures large pieces of equipment. As these units move through the factory, there are often times when numbers of workers are standing idle waiting for the next unit to arrive. The union representatives on production and screening committees have argued vigorously that management must improve its production scheduling before any substantial improvements in labor costs will appear. This management has not done.

It is unclear from our data whether management has been unreceptive to ideas in the production scheduling field or simply has found it impossible to make basic improvements. It is, of course, easier to balance production and keep all workers occupied most of the time when the factory manufactures a large number of small units than is the case when large units of varying types move through the plant. However, some of the large broaching machines manufactured by Lapointe present the same problem, and there the problem was solved. Whether it is unreceptiveness to what is proposed or inability to make changes, the result seems to be the same. It is difficult to stimulate workers to bring forward suggestions that would result in relatively small savings when they see the thousands of dollars that are wasted in the waiting time.

4. *Involvement of the total organization.* The Scanlon approach provides for a remarkably widespread involvement of people in the discussion of production problems. Workers become involved, but not only workers. We see engineers, production schedulers, accountants, and so on contributing their specialized knowledges. In fact, the work of the modern factory is so complex that the solution of any given problem often involves the specialized knowledges of several different types of functionaries. The Scanlon Plan provides for this flexible sort of involvement. At the same time, the involvement is not left completely to chance and spontaneous development in the various parts of the plant. A formal system is provided to bring suggestions up from department to screening committee and to management for action. The formal framework does not determine success, but it does provide a set of procedures through which the widespread informal activity can be organized and brought to a successful conclusion.

# PART IV

## A THEORY OF ECONOMIC INCENTIVES AND HUMAN RELATIONS

# 15

# Tools for Analysis

If our project has been successful, we have not simply presented a miscellaneous series of cases. Those cases fall into a theoretical pattern. We have sought to explain each case along with our description of it, but the building of a usable theory requires general statements in order to show explicitly the pattern into which the cases fit.

For this purpose, we need to use an abstract language that will not be limited in its meaning to any particular case. We need to work with a set of mental tools or concepts. We have no desire to give birth to a new set of elaborate technical terms. The terms we use will be simple and few. Some we have already used in the case discussions, but they will now be more specifically defined and utilized. In general, we follow the theoretical ideas developed by Eliot Chapple and Conrad Arensberg and elaborated by George Homans.[1]

Our main theoretical terms are four: symbols, sentiments, activities, and interactions.

*Symbols* are principally words or physical objects that come to stand for relations of man to man, of man to the physical world, and also for relations between man and physical objects and other men.

Piece rates or plant-wide incentive formulae are sets of symbols. Our research problem is to see how people react to these symbols.

*Sentiments* (or attitudes, we make no distinction between them) refer to the feelings people have toward each other and toward organizations such as union or management. People also have sentiments regarding the types of behavior that are expected or re-

[1] See George C. Homans, *The Human Group* (New York: Harcourt, Brace, 1950), for a full statement of this point of view. We differ with Homans on some points.

quired under various conditions. We use *norms* as a subcategory of sentiments to refer to types of behavior that are required of its members by a particular group.[2]

We are particularly interested in sentiments of conflict or cooperation. Under what circumstances do people feel that they are getting along well together? Under what circumstances do they feel that their relations are full of conflict? These days we hear much talk about the values of participation. We want to know under what circumstances people feel that they are really participating in an organization instead of just being passive members.

*Activities* refers to the physically observable things that people do. Man engages in a great number of activities that we will not attempt to explain here. Our chief interest will be in the activities connected with work in the factory and in those connected with making or withholding suggestions regarding efficiency of the organization. We want to know under what sorts of human conditions productivity goes up or down. We want to examine the effect of human relations upon the expression of ideas designed to improve the efficiency of the organization.

By *interaction* we refer to interpersonal contacts. This approach has a great advantage in that a large part of what we wish to study in interaction is open to our direct observation. We can observe who sees whom, how often the contacts take place and how long they last. We can note what sequences of interpersonal interactions take place in the carrying out of work or in the reaching of a management decision.

We can also note the initiation of interaction: When A and B get together, does A take the initiative in seeking out B or does B initiate interaction toward A? The identification of the parties, the measurement of the frequency and duration of interaction, and the frequency of initiation of interaction in any relationship can be observed and measured. We also want to look at an aspect of interaction that seems important, even though it is not always easy to observe and measure. This we may call the origination of activity. We are concerned here with observing a change in B's activity following interaction with A. And we do not mean simply

[2] Homans considers norms a category separate from sentiments. However, in practice the distinction does not seem important.

that B responds in conversation. We mean such things as that A gives B an order and B then changes his work activity, or that A brings a grievance to B and B agrees to take action on the grievance, and so on.

We do not imply that the quantitatively observable aspects of interaction are the only important aspects of interpersonal relations. However, we do believe that the quantitative aspects which are most readily accessible to our observation provide us with important data regarding the functioning of the human organization. We are concerned with discovering what pattern of interaction goes with a cooperative relationship in industry. We are examining relations between interaction and productivity. We are seeking to discover what pattern of interaction provides for the encouragement of the development of an expression of ideas for the improvement of the organization.

We are not dealing here in terms of cause and effect. Cause and effect thinking was abandoned many years ago in the natural sciences. We have come to realize, instead, that we are dealing with sets of mutually dependent relationships. This means that a change in one can be expected to lead to changes in others. Here symbols, sentiments, activities, and interactions form our theoretical system. According to this approach, change may be introduced in the observed data referred to by any one of these concepts and have the effect of introducing changes in the others. Sometime in the future it may be possible to state these relationships of mutual dependence in mathematical terms. In the present state of our knowledge we must be content with stating the relationships in general terms. The use of the concepts will, nevertheless, help us to a better understanding of the response of workers to incentive systems of various types.

# 16

## The Nature of Incentive Symbols

We shall begin by examining the nature of these symbols and the theories of motivation on which they are implicitly based.

Piece rates are based upon a reward-punishment theory of motivation. We assume that the individual is encouraged to perform desirable actions through the offer of reward and is restrained from performing undesirable actions through the threat of punishment. Under piece rates the offering and withholding of money is at the heart of this reward-punishment system.

The theory assumes that man responds as an isolated individual to rewards and punishments. This assumption will be discussed in the next chapter. Let us now concentrate upon the relation between the individual and the incentive symbols.

The basic problem is that human behavior is a good deal more complicated than this theory indicates. Psychologists and psychiatrists have demonstrated that a man's behavior cannot be understood simply in terms of the immediate rewards and punishments offered him. In fact, the very things he finds rewarding or punishing will be determined in large measure from his past experience. To cite an extreme example, we tend to take it for granted that physical pain is punishing and that therefore the individual seeks to avoid it. Nevertheless, throughout history there have been individuals and groups of people who have found it rewarding as a religious experience to submit to bodily pain.

But suppose we could overcome this difficulty. Let us assume that at least in the United States most people like money and consider the offering of it a reward and the withholding of it a punishment. Does that solve our problem?

Let us seek to answer this question by leaving the factory for a moment and consulting the findings of experimental psychologists.[1] While conditioning experiments have been performed primarily upon animals, they may provide us with some leads on human behavior.

It was the great Russian psychologist, Ivan Pavlov, who performed the classic experiments in this field. He worked with dogs, but other experimenters have achieved similar results upon other animals. In some of these experiments a piece of food served as reward and a mild electric shock as punishment. The sound of the bell was designed to indicate that food would shortly be offered, whereas a different sound signalized the approach of an electric shock. After only a few exposures to these auditory stimuli, the animal made the appropriate discriminations. When the bell sounded, and even before the food was offered, the animal would salivate and give other signs of anticipating a rewarding experience. For the other sound, it would crouch, lift up the leg that was to be shocked, or take some other apparently withdrawing or defensive reaction.

One condition should be noted in connection with its results. It has been found in various conditioning experiments that the animal does not continue indefinitely to respond in a vigorous manner to the stimuli. After repeated exposures, it reacts in a more lethargic fashion—as if losing interest in the whole business.

So far (if we overlook the condition just noted) the experiment seems to lend support to the reward-punishment theory. However, let us complicate the picture with reports on further conditioning experiments. In one case Pavlov presented to the animal two lighted disks of markedly different shapes. Upon presentation of one, food was forthcoming, whereas the other was followed by the shock. When the conditioned reflex had been established—that is, when the animal responded consistently and appropriately to each of the two symbols—Pavlov began to modify the shapes of the disks so that they became more and more alike. At first the animal reacted much as before. As the symbols became more similar, it continued making the appropriate behavior discriminations but with increasingly marked signs of agitation. Finally a point was reached

[1] See H. S. Liddell, "Conditioned Reflex Method and Experimental Neurosis," in J. McV. Hunt, *Personality and the Behavior Disorder* (New York: Ronald Press, 1944), pp. 389 ff.

where the animal failed to respond to either disk in the accustomed manner; instead, it displayed such signs of agitation as barking, panting, cowering, struggling to escape, and so on. Furthermore, it was found that this reaction was not a momentary one. The animal that had so broken down in the experiment could not be led to respond to the experimental stimuli again until after a rest of some months or even years. Its behavior outside of the experimental situation also showed signs of abnormality.

Other researchers have repeated the experiment and achieved the same results. In fact, psychologists speak of such experiments as inducing an experimental neurosis.

We cannot safely reason from analogy concerning the behavior of animals in a laboratory to the behavior of men in a factory. Research must be done at many intervening points before we can make such a jump on the basis of scientific evidence. Nevertheless, certain analogies may be suggestive.

The first stage of the conditioning experiments suggests that consistent association of a given symbol with a reward establishes an appropriate response to that symbol, whereas consistent association of another symbol with punishment establishes an appropriate response to that symbol. However, we note that even consistent associations, when repeatedly made, seem to have a "wearing off" effect. We seem to see this effect in the factory also. We hear many complaints from management that an incentive system that once stimulated a vigorous response seems now to be taken for granted and has little stimulating effect.

Our chances of eliciting desired responses with a reward-punishment approach depend upon our ability to establish a definite and consistent association between symbols that stand for rewards and the rewards themselves, and similarly in the case of punishments. We have seen what happens when the animal becomes unable to discriminate between the reward symbol and the punishment symbol. When a given symbol can stand for either reward or punishment, the animal's behavior becomes disorganized.

It is the thesis of this chapter that many piece-rate situations resemble much more closely the conditions of the experimental neurosis experiments than they do the experiments in which reward and punishment symbols are clearly differentiated.

We are not trying to say that factory workers are neurotic

individuals. We are simply suggesting that many incentive systems place them in a conflict situation where they are unable to determine whether the symbols presented them stand for expected rewards or for expected punishments or for some combination of rewards and punishments. We feel that some of the defensive and aggressive behavior of workers must be understood in these terms.

We do not mean that money ceases to be a reward for workers in the situations we have discussed. We mean two things:

1. Money is only one of a number of possible rewards and punishments that may be involved in the incentive situation. Money is not the only thing to which the worker responds. He responds to the total factory environment, and we have been exploring some of the other aspects of this environment that have an effect upon him.

2. The effectiveness of the money symbol depends in part upon a direct connection between symbol, action, and reward (or, as the psychologists call it, reinforcement). In the animal experiments we find this connection established. The animal can get the reward only when the designated symbol is presented to him. This is often not the case in industry. Roy has described in Chapters 3 and 7 some of the various possible forms of "cheating" which enable workers to get the money incentive without doing the work it is supposed to call for. This is not a unique instance. In our industrial research we have run across a number of cases where workers have made money by "writing" as well as by producing. In a situation of worker-management and union-management conflict, workers will still be motivated to make money, but if they can make it in other ways than through producing they will be content to do so. In fact, they may even derive special pleasure from being able to outsmart management in this way.

Confusion as to the behavioral meaning of the symbol also comes about because incentive symbols are so much more complex than the symbols that stand for food or electric shock in the conditioning experiments. It is not at all clear what connection there is between a given incentive symbol and reward or punishment as experienced by the individual. (Partly this is due to the fact that some people are much more interested in money than others. This aspect of the problem we shall explore later.) But even if we assume that all workers are interested in money, to some extent, we must note that it is not simply an amount of money that is offered. The dollar has meaning only as a price for a particular unit of production, and the attractiveness of the price depends upon the possibilities of production. This involves us in some difficult problems involving the determination of the nature of the symbols themselves.

### PROBLEMS OF WORK MEASUREMENT

Before a price can be set on a piece, work performance must be measured so that management can determine what standard of output to set. There are many difficult technical problems involved in such measurement. Industrial engineering experts disagree vigorously on a number of points concerning how the measurements should be made and the standards set. Furthermore, even when they agree on proper methods, they readily concede that actual practice in many if not most plants does not follow the recommended methods. These conflicts have been thoroughly discussed by men more expert than we on the technical side of time study, so there is no need to review their arguments here. We are simply concerned with emphasizing a human relations problem of work measurement that would remain unsolved even if all of the technical aspects of work measurement could be adequately handled.

We refer to the problem known as "rating." We have already noted that the time-study man does not simply measure work performance. He estimates at what percentage of normal efficiency the man under observation is working. A committee for the Society for the Advancement of Management has given us this definition: "Rating is that process during which a time-study engineer compares the performance of the operator under observation with the observer's own concept of normal."

After quoting the definition, William Gomberg[2] goes on to make these comments. First he quotes the definition of "normal" given by the Northern New Jersey Chapter of the Society for the Advancement of Management:

"The normal represents an unstimulated rate of production (or effort) that should be expected from a fully qualified operator. The fully qualified operator, being considered as one who has been working on a job long

2 William Gomberg, *A Trade Union Analysis of Time Study* (Chicago: Science Research Associates, 1948), p. 132.

enough to know it thoroughly and who possesses normal intelligence with enough education to perform satisfactorily the work assigned to him."

Gomberg makes this criticism:

Both of these definitions are meaningless. Rating for professional purposes should not be left to anybody's concept of normal if there is such a thing as a normal working rate. The second definition defines one word, "normal," the meaning of which we are attempting to investigate by equating it to a whole host of subjective words upon which it will be very difficult to get two men to agree. Such phrases as "fully qualified," "normal intelligence," etc., have no quantitative meaning as used in the definition.

We are examining here a most extraordinary procedure. The time-study man is observing and measuring one worker and at the same time comparing him with an imaginary worker. How, then, can the resulting figures be anything but a combination of fact and imagination?

To be sure, promoters of the time-study field have been developing films of various work movements which are designed to give the time-study man some guidance as to what he shall consider to be normal pace. So far these films seem to have provoked as much argument as agreement, so it seems doubtful that we will find a solution of the rating problem through such techniques.

Rating necessarily involves the time-study man in a guessing game. Where worker-management and union-management relations are reasonably good, the workers will not make extreme efforts to fool him and will probably demonstrate the job with a fairly respectable pace just a little on the slow side. Where the conflict is raw, workers are engaged in a constant effort to fool the time-study man as much as they possibly can. From their standpoint the problem is: can we fool him more than he allows for? This is hardly a foundation for a discipline that goes under the name of "*scientific* management."

### PROBLEMS OF RATE CHANGING[3]

If there were no changes in machines and processes, the problems of rate setting would be relatively minor. Setting the initial rate

[3] Much of the material in this section is from William Foote Whyte, "Economic Incentives and Human Relations," *Harvard Business Review,* March-April 1952.

would have the difficulties we have already discussed. But there would be ample time to make changes in the rate if experience seemed to show that it had been set too tight. The parties involved could then get used to a given rate that remained in force for months or years. Perhaps it would lose some of its motivating force, as we have seen in the conditioning experiment. Workers who discover short cuts might use them to get more leisure instead of more production. However, we would expect few rate changes to fight about, so this area of industrial life would proceed rather peacefully. Our problem is particularly difficult because American industry is so dynamic. New machines and processes are constantly being created. Old machines and methods are constantly being altered. The rate that is acceptable today may be obsolete tomorrow.

How does management meet this challenge of change? The problem has two aspects. There is first the problem of changing a rate when a mistake has been made in the rate-setting process.

Workers expect management to revise upward a rate that has been proved to be too tight. Can managers similarly expect workers to accept the downward adjustment in a rate that has been set too loose? The *Supervisor's Guide to General Electric Job Information* is interesting on this point. Note the following paragraphs (p. 51):

The fact that rate setters sometimes have been wrong and rates have had to be cut should be faced squarely by the supervisors.

No rate setter is perfect. However, it must be pointed out that these occasional mistakes are made on the up side as well as on the down side. No employee thinks it is wrong to adjust a rate upward when a mistake on the down side has been made.

There should be just as fair recognition of the necessity and right to make a downward adjustment in a rate as an upward adjustment.

This statement has a fair and reasonable sound. It seems just as fair to change rates set too high as it is to change rates set too low. But in practice how does management discover that a "mistake" has been made in rate setting? Workers have the impression that this discovery will take place only if they turn out exceptionally high earnings on the job. In fact, we know of cases where the industrial engineers were under instructions to take a new look at any job showing earnings over a certain figure. As to whether rate changes were then put into effect the record is not clear, but the regular appearance of these incentive engineers to check un-usually high earnings could hardly have failed to create the im-pression that it was dangerous to go beyond a certain quota.

If we move from possible mistakes in the rate-setting process to consider changes in job methods and content, the picture becomes still more complicated. Most union contracts provide for changes in rates based on changes in job methods and/or content. But we usually find the qualifying adjective "substantial" or "major" de-scribing the change. It seems generally agreed that management should not be allowed to change a rate on the basis of a trivial change in the job. If this were allowed, then management could make some trifling change in any job as an excuse for setting a new rate. In fact, we have heard workers in some plants charge that this was exactly the excuse that management manufactured and used.

In this connection it is interesting to note a comment by John Mills, an engineer:

Reward is supposed to be in direct proportion to production. Well, I re-member the first time I ever got behind that fiction. I was visiting the Western Electric Company, which had a reputation of never cutting a piece rate. It never did; if some manufacturing process was found to pay more than seemed right for the class of labor employed on it—if, in other words, the rate-setters had misjudged—that particular part was referred to the engineers for redesign, and then a new rate was set on the new part. Workers, in other words, were paid as a class, supposed to make about so much a week with their best efforts and, of course, less for less competent efforts.[4]

It is the function of the engineer to improve machines and methods so as to reduce the cost of production. Roethlisberger and Dickson have properly pointed out that low production on an in-centive job may call it to the attention of the engineers, who will then try to improve the cost situation by changing the job. Thus it is not only high production and high earnings that bring a job to the attention of the engineers. Nevertheless, we can expect the engineers to pay special attention also to jobs where worker earn-ings are exceptionally high. If the rate is demonstrated to be loose, then it is a natural invitation for the engineer to come in to see if he cannot institute a change which would justify changing the

[4] *The Engineer in Society* (New York: D. Van Nostrand & Co., 1946), p. 93.

rates so that management could get the same production for less money. It is not only the lure of cutting costs that operates here. Management is dealing also with problems in intergroup relations. If the rate for one work group is so loose that it permits them to make earnings well above that of their fellows at the same skill level, that situation in itself may lead to disturbances within the ranks of workers. One way of adjusting to this disturbance is through making a change in machine or work method and instituting a new rate.

Even if we leave out of consideration rate changes that are clearly motivated by management's desire to find an excuse to cut the rate, we still come face to face with major questions of judgment.

When does a change become a major or a substantial change? It is obvious that two men of equal good will and sincerity can hold different opinions on this point for many cases.

There is the further troublesome problem of a series of minor changes. It often happens in industry that a job will be modified step by step over a period of months or even years. No single change in itself would qualify as major or substantial, and yet the sum total of these modifications might change a rate that was average in earnings to one that was very loose. At what point in the series of minor changes should management be allowed to intervene with a new rate?

Even if all parties agree that the change in the job is so substantial that a new rate must be set, the problem is still far from a solution. Let us assume that the old job was yielding incentive earnings of 50 per cent over base pay. Let us assume that the average earnings figure on other incentive jobs was only 30 per cent above base. In setting the new rate for this group of workers, should the rate setter aim at a 30 per cent or a 50 per cent bonus?

The workers on the job and their union officers will naturally argue that the new rate should provide earnings equivalent to those under the old one. The management may well feel that the old rate was out of line with the general plant picture and that earnings on the new rate of 30 per cent above base are quite adequate. So, even if we assume that the rate setter would be able to predict accurately the earnings possibilities of the job—and we have seen how risky this assumption is—there is no easy answer to the question of what earnings he should aim to make possible. This situation opens up a wide area of conflict.

## STANDARD DATA: A WAY OUT?

Of course many students of time study have wrestled with the difficulties discussed here and have sought to devise various ways out. Some have seen a solution in the development of "standard data." The aim here is to make rate setting primarily a statistical problem rather than a problem of observation and measurement of particular workers in the department.

The aim is to catalogue all the various movements of the body that may be involved in work. The time-study researchers then time each movement repetitively as it appears in some task and establish a standard time for that particular movement. If this is done, the time-study man can begin his work with a table of standard times for all the movements he is to observe. Then he no longer has the problem of actually timing the man on the job. His problem is simply to determine what movements are used in the work process. He then looks up in his data book the standard time for each movement. He adds these times together and the sum gives him roughly the time that should be expected of a normal operator on a given unit of production.

The process, of course, is not so mechanical. The time-study man still has to make allowances for fatigue, and personal time—and these items in themselves can give rise to considerable argument, as they have a substantial effect upon the rate. The time-study man is also expected to determine whether the job is done under normal operating conditions, so that any peculiar difficulties are accounted for.

There are two main difficulties with the standard data approach. We have seen the problems involved in measuring performance to establish any given rate in the plant. The men who set up the standard data tables have presumably been able to make more observations in establishing their figures than the individual time-study man has time to make. We even may assume that they are better trained and more highly skilled. It seems doubtful, however, if these differences are sufficient to provide satisfactory accuracy. Furthermore, several experts have now come out with *different* sets of standard data.[5] Finally critics of the standard data approach have pointed out that the men who present the tables to the management and union public have been reluctant to present also the data on actual measurements that they used in establishing the standards for each movement. Until they come forward with the basic data, they should hardly expect others to agree that they have coped successfully with the problems of measurement we have discussed.

The other difficulty would remain even if the problem of measuring individual movements could be solved. The standard data approach assumes that the physical process of work is simply the sum of its individual parts. If this is so, then it does not matter in the slightest in what sequence the bodily movements are made. This flies in the face of both research and common experience. We know that efficient work involves a rhythmical coordination of bodily movements. That coordination depends in large measure upon the sequence in which these movements are arranged. Some movements flow into each other more readily than others. We are therefore forced to conclude that the physical side of the job is not simply a sum of the physical movements involved. The job will vary and should have different standard times according to the way the physical movements are arranged in sequence.

Some time-study authorities have recognized that the time for a given motion depends in part upon the motions immediately preceding and following it.[6] They argue that this difficulty can be handled through time study where the motion in question is timed as part of a particular sequence of motions. However, this brings us right back to time studies of particular jobs, which we were trying to avoid through the use of standard data.

This is not to say that the standard data approach is of no value. Since we find time study to be such an unreliable process at best, we cannot discard variations on this process simply because they too are unreliable. In a given plant the engineers may obtain better practical results through the use of standard data than through

[5] For a critique of the standard data approach, see Adam Abruzzi, *Work Measurement* (New York: Columbia University Press, 1952), especially pp. 123-126.

[6] See, for example, M. E. Mundel, *Motion and Time Study* (New York: Prentice-Hall, 1950), p. 363.

making all the measurements themselves and they will certainly do so at less hours of their own labor. However, the same problems that plague the work measurer in the department will continue to plague those who use the standard data system.

## ECONOMICS OF INCENTIVE RESPONSE

The proposition that everybody benefits through high production is almost an article of faith in the United States. To question this assumption may appear subversive and un-American. Nevertheless, we cannot accept the proposition on faith if we are to understand workers' response to incentive systems.

The high and rising standard of living of the United States might seem sufficient proof of the proposition, but here we must introduce a distinction between short-run and long-run results. We may agree that in the long run most people benefit from increasing production and yet in the short run an increase in production may involve hardships and difficult adjustments for quite a number of people. It has often been observed that man lives in the short run. He may, indeed, plan for a long-run future but he has to act and react to the situation that he meets on a day-to-day basis. To explain his reactions to incentive systems, we cannot be content with pointing out long-run results. We must examine specific situations.

Management's need to balance the production of the plant presents us with one limiting factor. Few incentive workers make a total product themselves. In nearly all cases the men in a given department simply produce parts of the total product. Suppose, for example, we are dealing with a plant that manufactures washing machines. Let us say that management plans its production in terms of fifty completed machines a day. Let us now give our attention to the men in the leg department. At four legs per machine, they will need to produce 200 legs in order to meet the daily quota of finished machines. Let's suppose they are on incentive and that they somehow decide to abandon restriction of output and do as much as they can. They raise their production of washing machine legs up to 250 per day. Now management has a surplus of 50 legs each day, and washing machine legs by themselves, we assume, have no market value. So what does management do now? Management may be happy with this increased rate of output and yet it presents a problem that can be solved only by laying off some of the workers in the leg department or by transferring them to other departments. In this situation some workers stand to gain through increased incentive earnings but others will lose money or at least have an adjustment to make elsewhere. Perhaps under the circumstances it is better to keep production at the existing level and not go all out after the incentive. (Note that this example resembles the case of the paint room where the dramatic response of the girls in that department created problems of balancing production as well as other problems of intergroup relations.)

Apart from this problem of balancing the production of various departments, can we say that high production is good for everybody? We must recognize first that too low a rate of production leads in most cases to fewer instead of more jobs. If costs are too high, management may have to curtail operations within a department or perhaps close down an entire plant. But does an increase in production beyond any given point mean more jobs or at least the same number of jobs and more money for the workers? That depends upon the company's position in the market and the conditions of supply and demand for the company's product and also upon management's price policy.

If demand for the product is insatiable—as it was for some products during the World War II years—then any stepping up of production by incentive workers certainly means more pay and does not cut down on the number of jobs available.

If supply and demand are more evenly balanced, then management faces a different situation. Let us assume that the company and its competitors are now producing all the units that can be sold at current prices. Now the workers in plant X step up production. What is management to do? Perhaps management cuts the price in order to take some of the business away from its competitors and maintain at least the same number of jobs with more income for the workers. In this situation the competitors, of course, may respond by cutting their prices so as to reestablish the preexisting competitive relationship. This benefits consumers throughout the country but doesn't necessarily maintain or improve the position of workers in plant X. That may well be the case. In our history such things have happened and are continuing to happen. Probably the best known case is that of Henry Ford, who in the beginning of the automobile industry cut his prices and succeeded not simply in taking away business from his competitors but in reaching a mass market for the product which would not otherwise have existed. But we cannot assume that this always and automatically happens. In considering their price policies, businessmen are constantly asking tnemselves whether a price cut which is then presumably met by competitors will mean more sales for everybody or will mean simply the same number of sales at a lower profit or something in between.

We are discussing here what economists call the elasticity of demand. Economists speak of an elastic demand situation when a small decrease in the price leads to a greatly increased sale of the product. Demand is said to be inelastic when a large price decrease leads to only a small increase in sales. The point is, we cannot assume that the demand for all manufactured products is highly elastic, nor can we assume that it is highly inelastic. The elasticity of demand varies greatly from product to product. Furthermore, it varies for the same product over different periods of time. This means that a price cut in situation A may have different effects upon sales and employment than would be observed for the same percentage cut in situation B.

Suppose, on the other hand, we assume that as productivity goes up management decides not to cut its prices—and this in a situation where supply and demand are in balance at the existing price. Perhaps through a high-powered advertising campaign the company can sell more of its products without cutting prices. In other cases, however, we shall find the company putting out the same amount of production with somewhat fewer workers. In such a case, then, we could have increased productivity on the part of workers leading to somewhat fewer jobs in this particular plant or department.[7]

There are other important factors that bear upon the relationships among productivity, prices, sales, costs, and profits, and level of employment. We do not go into them here because we are not attempting to present a comprehensive discussion of the economics

[7] However, if the firm is only one among a large number of manufacturers in this line and supplies only a small fraction of the market, it may be possible to maintain prices and still increase production.

of productivity. We are simply attempting to show that the relationship between worker productivity and the number of jobs available is not a simple one. Even if we agree that over the long run and for the economy as a whole increasing productivity leads to more rather than fewer jobs, we can point to many situations where there would be fewer jobs at least for the short run.

We are not assuming that workers make an economic analysis such as this, that they then decide that management's promises of more jobs with more production are not always true, and that they therefore decide to restrict production. We are concerned only with the relationship between the symbols of the incentive system and the experience that workers connect with these symbols. If the workers were firmly convinced that the symbols meant more earnings for everybody with more production, then we would not need to concern ourselves with the economic facts of the situation. However, worker interpretation of the meaning of these symbols depends upon the experiences they have actually had in industry. As it is, workers sometimes experience layoffs or transfers which they connect with too much production. (The economist might well point out in some of these cases that the increase in production and the layoffs and transfers were coincidental instead of cause and effect. But this coincidental appearance of the two phenomena suggests a connection in the minds of those who experience or who might experience layoffs or transfers.) If more production were always a rewarding experience, we could assume that workers would respond much more strongly to the incentive system. The problem of management, then, is to create conditions where the incentive will be rewarding in an economic security sense as well as in other ways.

As we have seen, this does not simply involve the relationship between the individual worker and the management that offers him the incentive. It involves the relation of worker to fellow workers, of department to department, of the plant to the company, of the company to its competitors. All these relationships have a bearing upon the success of the incentive system.

## CONCLUSION

As we examine the rate-setting process and the economic results of incentive production we are forced to conclude that the connections between the symbols and the promised rewards are neither simple nor consistent. This does not mean that the piece-rate symbol will evoke no response. It does mean that the response will be importantly influenced by the context of human relations within which the symbol is offered. Let us, then, examine further this human relations context.

# 17

# The Individual and the Work Group

Man is not born loving money. He has to learn to love it. This learning takes place in varying degrees in various parts of the world. In economically underdeveloped countries we find that the possibility of making more money does not lead people to do more work. On the contrary, they usually prefer to work a shorter number of days or hours to make the amount of money they have customarily earned. American and Western European businessmen have often been troubled by this phenomenon. Apparently the workers in these situations have not learned to want the consumers' goods that mean a rising standard of living. They are content to remain at the customary level. Factory work being unfamiliar to them anyway, they are quite happy to be able to maintain this standard of living by working a shorter time.

In our society too the response to money is a learned response; nor is it uniform. Americans in general, including factory workers, seem to have a stronger interest in making more money and in the things that money can buy than seems to be found in most other parts of the world. Even in the United States, however, among factory workers there are a great many variations in this response to money, as Dalton has so well demonstrated. We must recognize also that money is not the only reward nor lack of money the only punishment available in any given situation. We can expect almost any American who is offered more money without any compensating dissatisfaction to respond to the money. The problem is that other rewards and punishments always go along with it. Different individuals strike different balances between rewards and punishments, including money.

The response to money in the factory, however, should not be considered as the response of an isolated individual. The factory worker reacts to management as a member of a group. The work group in the factory, like groups of people outside the factory, tends to develop its own norms or standards of behavior. Not all the behavior to be observed in any given group is covered by the group's norms, but we can assume that the areas of behavior of greatest concern to the group will have established norms. In the factory, production is an important part of the activity of the group. Therefore, it is inevitable that certain understandings should arise as to the nature of a fair day's work. (It is not inevitable that these norms should be set low. Whether they are set low or high depends in large measure upon the relations between this group and the larger organization. This we shall discuss in following chapters.)

While recognizing the importance of the work group in industry, we should not assume that every worker acts as a well-integrated member of some work group. Sociologists have pointed out that the individual does not necessarily identify himself with the people immediately around him. They speak of reference group theory to explain this phenomenon. The individual in the course of his social experience learns to respond to the norms of some group or groups, but he may find himself, for example at work, associating with people whom he does not consider part of his group at all.

Dalton has pointed this out in his discussion of the rate buster. There we found nine individuals in a department of some three hundred who did not abide by the group norms in production—and in various other forms of behavior. One of these men led an active social life outside the plant but associated with middle-class people and seemed to look upon fellow workers as beneath him and not worthy of any group loyalty. The other eight men were inactive socially outside the plant. For them the reference group seemed to be simply the family. Groups that they had been part of in the past had been drawn from a different social level from that represented by fellow workers and they simply felt no compulsion to abide by the norms of such workers. Since these men had in effect declared themselves outside the work group, the customary forms of social pressure, including threatened ostracism, could hardly have any effect upon them. These men actually took pride in *not* being part of the work group.

Such men are extremely individualistic and highly acquisitive. Apparently they represent only a small minority even in such a supposedly acquisitive society as our own. Perhaps management would benefit if there were more people like this; on the other hand, the gains in production would have to be balanced against the extreme difficulties of building an organization with people who were determined not to fit into any organized group. It is idle to speculate as to what would happen if there were more rate busters. We should only note in passing that the theory on which the whole incentive program is based apparently applies to only a small fraction of the population.

Even as we observe most workers abiding by group norms of production, we should not assume that this acceptance of the norms is easily or happily accomplished. Dalton has presented us a picture of one factory department that may well apply to many others. There we see not one uniform response to the incentive, but people divided into three categories. The bottom producers, who hardly ever make incentive pay, have accepted the satisfactions of group membership and have renounced the incentive altogether. The rate busters have renounced the work group and devote themselves entirely to getting as much out of the incentive as they can. Most people fall between these extremes (50 out of 84 in Dalton's sample). They want to be part of the group and still they want to make more money. When they reach the ceiling on production established by the group norm they hold back, but they hold back reluctantly. It is these people who chiefly experience the frustrations of the incentive system. Can it be only coincidental that Dalton found all his ulcer cases in this middle production group?

### WHY RESTRICTION?

Let us return now to the question of restriction of output. In the preceding chapter, as we examined the relationship between the incentive symbols and rewards experienced by workers, we considered one aspect of that problem. In following chapters, as we deal with intergroup relations and with the relations of the group to the total organization, we shall take up other aspects of restriction. Here we shall focus upon a source of restriction that seems to lie within the group itself.

Our thesis here is that restriction of output under some circumstances contributes to the stability of relations among individuals in the work group. A group is not simply an undifferentiated aggregate of associating individuals. Groups have their own structures, with leaders and followers and varying levels of status or prestige separating them.

What are the sources of status in the work group? The job that a man holds is, of course, of prime importance. Jobs are ranked by management and workers in terms of their relative importance in the department. Even if we assume, however, that the people under discussion all hold the same job, we find at least two important sources of status distinction:

1. *Production performance.* What sort of worker the man is is important to fellow workers. They evaluate the skill, speed, and versatility with which he works.

2. *Interpersonal skill.* The leader in this area is a man whom others turn to for advice. It is he who brings up ideas that others act upon. It is he whom other people seek out for social or other discussions.

These two sources of status may fit together, but this will not necessarily be so. In fact, we may well find them pointing in different directions. Consider the following case, which, though not drawn from an incentive situation, will illustrate this point:

The department manufactures fine glassware. The men work in teams of from six to eight. This is a hand operation taking a high degree of skill and also requiring close cooperation among team members. The appointed leader of each team and the highest skilled man is known as the "gaffer." At the time we began our study, Paul DeSantis was recognized as the top prestige gaffer of the twelve who worked on two shifts in this department. He was a man in his mid-fifties with more than thirty years' experience in the trade. He received the most difficult job assignments from management because he was recognized as the most skillful and versatile gaffer. However, he was also a rather slow worker.

This presented no problem as long as DeSantis was working on pieces which no other work team produced. However, as management introduced new pieces into production, some of the pieces that had been done by DeSantis' team exclusively were now assigned to the work teams of Jack Carter and Ralph Orlandella, two much younger men who had only recently attained the position of gaffer.

These men had risen rapidly to the top in a period when production was expanding, so that the number of teams was doubled at a time when the old-time craftsmen were retiring or dying off. The old men in the department considered Carter and Orlandella as upstarts who were not really qualified glassworkers. The young men in the department, on the other hand, were encouraged to find men like themselves moving up and tended to gather around the young gaffers.

At first Carter and Orlandella had difficulty in doing the pieces that had been assigned to them from DeSantis' team, but in time they mastered the technical problem and developed the necessary skill and coordination of their team members. When they had mastered the jobs, they built up production to the level that had been attained by DeSantis and then began to move above his previous records. This was a conscious bid by the young gaffers for management approval (and possible pay increases) and for prestige among fellow workers. The young gaffers pointed out to their friends that they were showing that they could produce just as good pieces as DeSantis had turned out and more of them. DeSantis and other old-timers reacted against this challenge. Some of the old men refused to give technical advice that the inexperienced men badly needed, or gave misleading advice. The old-timers could not fail to acknowledge that the young men were getting good production but they deprecated this record by saying that the quality was poor and would never have been accepted when management in the old days had higher standards. Furthermore, DeSantis tried through intermediaries to get the young men to slow down. The argument they were to present was "Why do you want to kill the job? Seven an hour is a fair day's work."

Why this pressure to keep down production? DeSantis and his friends were talking just as do incentive workers when they warn their fellows that management will cut the rate if they produce too much. But there was no threat of rate cutting because there were no incentive rates. The rising production of the young men, furthermore, presented no possible economic threat to DeSantis because he was at the top of the rate range for the position of gaffer. He could go no higher except through general increases negotiated between union and management. On the other hand, long-standing company policy and the union contract protected him against wage cuts or layoffs, for his seniority was among the highest in the department.

He was saying in effect to the other men: if you work faster, management will expect everybody to work faster. There may, indeed, be some physical substance to this argument quite apart from the money to be gained or lost. There are important satisfactions in maintaining a customary work pace. However, the strong feelings manifested on both sides in this situation can hardly be attributed to questions of work pace and fatigue. The rise of the young men presented a threat to the status of DeSantis. He had held the unquestioned top prestige position. He was recognized as the most skilled and most versatile man. It was he to whom people turned for advice and it was he whom people watched when he had a particularly interesting job and they could take a moment from their work.

Now Carter and Orlandella were narrowing the gap in skill between themselves and DeSantis. They equaled DeSantis or even surpassed him in speed of production on certain pieces. Their status in the department rose. Especially the younger men gathered around them and followed their progress with interest. Thus we see that even in a department where skill is on a handicraft basis the speed of production can have an important effect upon the status of workers.

Let us turn from that actual example to a hypothetical situation in an incentive department in a mass production plant. In this department Al Collins holds the highest informal status. He is a man who is turned to for advice. He is respected also for his skill on the machine. At this time the group norm has established a ceiling of total earnings at 130 per cent of base pay. Now let us make a completely impossible assumption: that without any other changes in this situation the ceiling is suddenly removed and each worker tries to see how much he can produce. Will Al Collins now turn out to be the top producer? Not necessarily so. Maybe he has the skill to turn out the highest quality product, but management is not now emphasizing quality except within certain limits set by inspection standards. Now Al Collins is a man who can perform what turns out to be a lot of unnecessary fancywork on the machine, but he is not a particularly fast worker. When the ceiling goes off, he finds that, try as he will, he can only average about 130 per cent, just 10 points above his former average. On the other hand, Tom Jones, who was formerly a mere nobody in the department, has no trouble in building his average up to 180 per cent. Furthermore, he is not reluctant to let other people know how he is doing and even begins giving production tips to men who had formerly looked to Al Collins for advice.

Now, instead of being toward the top in production as he was under the ceiling, Collins finds himself in the middle. At the bottom are several workers who average about 110 per cent. They are upset too because their performance did not look bad when everybody was keeping under 130 per cent. But when a number of men are producing between 130 and 180, 110 looks poor indeed and these fellows feel that the foremen may be looking for ways to get rid of them even if they have seniority to protect them against layoffs.

Al Collins is not in such an economically threatened position. We can assume that his 130 per cent average is quite satisfactory to management. However, the social balance in the department has been upset. The former leader of the men is shown up as only an average producer, while the top producer turns out to be someone who had little prestige in the department before.

This hypothetical example, together with the case from the glassworks, points out a function performed for the work group by restriction of output. It prevents the competition among the men which would disturb established interpersonal relations. If the ceiling on production is kept at a point where most workers in the department can reach it, then it is possible for a man like Collins to attain a leadership position in the department through exercising the sort of social skill that wins leadership outside the workplace.

If this partial explanation of restriction is valid, we may find that it also suggests a partial explanation for the breakdown of restriction in a successful Scanlon Plan situation or in other instances of active union-management cooperation. A program for bringing up suggestions toward improvement of production, together with a functionary charged with this responsibility in the department, provides Collins and others like him with an additional source for the support and improvement of status in the department and in the plant. We have pointed out in our discussion of the Scanlon Plan that it does not simply channel individual technical suggestions to the top. The most important suggestions coming up are those which involve complex relations of man to man, of man to machine, of machines to each other, of department to department, of work group to the entire plant, and so on. To develop such suggestions in such form that they can be applied in practice requires a high level of leadership skill. This leadership skill is to be found in men like Al Collins, who have already shown themselves to be informal leaders within the department. Before the advent of cooperation, however, Collins exercised his leadership unrecognized by management or, if management has recognized it, management has probably considered him a troublemaker and wondered how he could be disciplined or perhaps eliminated from the work force. Now the cooperation program provides him with official recognition from management and union as well as from the work group. His status in department and plant then comes to depend more and more upon his activity in the social system than upon his production achievements. As this shift takes place, he does not need to feel threatened if other workers outproduce him. If he uses the intelligence and social skills that have enabled him to become an informal leader in the department, in order to build up the cooperation program, he can be recognized as the man in his department who is making the greatest contribution to the group and to the plant-wide effort. Under such circumstances, it is not necessarily the top producers who are the heroes. We suspect that the ones who receive the greatest recognition are those whose leadership activity makes the high production possible.

# 18

## Intergroup Relations

The factory is a social system. The parts of the system are the relations existing among the people making up the organization. These parts are mutually dependent. A change in one part or set of relations will not be limited in its impact to that particular part but can be expected to have repercussions in other parts of the organization.

That is an elementary statement of the thinking underlying the field of human relations in industry. No one will disagree with such a general statement. However, many people can accept the statement in general without grasping its implications. It is this examination of implications that we are undertaking in the present chapter. This chapter demonstrates clearly that the factory is indeed a social system having its own equilibrium conditions.

This means that management cannot afford to be satisfied with success achieved in introducing an incentive at one point in the plant. The impact of this incentive will be felt not only in the department immediately affected but also in neighboring departments and perhaps throughout the plant. In fact, in the paint room case reported by George Strauss and Alex Bavelas, we have seen that management can be defeated by its very success in introducing an incentive in one department.

Individual or group incentives may introduce two types of disturbances to the equilibrium of the plant:

1. *Changes in relative economic status.* Leonard Sayles has presented us several cases of this type. The groups affected are not directly dependent upon each other in the work flow, but the introduction of an incentive changes established economic status relations. People in group A have been receiving more pay than people in group B. But now an incentive is introduced into group B so that now group B members earn more money.

2. *Changes in work flow as well as in relative economic status.*
Here, in addition to the type of change noted above, we deal with
work groups or departments related to each other in the work flow.
In cases described by Arensberg, Sayles, and Strauss we have an incentive introduced into a department where the departments preceding or following in the work flow are not on incentive. In the
case of the preceding department, supervision or the incentive workers themselves may apply pressure to turn out production so that
the incentive people have enough to do to make their quota earnings. In the case of the following department, the workers there may
face a suddenly increased work load. In either case, the people in
an adjoining department are under pressure to do more work without additional compensation. They are naturally resentful against
both the incentive workers and management.

Conflicts such as these may be looked upon by management as ac-
cidental or abnormal. Actually they are completely normal and
predictable events if management follows its customary practices.
In fact, we can say that in many plants a conflict between the job
evaluation system and the incentive system is built into the organization.

Management has recognized that untold difficulties arise if rates
of pay for various jobs are only haphazardly related to each other.
In such a case the workers are confused as to where they stand, and
they cry out against favoritism. Furthermore, management has no
adequate defense against union grievances on inequities in pay.

To meet these problems, management develops a job-evaluation
program. This involves a careful study of all the jobs in the plant,
assessing the degrees of responsibility, skill, difficulty, and importance of the jobs so that they may be rated and compared. Management seeks to work on an orderly scale of jobs and sets wage
rates so that the jobs high on the scale will pay more money than
those at lower points.

When the job-evaluation program upsets traditional relations
among jobs, workers and union officers protest, of course. They
may object to the methods used by management in job evaluation,
they may object to certain of the conclusions drawn, and they may
express a desire to participate in the evaluation process. However,
all these are objections to the means and methods used, and not to

the general objective. Workers and union officers would agree that it is important to have an orderly arrangement of jobs so that the individual can place himself in the social system of the plant. They also believe firmly that the jobs which are evaluated higher should pay more than the jobs which are evaluated lower.

Workers, union officers, and management are not dealing here with a technical problem alone. The decisions made regarding the arrangement and relative values of the various jobs tend to place the jobs in terms of a prestige scale in the plant. We are talking about what the sociologist would refer to as a *"status system."* All our work in sociology suggests that the status system of an organization is an exceedingly tough organism. It is tough in the sense that changes are not readily introduced into it and also in the sense that, when changes are introduced, serious repercussions may take place.

Let us assume that management has installed its new job-evaluation program and let us make the perhaps rash assumption that the program has been reasonably well accepted by workers and union officials. But now management introduces an incentive program into the plant. There is nothing that can so surely upset the relations so carefully established in the job-evaluation program.

When incentive workers begin to make more money than nonincentive men on jobs that outrank them in the job-evaluation scheme, management seeks to explain the disturbance by saying that the incentive workers are working at an incentive pace and therefore deserve more money. As Sayles points out, however, this argument does not go over well with workers. The nonincentive people are inclined to look at incentives as just so much gravy and to feel that they have a right to get on the gravy train too.

When both work groups A and B are placed on incentive, the incentive rates are supposed to be set in a manner so that the existing pay differentials will be maintained. But we have seen that the rate setters are not so accurate that we can have confidence in this outcome. One group may get a tight rate and the other group a loose rate. Likely as not, it will be the group that receives higher base pay according to the job-evaluation plan that will get the tight incentive rate, so that the incentive system will serve to reverse the earnings relations between groups A and B.

Reversals of positions established through job evaluation may take place at any point in the plant. The most general and persistent problem involves relations between production workers and maintenance, toolroom, and other workers who are not in production. The maintenance and toolroom people consider themselves skilled craftsmen. While the production worker may be hired right off the street and put on the machine with only a few minutes or a few hours of training, the craftsmen have their apprenticeship programs so that the new man must go through a long learning period before he is considered qualified as a craftsman. However, the performance of production workers can be measured, whereas it is difficult, if not impossible, to measure the work of the craftsmen. Therefore, we commonly find incentive systems developed for production workers whereas the craftsmen receive only their base pay. Furthermore, the introduction of an incentive in production by stepping up production activity may lead to increased pressure for work on maintenance people, thus aggravating the problem.

We thus find a supposedly high-status craftsman receiving less pay than his unskilled fellow worker and also being under pressure to do his job so that the incentive worker will always be able to make those incentive earnings. This kind of situation generates terrific pressures inside the union and these, in turn, are directed against management. The union does not negotiate only for an across-the-board wage increase. The union negotiators demand that management raise pay in certain maintenance classifications in order to eliminate alleged inequities. What are these inequities? The union may claim that the craftsmen in the plant are not receiving as much pay as craftsmen in the same trades in other plants. Union and management may each undertake area studies to compare the pay of craftsmen in this plant with those outside. Generally the union study demonstrates that its craftsmen are underpaid in terms of area rates, whereas the management study indicates that the pay of the crafts is pretty well in line. Even so, management may yield to the raising of rates in the maintenance department because the management negotiators recognize that the problem does not primarily involve inequities between the craftsmen in the plant and those outside. The union negotiators may indeed be concerned about these comparisons with the outside world, but they are probably much more concerned about pay relations between their own production and maintenance workers. The union negotiators need these inequity adjustments in order to ease the conflict within the local union. If the negotiators cannot keep bringing back "inequity" adjustments for the nonproduction workers, they may find these groups splitting off and joining craft unions.

The worker thinks of his pay in relative terms. He is interested in the absolute amount he received, of course, but whether this absolute amount seems good or bad to him will depend upon where it places him in relation to those people with whom he compares himself. In recent years in the big negotiating sessions in the major industries, we have come to take it for granted that the settlement reached by the automobile workers will be compared with that received by the steelworkers and so on. Union leaders are especially concerned with such outside comparisons and rank-and-file workers seem to be concerned also, although certainly to a lesser degree.

The worker compares himself primarily with other people in his plant—with the people he knows and talks with or at least sees or hears about.

Let us see if we can now place these relationships in a more systematic, theoretical statement. Let us say that the workers' *position* in the plant is a function of two factors: his *economic status* and his *social status*.

*Economic status* we define as average hourly earnings. In cases where economic security is important, that is, where workers on one job are much more subject to working short time or being laid off than on another, our formula would have to be considerably complicated. However, let us assume for the sake of illustration that we can deal simply with average hourly earnings. This, of course, is a measurable quantity, so that we can rank people in the plant in terms of economic status.

*Social status* is a more complex item and is not so readily defined. We mean by social status the prestige people attach to jobs in the plant. This prestige comes from the skill required by the job, from its importance in the production process, from the seniority that people have to have in order to hold the job, from the money the job pays, and from other factors.

Note that there is an overlap between these two concepts, since social status is affected by the money the job pays. On the other hand, the pay rate or earnings never completely determines the prestige attached to a job.

Social status is subjective in the sense that we are dealing with the evaluations that people have of the various jobs. However, we find that these evaluations vary little from individual to individual. There tends to be fairly general agreement in the social ranking of jobs. What this social status is we can readily determine through asking a sample of workers to give us their own rankings of the jobs around them.

*Position, economic status,* and *social status* are all relative terms. We are thinking of where the individual stands in relation to other people in the plant.

When the economic status and the social status of the individual are in line with each other, then the individual's position in the social system is clear and unequivocal. Furthermore, he tends to be satisfied with it.

If there is a discrepancy between economic and social status, the individual will feel that something is wrong and that something must be done to bring the two in line. Since both types of status are relative, it follows that the individual's status can change without any change in his pay or in the nature of the job.

Let us assume that we have two work groups A and B, with group A having the higher social status and also the higher economic status. Then management introduces an incentive scheme for neighboring work group B so that the total earnings and therefore the economic status of work group B is now higher than that of work group A. The men of work group A have higher social status but lower economic status. They respond to this imbalance by demanding more money in some form so that their economic status will once more be in line with their social status. If they succeed in reestablishing their former relative economic status, then their social status is protected and their problem is solved. If they fail to get such a financial adjustment, then over a period of time the disparity of earnings in favor of job B over job A will so affect the prestige of job A that workers will no longer look upon it as the superior job. As these evaluations change, we say that the social status of the job changes and in time we may find that job A ranks below job B in both economic and social status. In such a case workers may no longer be willing to "promote" from job B to job A, thus presenting management with a difficult problem. Or, people on job A, if they have higher seniority, will try to bump into job B, thus presenting the union with a difficult internal problem.

In the case just described group A can maintain its social status either by increasing its own earnings or by decreasing the earnings of group B. If the adjustment is made through increasing the earnings of group A, the people in group B will make no protest. The increase will simply preserve the existing status relationships. If the adjustment is made through decreasing the earnings of group B, there will, of course, be vigorous protests on the part of group B members. They would not previously have demanded that they receive more pay than group A workers. But, since they have been receiving more pay, they buttress their position with various rationalizations to the effect that they have been working hard, that their job is really more important to the plant, and so on. For this reason management finds it difficult to iron out "inequities" in anything but an upward direction.

This sort of formulation seems to apply when we are dealing with jobs not directly related to each other in the work flow. It applies with even more force where the jobs are so related. In such workflow cases, the change in the symbols of economic and social status leads to changes in activity and also perhaps in interaction. That is, one group may have to do more work than was before expected (change in activity) or one group may be under pressure (change in interaction) from supervision and from the adjoining incentive workers to increase its work efforts.

When individuals are dissatisfied with the discrepancy between economic and social status, they do not keep this dissatisfaction to themselves. We can say that the change in *symbols* leads to a change in attitudes, or *sentiments,* and that that in turn leads to changes in *activity* (affecting production) and to changes in *interaction* as the workers affected complain to the foreman, the union steward or the union officers, and perhaps to anyone who will listen to them. The response by management or by union officers or the failure to respond to such complaints will not only affect the economic and social status of the aggrieved workers, it will also affect their sentiments toward the union and toward management and the future interactions they have in both directions.

## CONCLUSION

We see here how incentive systems of traditional types disrupt the equilibrium of the social system. In a dynamic economy such as ours we cannot expect to preserve complete stability in the social system. Changes will necessarily be introduced through technological advances and the conditions of the market place. However, some degree of stability is necessary both for maintaining the morale of the organization and for getting out the production. We may well ask whether some organizations can afford the almost constant disturbances of equilibrium that some incentive systems provide.

We are not suggesting that the relative statuses of jobs in the plant should be fixed and not subject to change. There may be cases when a change is necessary and should even be planned for. For example, let us assume that the market for product X is declining, whereas in an adjoining department the company is going into production on product Z which it expects to be of great importance to the company's future. In such circumstances it may be quite appropriate to shift the status balance between the two departments so that jobs in department Z become more attractive, and workers are willing to transfer out of the declining department in order to work on product Z. Such a change can be planned for. However, the changes in status relations that we have been discussing are those which have not been planned for by management. In some cases they may disrupt production as well as lead to interpersonal tensions. Perhaps the manager of the future will learn to plan in terms of the equilibrium of the social system and not exclusively in terms of technology, rates of pay, and various other items which together affect this equilibrium.

This discussion of intergroup problems focuses attention on one important advantage of the plant-wide incentive approach. This plant-wide approach does not eliminate such intergroup inequities as may be thought to exist; however, it does not create new inequities and new intergroup struggles. It does not create a unified plant, but it does provide an approach with which such integration can be achieved.

# 19

# The Structure of Interaction

The researcher had been trying to discover how it was that union and management were getting along most harmoniously after they had been through a bitter conflict. He was still quite baffled by the problem when one day he happened to be talking about the plant to a representative of home office top management.

"Well, at first I couldn't understand it," said the management man, "but now I think I've got it figured out."

Bursting with curiosity, the researcher asked for an explanation.

"Well, I think the answer is, they learned to trust each other."

The researcher was momentarily stunned by this answer, but when he had recovered his composure he said, "That seems to be true, all right, but how did they learn to trust each other?"

The management man had no answer to this question. The research man has been trying to answer this question and others like it ever since.

This incident poses the research problem. Many times we hear such explanations: that people are getting along together because they have learned to like or trust each other, that workers have stopped holding back on production because they have come to believe in high production, and so on. Always these reported answers should lead us to ask the next question: how did the people come to feel as they do? In other words, we cannot explain anything by simply reporting that people have positive sentiments or attitudes toward each other. Sentiments change and sentiments alone do not change sentiments. If, then, we are to explain changes in sentiments toward the company and toward productivity we shall have to search elsewhere for our explanation.

In searching for some more tangible and objective factor to explain changes in sentiments and behavior, we are going to examine what we call the structure of interaction: the organization of interpersonal relations.

It is the thesis of this book that response to incentives depends in large measure on the organizational context in which they take place. Accordingly, we have been examining relations between the individual and the work group, we have looked at the relations of groups to each other, and now we are looking at the total organizational framework. When we talk of the structure of interaction we are assuming that the relations among people in an organization are not haphazard; on the contrary, that they are definitely patterned. We are also assuming that when we discover what this pattern is we can also explain the response of workers to incentives and their sentiments toward management.

How do we change sentiments and activities? How do we build sentiments of cooperation when conflict existed before? How do we change the activities of people in production and in making suggestions about production? The general answer to these questions is simple: *we change sentiments and activities through changing interaction*. And we change interaction through changing the symbols that are presented to the people in question or through changing the work flow or organization structure. To put the answer into practice is, of course, not so simple, and there remain many points on which further knowledge is needed. However, through examining reactions of time-study men and of workers we can see certain ways in which interactions can be changed in order to lead to changes in sentiments and activities.

## THE TIME-STUDY MAN IN THE SOCIAL SYSTEM

As we have been examining the structure of interaction in the plant, throughout this book, we have given little direct attention to the role of the time-study man. We have seen him simply as someone to whom workers react. Now let us place him in the social system and examine further the role he plays.

For any individual or group incentive system, the time-study man is obviously a most important figure. However, we find that his status in industry is hardly commensurate with the importance of his functions. This was remarked upon forty years ago by R. F. Hoxie in his classic study on *Scientific Management and Labor*.

After looking at time-study operation in many plants, including some which were supposed to be the best in their field, he had this to say:

Indeed, time study and task setting were almost universally looked upon as primarily mechanical tasks in which the ability to analyze jobs and manipulate figures rather than broad knowledge and sound judgment were regarded as the essential factors. Naturally, therefore, the time study men were found to be prevailingly of the narrow-minded mechanical type, poorly paid and occupying the lowest positions in the managerial organization, if they could be said to belong at all to the managerial group. Nor does the situation seem to promise much improvement. For the position and pay accorded to time study men generally are such as to preclude the drawing into this work of really competent men in the broader sense. Aside from a few notable exceptions in the shops, and some men who make a general profession of time study in connection with the installation of scientific management, this theoretically important functionary receives little more than good mechanics' wages, and has little voice in determining shop policies.[1]

Perhaps the status of the time-study man has improved over the past forty years, yet fundamentally the same statements could be made regarding many situations today. The time-study man stands at the bottom in the status hierarchy of the engineering specialties. The man who designs new machines or processes holds much higher status than does the man who works with clipboard and stopwatch. Furthermore, many time-study men today are not college graduates in engineering at all, and this naturally puts them at a disadvantage in dealing with the college-trained management men. Finally, time-study men spend a large part of their time out on the factory floor in contact with workers. Here we are not concerned with whether the time-study man does or does not get along well with workers; we simply observe that the prestige or social status the man occupies tends to be strongly influenced by the status of the people with whom he is associating. Workers being the bottom status group in industry, association with them can hardly build up for the time-study man the sort of position that the importance of his function would seem to call for.

The time-study man's problem is, of course, not simply one of

[1] R. F. Hoxie, *Scientific Management and Labor* (London: D. Appleton & Company, 1915), p. 57.

low status. He also seems to have a most unclear and insecure position in the social structure. In many plants time-study functions are not tied to the production organization people at the department level. Just how the time-study man is to relate himself to workers, foremen, production superintendents, and so on is not at all clear. Since his job calls for him to work in various parts of the plant, the time-study man does not have the opportunity to build up the sort of stable relationship that may exist between the foreman and his workers. If the time-study man does not come around on any regular basis, if his plans are completely unpredictable to the people in the department, then workers and even foremen will look upon him as a threat to the stability of their situation. Thus the rates determined by the time-study man may not only be rejected by the workers, but they may also be at least tacitly rejected by the foremen. And when the union puts on pressure to loosen a given rate, management itself may be divided as to the merits of the rate. Often the figures of the time-study man are discarded in order to reach such a compromise on a rate as will allow production to move ahead. This further weakens the position of the time-study man.

The position of the time-study man is difficult at best. But we have among our cases one example that suggests ways in which his unclear position may be clarified and his security built up. In the Inland Steel Container Company case we noted certain marked changes in the structure of interaction that concerned the time-study man. No longer was he to be a free-wheeling, apparently autonomous agent who carried the threat of change with him wherever he went in the plant. Instead, management decided that he should not enter a department for purposes of making a study unless he had written approval by one of two production management officials. Furthermore, he had to present this clearance to the foreman in whose department he was to work, and the foreman then took the initiative in bringing in the union steward so that the three of them could discuss the work that was to be done. Then, before the work was started, the foreman and steward would accompany the time-study man to the worker or workers whose jobs were to be studied so that the next steps could be explained to them.

What is happening here? Basically the change involves tying

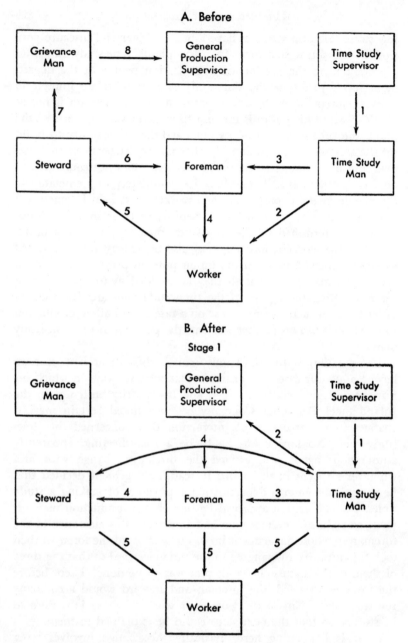

Fig. III. Time Study Men in the Structure of Interaction

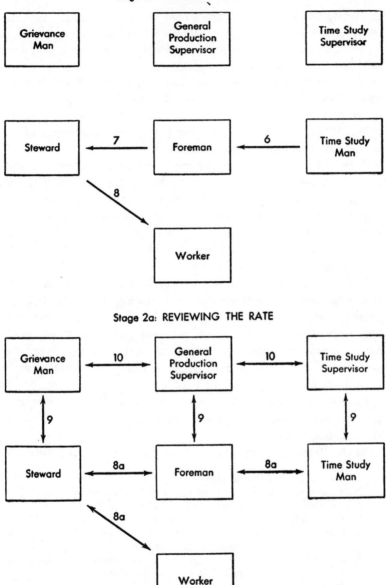

Stage 2: ACCEPTING THE RATE

Stage 2a: REVIEWING THE RATE

Fig. IIIB, *Con't*

the time-study man in with the already thoroughly established and well-grooved channels of interaction in the production organization. The workers may not particularly like their foreman but at least they have a chance to get used to him. It is, then, much less threatening to have the time-study man introduced through the foreman and through the union steward than it would be if he just operated on his own.

We noted, furthermore, that the prescribed interactions of the time-study man did not end with the beginning of the study. He was required to present his proposed rate and the figures underlying it to the foreman for approval before the rate was put into effect. Here we see a linking together of symbols, activities, and interactions. Where the foreman has no power to accept or reject a rate he is in effect responsible for production activity in his department without having any control over the symbols that have important effects upon this activity.

The significance of these changes can best be understood by representing them in diagrammatic form (see Fig. III). The diagrams must necessarily be highly simplified, for they can only represent typical sequences on interaction, whereas each actual case would have its own variations. However, the changes between the two periods of time are sufficiently great so that the individual variations from case to case may be overlooked.

Here the direction of the arrows indicates the direction of origination of activity, and the numbers represent the sequence of interactions through time.

In the *Before* diagram (A), we have the following sequence:

1) Time-study supervisor assigns task.
2) Time-study man observes worker. (Of course, this may happen several times and for an extended period of time.)
3) Time-study man announces rate to foreman.
4) Foreman announces rate to worker or workers.
5) Worker(s) calls on steward to raise grievance.
6) Steward grieves to foreman. (As foreman is powerless to change rate, steward probably spends little time with him.)
7) Steward takes grievance to his grievance man.
8) Grievance man takes grievance to general production supervisor. Higher levels of both organizations may be involved later.

In the *After* diagram (B), we have the following sequence:

In stage 1:
1) Time-study supervisor assigns task.
2) Time-study man gets written authorization from general production supervisor.
3) Time-study man presents authorization to foreman.
4) Foreman calls in steward to discuss plans with him and time-study man.
5) Time-study man, foreman, and steward go together to explain study to worker (s).

   Stage 2 represents the situation when the rate is accepted without question:
6) Time-study man presents rate to foreman for approval.
7) Foreman presents rate to steward for reaction.
8) Steward presents rate to worker. No protest.

Stage 2a occurs when the rate is not accepted by foreman or steward. Here the two-headed arrow indicates a situation where activity may be originated in either direction, on the basis of discussion.

8a) Worker and steward discuss rate.
Foreman and time-study man discuss same.
Foreman and steward discuss objections to the rate.
9) Time-study man discusses rate with his supervisor.
Foreman discusses rate with his supervisor.
Steward discusses rate with grievance man.
10) Grievance man and general production supervisor discuss rate. General production supervisor and time-study supervisor discuss rate. (In a situation such as Inland Steel Container Company, we may have a three-cornered discussion here with more than one level of personnel involved also.)

We are not recommending that the Inland Steel Container Company arrangement of the time-study man's relationships be applied in every factory. The effectiveness of any one type of interpersonal relationship will depend upon the whole organizational context of which it is a part.

With this illustration we are trying to make just one general point. The problems of conflict surrounding time study cannot be resolved through explaining to people the purpose of the function and trying to persuade them to have more favorable sentiments (attitudes) toward it. Sentiments are not changed through such a direct approach. They change with changes in the structure of interaction. Such changes are not the "intangibles" so often thought to constitute human relations. They can be observed, and measured, and represented in diagrammatic form. We have used one such diagram to illustrate the magnitude of change in the structure of interaction in the Inland Steel Container Company case.

## AT THE BOTTOM OF THE PYRAMID

For all the attention some managements may give them today, workers are still at the bottom of the industrial pyramid. They are the only people in the production organization who receive orders and who have no one below them to whom they can give orders. Management is constantly originating activity for them. In many cases they have little opportunity to originate back to management. In or outside of industry, when this one-sided origination situation exists, we find the people in the bottom position developing some resentment against the people who are always originating for them. Consciously or unconsciously they build up a self-defense organization to resist the changes that management is imposing. It is in this way that Roethlisberger and Dickson explain restriction of output in the Hawthorne case.

In effect, workers are trying to achieve some control over their jobs and over their own fate in the department. They are trying to work at a pace comfortable for them instead of one imposed by management. They try to build up a stable production situation on the assumption that if production is stable management will not be able to press for more production. If the worker put out 150 units yesterday and puts out only 100 today, he fears that the foreman will want to know why he is not putting out 150 every day. To protect himself against such pressures he prefers to put out 125 regularly, or, still better, he would like to produce 150 when conditions are right and he feels like producing, but only turn in for credit 125 units and keep the other 25 in a "bank" where they can be pulled out for credit on a day when he has made only 100.

As we have seen in the situation discussed by Donald Roy (pages 20 ff.) the workers get satisfaction out of taking conspicuous leisure. They work hard to reach their quota, but then take the time gained to flaunt their independence of management pressures. These pressures will be felt as long as activity is originated primarily, and almost exclusively, downward upon the workers.

If sentiments and activities can be changed through interaction, this conclusion suggests a rechanneling of interactions so that workers can increase the frequency with which they originate up the organization. These upward originations can take two general forms: grievances and suggestions. These two types of communication serve in part the same functions and in part different functions.

It has long been recognized that it is important for worker morale and for union-management adjustment to have channels open so that grievances can be readily raised and dealt with. Many management people have learned not to limit these upward originations to grievances according to the strict wording of the contract. They have come to be willing to listen to complaints which have no standing in the contract and to take action on those complaints when it seems reasonable to do so. In other words, they recognize that it is important for workers to have opportunities to raise complaints of all sorts and to be able to get action on some of these complaints.

Suggestions perform something of the same function. Suggestions are another way through which workers can originate activity for management people.

Except in the literal wording of the contract, we cannot make a sharp distinction between grievances and suggestions. Both are attempts to originate activity for management. Both may imply criticism of management action, although this is explicit in grievances and only implicit in suggestions. However, grievances represent attempts to get management to reverse actions already taken, whereas suggestions are proposals for new actions that management may not have considered. It is this difference between them that we will examine further.

While it is crucial for the success of cooperative programs to build up origination of activity from workers through their union to management, this change alone is not enough. We need also to build up originations from management to the union at all levels in the plant.

In some cases we find that it is an established management policy not to originate activity directly for the union. In other words, management conceives of the union as a watchdog of the contract. Management transmits its orders and directions to the work force right down the line of authority from plant manager through foreman to worker. The union, then, has a function to perform only when it challenges decisions that management has made.

This managerial approach has two consequences: It provides the union stewards and officers with so little scope for activity that they must be constantly seeking to find ways to challenge management's authority through the grievance procedure. In the second place, this approach limits union-management interaction to those situations in which the union is challenging management's decisions. If those are the only interactions between union and management, they inevitably tend to build up a defensive reaction on the part of management people. They come to see the problem as one of maintaining management prerogatives against the onslaught of the union. In such situations no cooperation between union and management is possible.

Here we are looking at the structure of interaction in order to predict the sentiments we will find between union officers and management people. Our theory gives us certain simple data to seek in order to determine the state of the relationship. If we find that interactions between union officers and management people are limited entirely to attempts on the part of the union to originate activity for management, then we can expect to find friction and conflict separating the parties. This analysis may be applied more specifically to particular points in the two organizations. We may find top management and foremen originating for the union while middle management people are entirely in the defensive position. In this case we can predict that the hostile sentiments between the two parties will be concentrated at this middle management point.

The structure of interaction resulting when management pursues the watchdog theory of union functions can be illustrated as in Figure IVA. Here the arrows indicate that contacts between union officers and management are limited to union challenges to management actions. With the union constantly seeking to originate activity, management assumes a defensive position.

To build cooperation, then, it is necessary for management to abandon its defensive position and develop a regular pattern for originating activity for the union. However, standing by itself, this prescription is oversimplified and misleading. In fact, it may lead management down another road to the breakdown of cooperation.

There are a number of cases in which management, in seeking cooperation, is active in calling upon top local union leaders for help. In some of these cases the union leaders, meeting frequently with top management, become convinced of the sincerity of purpose and soundness of judgment of management officials. They then seek to support management's decisions through originating activity

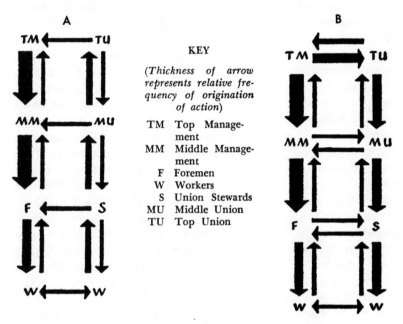

**KEY**

*(Thickness of arrow represents relative frequency of origination of action)*

TM  Top Management
MM  Middle Management
 F  Foremen
 W  Workers
 S  Union Stewards
MU  Middle Union
TU  Top Union

Fig. IV. Structure of Interaction Between Union and Management:
A. Management on the Defensive; B. Cleavage Within the Union

down the line to the rank-and-file union members. If these increased pressures from above in the union are not compensated for by increased originations from the rank and file to high union officers, then we can expect to observe an estrangement between members and leaders, which may lead to an overturn of the leadership, Figure IV B represents such a situation.

This does not mean that management must avoid asking for action from union officers or that union officers must avoid increasing their originations for rank-and-file members. It does mean that the responsible officers need to recognize that such a change—without other compensating changes—will upset the balance of the social system. The problem is one of adjusting for changes in down-the-line activity with changes in up-the-line activity, or vice-versa.

In the Lever Brothers case, we observed a sharp drop in up-the-line activity within the union at the same time that the union leaders sought to maintain their accustomed frequency of down-the-line activity. It was this imbalance which provided us with our explanation for the overturn of the union leadership.

In the Inland Steel Container Company case we observed a high level of down-the-line activity within the union, but we also saw the rank and file originating actively for the leadership. For example, the problem of the punch press department manifested itself through numerous daily originations of workers to their union leaders. Eventually Columbus Gary responded to these pressures by taking the initiative with management in proposing a new plan for the assignment of jobs. He then called a meeting to present the plan to the workers. But before final decisions were reached, the rank-and-file workers had an opportunity to decide on the ranking of the jobs in the department. It is this active involvement of rank-and-file members, this skillful balancing of up-and-down-the-line activity in the union, that gives us part of our explanation for the remarkable level of cooperation we have observed in this case.

As we look at cases of active and effective cooperation, in structural terms, we come to four general conclusions:

1. There must be frequent opportunities for union officers, at all levels, to originate for their opposite numbers in management. This includes the handling of grievances, of course, but it must also involve the encouragement of a union-management flow of suggestions.

2. Within union and within management there must be a flow of originations upward as well as downward. We have just discussed the problems that arise within the union when originations are channeled too strongly in a downward direction. In the Inland Steel Container Company case we have seen how the channels for upward origination within management were opened up in the early stages of the transition from conflict to cooperation. It does not seem pos-

sible that such a transition in union-management relations could have taken place if John Gossett had continued to direct the management in an autocratic manner.

3. Management must originate activity for the union at various levels of the organization. Here it is unrealistic to draw a line separating potential grievances from potential suggestions. Management presents problems—sometimes complex problems—to the union. These union-management discussions, backed up by discussions within management and between workers and union officers, develop the suggestions that lead to both greater efficiency and higher morale. In some of the Scanlon cases we have seen instances of problems that could not be solved through suggestions until management had taken the initiative in posing these problems to union representatives. The Inland Steel Container case also is full of such examples.

4. The cooperative relationship depends upon maintaining reciprocity in the origination of activity within management, within the union, and between union and management. Cooperation requires a regular and continuing pattern of interaction. The pattern cannot be interrupted and then resumed after a space of time as if nothing had happened—for something will have happened. In the Lever Brothers case we saw that the inability of the parties to agree upon a new goal for cooperation led to a radical change in interaction, and that, in turn, led to the overturn of the union leadership.

This does not mean that a given pattern of interaction must be maintained indefinitely without any change. In a dynamic society like ours there will inevitably be changes. In the case of changes, the questions are these: How sudden are the changes? How drastic are they? And to what extent are they balanced by other and compensating changes?

The last question gives us one key to effective leadership in management or union. The leader recognizes that if he (or circumstances) imposes a substantial change in one channel of interaction, he cannot expect to hold all else constant. If he wishes to maintain the existing level of activity and cooperative sentiments he must seek to introduce compensating changes in other channels of interaction.

This prescription is not so precise as we would like to make it. When we talk about interactions we are dealing with phenomena that can be observed and even measured. In laboratory situations precise measurements have been made.[2] In the study of complex organizations we have not reached this point of precision. When we say that union officers must originate frequently for management, we do not know just how often that means. When we say that an increase in down-the-line activity must be compensated for by an up-the-line increase we do not know how great an increase can take place in one direction before a compensating change is necessary, nor do we know what magnitude of change in one direction is required to compensate for a given amount of change in the other.

We are saying, in effect, that we are dealing with quantifiable variables that we have not yet quantified. From a scientific point of view, this is a sweeping confession of ignorance. Still, this need not leave the management or union official without resources. Enough research has been done to tell us where to look to find our answers. We know that the level of activity and the character of existing sentiments in an organization depend upon the pattern of interaction in that organization. We know that changes in interaction lead to changes in activity and in sentiments. At least then the responsible official can give close attention to the interaction pattern prevailing around him. When he sees changes being introduced into that pattern he can expect to witness changes in activity and sentiments. The man who knows, even in a most general way, what to expect is far ahead of the man who is constantly surprised at disruptions of activity or explosions of hostile sentiments. The man who can see ahead to anticipate problems can establish better control over those problems.[3]

[2] For a discussion of the work done particularly by Eliot Chapple along this line, see W. F. Whyte, *Modern Methods in Social Research*, pp. 53-60. Published by the Office of Naval Research.

[3] Some of the charts and the theoretical outline for this chapter are taken from W. F. Whyte, "Patterns of Interaction in Union-Management Relations," *Human Organization*, Vol. VIII, No. 4 (Fall 1949).

On the subject of the effect of human relations on worker reactions to incentive systems, see an unpublished study by the Survey Research Center, University of Michigan.